ALREADY COMPROMISED

Christian colleges took a test on the state of their faith and **THE FINAL EXAM IS IN.**

Ken Ham & Greg Hall

with *Britt Beemer* of *America's Research Group*

First printing: May 2011
Fourth printing: October 2012

Master Books®, P.O. Box 726, Green Forest, AR 72638
Master Books® is a division of the New Leaf Publishing Group, Inc.

ISBN: 978-0-89051-607-2
Library of Congress Number: 2011926096

Cover design: Joseph David Advertising, jdausa.com
Photo credit, pages 8, 10, and 11: Shutterstock.com

Unless otherwise noted, Scripture quotations are from the New American Standard Bible.

Please consider requesting that a copy of this volume be purchased by your local library system.

Printed in the United States of America

Please visit our website for other great titles:
www.masterbooks.net

For information regarding author interviews,
please contact the publicity department at (870) 438-5288

Master
Books®
A Division of New Leaf Publishing Group
www.masterbooks.net

Endorsement

I have no doubt that the average church member would be shocked and outraged to discover how many supposedly evangelical colleges and universities have more or less given up their commitment to biblical inerrancy and the authority of Scripture—especially when dealing with the early chapters of Genesis. I'm grateful for this important work by Ken Ham and Greg Hall, documenting the many compromises that have ravaged the Christian academy. *Already Compromised* is a much needed wake-up call and a summons to arms for faithful, courageous Bible believers. We need to stand up, declare our faith, and defend the truth of Scripture courageously. The stakes are high and the battle may be more fierce than ever, but God will bless those who honor His Word. May He bless us with clear, unwavering voices.

—John MacArthur
Pastor of Grace Community Church
President of The Master's College and Seminary
President, Grace to You ministry

Dedications

This book is dedicated to our young people in the Church. Be bold and
uncompromising regarding the authority of the Word of God!
—Ken Ham

For my family:
My love, admiration, and appreciation for you
knows no limit.
— Greg Hall

Acknowledgments

- Britt Beemer and America's Research Group. Thanks for your
  amazing work. By putting statistics to our concerns, you prove what
  we see and sense.

- AiG . . . Steve Ham and Terry Mortenson.

- Roger Patterson and Bodie Hodge for reviewing this book.

- Alane Richardville, for help with research.

- Tim Dudley, Laura Welch, and the team at Master Books. Thanks
  for your personal dedication to the cause and your professional
  devotion to excellence in publishing.

- Todd Hillard, our editor/writer, who ds and our thoughts and
  crafted them into a cohesive message.

Contents

Introduction

The Rise and Fall of Higher Education

Ken Ham

founder and president of Answers in Genesis

Early every fall, one of the great American traditions takes place from coast to coast. Planes take off, trains depart, and compact cars stuffed full of bikes and clothes and computers pull out of driveways. At the end of the journey, teary-eyed parents hug their children in the parking lots of dormitories, say one last goodbye, and then turn around, leaving their child on the threshold of one of the most important milestones of life: college.

Higher education, of course, has done much good for our society. It is the reason we enjoy many life-enhancing blessings. Through education we have learned to prosper in so many ways. Our lives have been transformed by medical advances and technology. We have learned to build the economy of the world. We feed the hungry and heal the sick. We build buildings and cities and nations. We explore the universe. The advances now realized by humankind have been made possible by education.

The American higher education system used to be the envy of nations around the world, but in several profound ways, it is not making the grade. Many Christian parents are concerned about the secular forces at work in public schools and concerned about the worldly environment that festers without restraint on most campuses. So early every fall Christian parents engage in another great American tradition: they shell out hundreds of thousands of dollars to send their children to a Christian university, Bible college, or seminary. In good faith they entrust their "heritage from the LORD" (Ps. 127:3; NKJV) to the professors and administrators they believe will protect their children and train them in the truths of the Scriptures and nurture them in their young adult faith.

The students themselves enter eagerly, committed and excited to begin their training — often with a view of being involved in missionary work, becoming a pastor, or in some way use their educational training to be a more effective witness for the Lord Jesus Christ. Both parents and students enter the whole experience with high expectations. What they don't know is that, like the secular schools they wish to avoid, and like the majority of the great Christian institutions of higher learning of the past, a growing number of the Christian schools they attend are . . . *Already Compromised*.

The Ivy League Legacy

Seniors of secular and Christian universities graduate as different people; much different than the wide-eyed, impressionable freshmen who entered. But sadly, in many instances, the changes are not all positive. The reasons are many, but the trends are now well documented. It's almost as if there is an

entropy taking place on campus — a moral and theological slippery slope that seems to take institutions in the wrong direction — usually taking the hearts and minds of naïve students with them. Like the proverbial frog boiled to death in a pot of slowly warming water, universities often end up far, far from their intended purpose.

Harvard

Harvard University was established in 1636 and is the oldest institution of higher learning in the United States. Would you be surprised to find out that it had its roots in a strong Puritan philosophy? It was never affiliated with any denomination, but many of its early graduates went on to be clergyman throughout New England.

Conflict arose, however, between Harvard's sixth president, Increase Mather, and the rest of the clergymen. Mather was deeply concerned that Harvard was becoming increasingly liberal, lax in its theology, and vague in its church policy. But his warnings went unheeded. Harvard's curriculum became increasingly secular through the end of the 1700s and was taken over by the Unitarians in 1805, resulting in the secularization of the university. By 1850, it was known as the "Unitarian Vatican." Charles W. Eliot, who was president between 1869 and 1909, eliminated Christianity as the dominant foundation of the curriculum in order to accommodate Transcendentalist Unitarian beliefs. Currently, Harvard Divinity School embraces a wide spectrum of religious belief. From meditations in the Buddhist tradition to the "Seasons of Light" — a multi-religious festival held each December — Harvard Divinity School strategically encourages an atmosphere of religious pluralism where almost any belief is encouraged, not just tolerated.

Yale

Yale, founded in 1701 in Connecticut, is the third oldest university in the United States. Its original purpose? To establish a training center for clergy and political leaders of the colony. A group of ten Congregationalist ministers, called "the founders," met in the study of Rev. Samuel Russell and donated their books for the school's first library. Like many universities and educational institutions, Yale came into its own during the Great Awakening and the Enlightenment. Presidents Thomas Clapp and Ezra Stiles pursued both religious and scientific interests as they studied Hebrew, Greek, and Latin — languages that were essential for the study of the Scriptures.

In 1872, however, a professor of economics and sociology named Graham Sumner began to use a textbook by Herbert Spencer that supported a naturalistic, agnostic view of the world. President Noah Porter objected, concerned that it would cause religious and moral harm to his students, but Sumner continued to teach until 1909. The compromise had begun.

A few decades later, President James R. Engel and psycho-biologist Robert M. Dierks were creating research programs testing the outer boundaries of naturalistic, humanistic theory. In one study, they analyzed the sexual behavior of chimpanzees, hoping to discover the evolutionary roots of human development. Today, little residue can be found of the school's former foundation of faith.

Princeton

Princeton University was founded in 1746 to train ministers for the Presbyterian denomination. For several decades, the college was the religious capital of Scottish and Irish Americans, helping build the spiritual foundation for the emerging nation of immigrants.

John Witherspoon became the sixth president of Princeton in 1768 and led the transformation of the college into a school that would equip the "revolutionary generation." At the same time, significant changes were taking place in the school's philosophy of morality as well as the school's devotion to what they called "natural philosophy." Witherspoon's view of morality was

more influenced by the Enlightenment and the ethics of philosophers than the Christian virtues espoused by Jonathan Edwards. He still supported "public religion" on a social level, but he did not believe that it was the only source of virtue. He believed that all human beings could be virtuous independent of God. There was opposition at first, but the momentum was strong and the school began to fragment.

Princeton Theological Seminary was established in 1811 — officially separating the secular and religious focuses of the school. In the late 1860s and 1870s, debates between the president of the college, James McCosh, and the head of the seminary, Charles Hodge, focused on the rising conflict between "science" and religion and Darwin's evolutionary model. Significantly, President McCosh became one of the first religious leaders to publicly endorse evolution.

In the next decade, President Francis Landey Patton came under fire for his traditional views and administrative methods. He insisted on a structured Christian education program, but many felt that approach limited academic freedom. In 1902 Patton was forced out of the presidency.

Liberal Christians dominated Princeton in the early 20th century. Evangelist Billy Sunday was not allowed to preach on campus, but liberal theologians had an open door to influence the university as it became a "modern" institution. Soon even the liberal Christian leaders lost their influence as it was eroded by secularization. By the 1920s, Princeton had ceased to be a Presbyterian institution. Evangelist Charles Templeton, a founder of Youth for Christ International, and crusade partner of Billy Graham, abandoned his faith during his years at Princeton Seminary starting in 1948.

Dartmouth

Dartmouth College was established in 1769 by Puritan Congregational minister Eliezer Wheelock. Dartmouth was the last university to be established in America under colonial rule and is the nation's ninth oldest college. Wheelock was inspired by Mohegan Indian Samson Occom. Occom had become an ordained minister after studying under Wheelock. He later went to preach to the Montauk Indians on Long Island. Wheelock's desire was to see a training school for Native Americans so that other Mohegans could be trained to reach their own people with the gospel. For this new school, he chose the motto *Vox Clamantis in Deserto*, a Latin phrase that appears five times in the Bible and is translated "the voice of one crying in the wilderness."

He chose a seal that strongly resembled the seal of the Society for the Propagation of the Gospel — a missionary society started in 1701 in London. Among its most famous alumni is Daniel Webster, who was purported to be able to recite the entire Bible, chapter and verse.

But that was then. Now, 240 years later, Dartmouth has established itself as a

premier in the university of the Ivy League but shows little or no expressions of its spiritual legacy.

History Repeating Itself?

This is the legacy of the Ivy League, and many of us have become concerned that the same trends are taking place today among Christian institutions that were founded on the same values and principles as these historic schools. The blatant disregard for the Bible and God is obvious on the secular campus, but even more disconcerting is the significant level of compromise we sense taking place among "Christian" institutions — most of which started with intentions as strong as the Ivy League but now show clear signs of the same decline.

How bad is it? We wanted to find out for certain, so we turned again to Britt Beemer, founder and president of America's Research Group (ARG), a nationally recognized surveying and marketing firm (americasresearch-group.com). When we were considering building the Creation Museum, we asked Britt for his advice. He took down all the pertinent information and went to work with his surveys and number crunching. What he came back with astounded us: ARG thought that 400,000 people would be willing to visit a museum like this in the first 365 days. The actual number turned out to be 404,000! He has done exceptional work for us in the past, including the survey for the book *Already Gone: Why Your Kids Will Quit Church and What You Can Do to Stop It*.

That study dealt with the two-thirds of the young people who grew up in the Church who are leaving when they reach college age. But this research indicates a far greater failure — a failure in regard to those who train the trainers who influence the minds of the coming generations — a failure at the level of the "shepherds" in many of our Christian academic institutions.

Over and over again, the Israelites were warned not to contaminate the purity of God's Word with the pagan religious ideas of the day. Jeremiah warned, "Do not learn the way of the Gentiles" (Jer. 10:2; NKJV). The Israelites were to be a nation to shine the light of God's truth to all the other nations. However, they contaminated their culture by adopting the pagan religion of the age into their thinking. This contamination basically destroyed them.

We contend (and scientifically conducted research will back this up) that many of the professors at many of our Christian institutions today have exhibited a behavior no different than those of the compromising Israelites. They have, by and large, adopted the pagan religion of this age and contaminated God's Word, thus contaminating the thinking of those to whom they impart their teaching. And we also contend, as the research will clearly show, that there is almost what one could call "deceptiveness" in the way some of these shepherds use language. Subtle twists in semantics clearly show up in their attempts to allay the fears of the unsuspecting parents in regard to what their children are really being indoctrinated in.

In Part 1, I will walk you through the research conducted by Britt Beemer and America's Research Group. After interviewing more than 300 presidents, vice presidents, religion department chairs, and science department chairs from 200 different colleges, we discovered great cause for concern in the curriculum, conflict between departments, and confusion among the leaders on many levels.

As the numbers came in, our concerns were not only confirmed, they were intensified. As I share the results of the survey, President Greg Hall gives a heart-piercing account of "the battle for the mind" that is raging on college campuses today — both secular and Christian. Greg is the president of Warner University. Not only does he know the ins and outs of both secular and Christian higher education, he also knows the heartache and the joy that comes with maintaining an institution of higher education that upholds the authority of Scripture. Greg has a tremendous heart and a tremendous passion for students. His love for God and his commitment to the Word is obvious in his life and in his career. His insights will lead us through the war of the worldviews between naturalism and Scripture and why the outcome of these battles is so important for our children and our society.

Our research shows that an "uncertain sound" is emanating from many of our Christian colleges. The authority of Scripture is being undermined at many levels, and the voices of naturalism, agnosticism, and even atheism are permeating the eardrums of generations of young people who become the leaders of tomorrow. And as they step into those leadership roles, most do not have the certain sound of the trumpet of truth to advance the battle as it should be fought. What do we do about it?

In Part 2, Greg and I will leave you with a personal challenge and an action plan that can help protect your children and begin to initiate changes in the system as a whole. You'll find guidelines for choosing the best schools for your children and questions to ask to verify what they are really teaching. Finally, we will offer students a "Spiritual Survival Kit" that will equip them to thrive, and not just survive, during the college years.

I believe that this book will prove to be even more controversial than the study we did for the book *Already Gone*. It's factual, but it's also personal. As fathers, both Greg and I have had to decide which colleges are best for our kids. Knowing that compromise (to one degree or another) awaits our kids, we had to contend with where to send them and try to prepare them for battle and encourage them to keep their guard up. All we can hope and pray is that if one person is saved or has his or her life changed, or parents can be equipped to help protect their kids from blatant faith-destroying compromise because of the research in this book, we believe that's enough. All we ask is that this book might be a guide and a defense for the truth as our children leave our homes and begin to walk through a world and an educational system that is *Already Compromised*.

Want to know which colleges were contacted as part of the ARG study? Visit www.creationcolleges.org and also find a growing list of Christian colleges we recommend you search out.

PART 1

An Uncertain Sound

For if the bugle produces an
indistinct sound, who will prepare
himself for battle?

— 1 Corinthians 14:8

Chapter 1

Concern for the Curriculum

Ken Ham

Let not many of you become teachers, my brethren, knowing that as such we will incur a stricter judgment (James 3:1).

This book really began with a hunch — one of those hunches that comes from repeated observation over 30 years — but nothing that you can objectively put your finger on. As part of my ministry through Answers in Genesis, I travel extensively, meeting with families, churches, and educators.

When the topic of parents' and students' experiences in colleges and universities comes up, I hear a lot of good; and I also hear a lot of bad. I hear far too many stories of well-meaning parents who have sent their children off to college with the highest of hopes, only to have them return skeptical, disillusioned, and uncertain about their former faith. Many of them leave the faith of their family altogether. I have also met with students at Christian institutions where I have spoken, and I hear from their own mouths what certain professors teach them and which books they are encouraged to study.

At one Christian college, I met with the chaplain before I was to speak at chapel. The chaplain told me, "We aren't narrow-minded like you young earth creationists at this college — we allow all views here."

I said to him, "Oh, I consider the view of taking a strong stand on six literal days and a young earth as the correct biblical view, and the other views are incorrect. Do you allow that view?"

The man replied, "No, because we allow all views." Of course, he didn't realize he was actually saying they do not allow all views, as they didn't allow mine. He thought they were being neutral, but as we will discuss, there is no neutral position.

Before speaking at another well-known conservative college, a person high up in the administration spoke to the students — basically giving them a disclaimer in regard to what I was going to teach them. I found out later from the students that, to their knowledge, I was the first person ever to be given a disclaimer in chapel — even though there had been speakers who would be considered somewhat liberal in their theology!

At another (what is considered to be) conservative Christian college, I was ushered into the president's office, where he began to "dress me down" in regard to our stand on six literal days and a young earth. He wanted me to know he did not approve of what I believed and was upset with my being at the college. (There were other reasons why I was actually invited to speak.)

At a conservative Bible college in Australia, the president asked me into his office, where he proceeded to admonish me because I had spoken against the gap theory and millions of years.

Yes, I knew that something was happening out there. Over the years I've been engaging in an increasingly heated debate not only with secularists, but also with Christian brothers and sisters involved in Christian higher education. . . . those were the administrators and professors at respected and trusted Christian colleges and universities. My concerns continued to grow, but before I spoke too "loudly" I wanted to make sure that I could prove it. When we produced the book *Already Gone*, we were simply verifying what everyone was already experiencing: Christian students, who grew up in evangelical churches, are leaving the church at an astounding rate. We had some ideas from experience as to why this was happening, but we set out to use statistically valid, professionally conducted research to determine what was happening. Our findings were very controversial.

I expect that this study will be far more shocking because people don't know that in most cases, their child's education at Christian institutions is "already compromised." Sometimes parents aren't even aware of this until their student's junior or senior year — when the discussion around the dinner table during the holidays reveals that there have been problems from the very beginning. What is the core of that problem?

A blind man cannot guide a blind man, can he? Will they not both fall into a pit? A pupil is not above his teacher; but everyone, after he has been fully trained, will be like his teacher (Luke 6:39–40).

When parents and students willingly submit themselves to a teacher, accepting him or her as authoritative, accepting what he or she says as truth, they *will* become like that teacher. Because of that, we felt strongly compelled to find out what is really being taught in colleges and universities today. Our primary focus of study, however, was not secular institutions. For the most part, secular institutions are rather upfront and honest about what they teach. As you will see, their goals and objectives have been clearly stated.

But this is not often the case in the Christian institutions. Because parents and students make assumptions about the beliefs of their Christian teachers that may or may not be true, we wanted to get an objective, quantifiable picture of what is really being taught in the classrooms. And, as we will show, we can't accept that the terminology being used by administrators and professors at such institutions means the same to us as it does to them! That is scary!

Review of the Survey

The goal of the survey conducted by America's Research Group and Britt Beemer was to survey 200 different Christian institutions of higher learning through interviews with people in four different positions:

- the president of the university
- the academic dean/vice president
- the head of the science department
- the head of the theology/religion department

Not every school used the same titles to describe these positions;[1] however, we are able to easily categorize them appropriately by their function. In a perfect world, we would have interviewed 800 people. Virtually everyone that we could reach wanted to answer the questions. The problem was getting to them — some were on sabbatical and some of their staffers filtered us. But once we actually got through to them, we had less than 40 people turn down the opportunity to be interviewed.

In the end, we were able to interview 312 people. Of these, 223 were from schools associated with the Council for Christian Colleges and Universities (CCCU), a group of over 90 colleges that require all of their professors to sign a personal statement of faith. The other 89 respondents were from schools that were "religiously affiliated" through an association with a religious denomination.[2] (These two groups responded in very similar ways to survey questions, by the way.) The only real difference in their demographics is that Catholics labeled themselves as being religiously affiliated and Baptist colleges tended to be members of the CCCU. Other than that, these two distinctions simply confirm that we have a good cross section here of a number of different denominations from different backgrounds — more than plenty to make generalized considerations according to the data.

So out of a potential of 800 people, we had a sample size right at 40 percent. That was much higher than anyone expected we would be able to get. This response rate gives us an error factor of about +/- 2.5 percent. (Statistically, that means that if we say "50 percent," the actual number across the whole country is somewhere between 47.5 percent and 52.5 percent. Because of this small error factor, we will be rounding all of our results to a 10th of a percent.)

Many of our questions required simple yes or no responses. Others were more open-ended and each person was allowed to give one response to the question, their number-one answer. So the data you see on the open-ended questions is not word-for-word, but rather grouped together with other similar responses.

The survey went very well. We were allowed to get not only a big picture view of what's happening on the Christian college campus, but also insights into specific issues that should be of concern for everyone involved. Let's take a quick look at the big picture responses. In upcoming chapters, we will dissect them in much more detail.

New Testament Agreement / Old Testament Dividing Lines

We were pleased to find nearly 100 percent agreement on some important New Testament issues:

- Do you believe in the virgin birth of Christ? Yes: 99.0%
- Do you believe in Christ's substitutionary death on the Cross? Yes: 99.0%
- Do you believe in a literal heaven and hell? Yes: 96.5%
- Do you believe in Christ's Second Coming? Yes: 99.0%
- Do you believe in the bodily Resurrection of Christ? Yes: 99.0%

But the minute we stepped into the Old Testament, division began to arise. The more detailed the question, the clearer it became that there were serious problems.

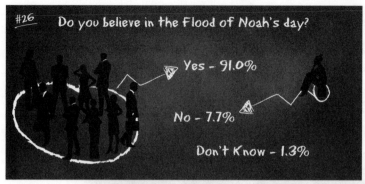

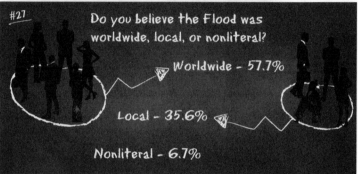

Immediately we see a rift forming over the historical account of Noah and the Flood, but that was just the tip of the iceberg. When we started to look at issues regarding creation and evolution, the issues became more pronounced. Once more, the more detailed our questions became, the deeper the division became.

Q13: Do you believe the Genesis 1–2 account of creation is literally true?

• Yes: 83.0%   • No: 14.7%   • Don't know: 2.2%

It's clear that we have some confusion here. We are beginning to see a trend that concerned us throughout the entire survey: *people didn't always mean what they said.* For example, 83 percent said that they believe Genesis 1 and 2 are literally true. But when we asked whether they believe God created in six literal days, only 59.6 percent answered yes. That means about 23 percent are either confused, wrong, or just haven't thought this through. Or it could also be how people in a postmodern culture determine the meaning of words. I have realized over the years that many professors will sound like they believe in a literal Genesis, but what they mean by the words is not what I (and many others) understand them to mean. This is a major issue we will deal with in this study.

Questions 16 and 17 are virtually the opposites of each other (with 16 being positive and 17 being negative), but almost 10 percent of the people answered yes to both questions, indicating that they believe in six literal days of creation and they don't believe in six literal days of creation! These concerns continued to grow as we gathered data about what they teach about evolution.

#6 What does your institution teach about evolution?

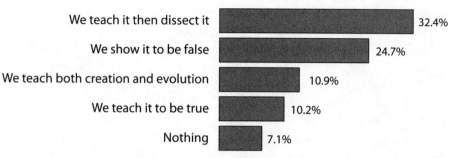

We teach it then dissect it	32.4%
We show it to be false	24.7%
We teach both creation and evolution	10.9%
We teach it to be true	10.2%
Nothing	7.1%

This was an open-ended question. These five answers accounted for 95 percent of all the respondents, with more saying that they "teach and dissect" evolution. That word "dissect" is interesting and requires some further investigation (9 percent of them used the same word when describing how they teach the Bible!). I would like to give them the benefit of the doubt. We hope they mean that they (1) explain the idea, (2) give an accurate critique of the idea's strengths and weaknesses, and (3) show how it is absolutely contrary to the authoritative account in God's Word. At least I hope so — but the further we look into the answers to the questions, the more I have my doubts.

I don't think there's anything wrong at all with "teaching evolution" as long as it is put under the same scientific and biblical scrutiny that any idea would be. On the other hand, "dissect" might mean "we teach and let them decide." That is a big concern. Are they presenting the issues loosely and just letting students decide what is true? Or are they explaining all the facts and pointing to the definitive conclusion that evolution is false and creation is true? That's a big question, and the answer hinges on the fundamental difference between relativism (no absolute truth, i.e., people decide their own truth) and the biblical worldview: *is there absolute truth or is there not?*

Twenty-four percent said that they teach evolution to be false. Not a lot. In the next two responses, we see that at *least* 20 percent of Christian colleges are teaching evolution as a viable option and another 11 percent admit to teaching evolution as truth. That's more than 30 percent. If we add to that a portion of those who are in the "we dissect it" category (who probably aren't taking any sort of stand in favor of creation), this number could be much, much higher. The answer "nothing" is a concern as well. To teach nothing about evolution, when it is the dominant worldview theme in our culture that is in opposition to biblical creation, leaves students vulnerable and ignorant.

#14 Would you consider yourself to be a young-earth or old-earth Christian?

Old earth – 49.0%

Young earth – 42.3%

Neither – 8.3%

Don't Know – 0.3%

This number turned out to be quite a bit bigger than we had expected — 42 percent say that the earth is young. I'm actually fairly encouraged by that because it doesn't seem like that many people are taking a stand on the issue publicly. My guess is that many of them feel intimidated because of academic peer pressure and are "closet" young-earth creationists. If the system is already compromised, individuals within the system will feel pressure to compromise or hide their position in order to keep their jobs and advance their careers. One continually risks rejection when taking a stand on this issue (as has been documented by others).

They also need to be published in academic journals to have respect in the community. By taking a stand on the age of the earth (and evolution) one can "slit his or her own throat" when it comes to advancement. Tragically, in both secular and Christian institutions, people will be more dedicated to their academic discipline in order to get published in the journals than they are to the institution and its beliefs. They have to look good within their field of study, even if it doesn't reflect the values of the school.

At one seminary where I spoke, I asked the head of the seminary (who invited me as he had the same view of Genesis as I do) why so many professors in such institutions would not take a stand on six literal days (no death before sin, young earth, etc.). He told me that a lot of it had to do with peer pressure and being published in the academic journals. He said if someone is labeled as a literal six-day, young-earth creationist, they basically could not get published in such journals.

Still, we were encouraged by the number of people who said they believed in a young earth.[3] But as we evaluated the survey as a whole, another "hunch" was clearly confirmed . . . and when it comes to Christian colleges, this clearly has become one of our greatest concerns.

"Newspeak" and the Old Testament

In his stunning book *1984*, George Orwell introduced a concept called "newspeak," in which characters in positions of power began using terms and phrases that sounded right to the masses — when in fact, they meant something very, very different. I've been concerned that the same sort of thing is happening in Christianity, so we began comparing what teachers claimed they believe about the Bible, and tried to determine what they actually mean by what they teach.

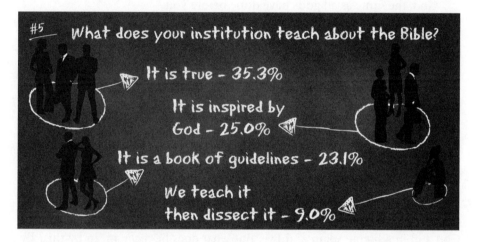

#5 What does your institution teach about the Bible?

It is true – 35.3%

It is inspired by God – 25.0%

It is a book of guidelines – 23.1%

We teach it then dissect it – 9.0%

These first four responses accounted for 92.3 percent of all the answers. What was the fifth most popular answer? Five people, or 1.6 percent, made it clear that they teach the Bible to be false. At least they are honest about it! And further, this is supposed to be a Christian college!

Our question is this: what do they mean when they say "true"? Because when you correlate these answers with the answers they gave on other questions, you quickly find out that people don't necessarily believe the Bible is "literally" true.

There's a postmodern influence here about what "true" means. Unfortunately, many people believe something is "true if it works for you." This allows the speaker to put a spin on his or her words, making them sound acceptable even though they really mean something totally different. Politicians do this all the time. When forced to explain what they really mean, they will dodge the truth by saying things like "it depends on what your definition of 'is' is."

The cults do this as well. The Mormons, for example, have become masters at using words that *sound* like Christian terminology, even though they *mean* something *entirely* different. And the masses (most Christians included) think their usage of these words means the same thing the Bible does. For example, Joseph Smith, the founder of the Mormon church, said:

> God himself was once as we are now, and is an exalted man. . . . We have imagined and supposed that God was God from all eternity. I will refute that idea. . . . He was once a man like us. . . . ere, then, is eternal life — to know the only wise and true God; and you have got to learn how to be gods yourselves and to be kings and priests to God, the same as all gods have done before you.[4]

So when a Mormon says "God," he is really talking about one of thousands of gods that were once men and earned their way to be gods just as you or I can! Their definitions of "Jesus," "grace," "atonement," and "heaven" are equally different from the biblical view. This "newspeak" has allowed them entrance into mainline evangelical Christian circles, even though what they mean by what they say is absolute heresy according to the Bible.

Similar word-twisting, truth-skewing "newspeak" is going on in the debate over the creation account in Genesis. Dr. William Dembski is a research professor in philosophy at Southwestern Baptist Theological Seminary in Fort Worth, Texas, and a senior fellow with the Discovery Institute's Center for Science and Culture in Seattle. He *says* that he believes in the inspired, inerrant Word of God and in a literal Adam and Eve. But what does he *really* mean by this? By scrutinizing his own words from one of his latest books (*The End of Christianity*) we quickly discover that he believes in billions of years, evolution, *and* Adam and Eve. The mental gymnastics used are dizzying. Consider this one quote: "For the theodicy I am proposing to be compatible with evolution, God must not merely introduce existing human-like beings from outside the Garden. In addition, when they enter the Garden, God must transform their consciousness so that they become rational moral agents made in God's image."[5]

I go into much, much more detail on Dr. Dembski and others in appendix A: "Speaking of Newspeak." Please take the time to read it. There are many other inconsistencies in Dr. Dembski's beliefs, but what they show are the outrageous lengths some Christian academics will go to in order to try to reconcile billions of years and evolutionary ideas with the Scriptures, all the while trying to keep their belief in a literal Adam and Eve and the original sin while telling unsuspecting parents and prospective students that they believe in inerrancy.

Another example is Professor Bruce Waltke, acknowledged to be a world-renowned Old Testament scholar and considered to be a "conservative evangelical." But even this label, "conservative evangelical," is an example of "newspeak," for it just doesn't mean what it used to. He resigned his position at a "conservative evangelical" seminary (Reformed Theological Seminary in Orlando) in 2010 over the issue of his public endorsement of evolution.

Dr. Waltke made statements that became very public, especially through a video that had appeared on a theologically liberal website: The BioLogos Foundation. He subsequently asked for the video to be removed from the site, but not before his pro-evolution statement had become widely known. It helped lead to his resignation from the seminary. So what did Dr. Waltke say in that video? Well, here is one quote:

> I think that if the data is overwhelming in favor, favor, of evolution, [then] to deny that reality will make us a cult, some odd group that's not really interacting with the real world, and rightly so.[6]

As of the writing of this book, Dr. Waltke had a teaching position at what is considered to be a conservative evangelical seminary — *Knox Theological Seminary* in Florida.

So, what does "conservative evangelical" really mean?

In the end, we discovered from the research that it really doesn't matter what people *say*, it's what they *mean* by what they say that needs to be discerned.

Defining Terms Practically

In order to determine what people really mean by what they say, we used open-ended and closed-ended questions so we could compare answers.

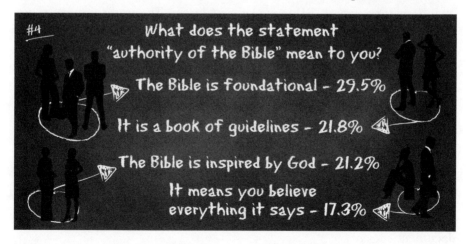

#4 What does the statement "authority of the Bible" mean to you?

The Bible is foundational – 29.5%

It is a book of guidelines – 21.8%

The Bible is inspired by God – 21.2%

It means you believe everything it says – 17.3%

The remaining 10 percent used words like "priority," "inerrant," or "expertise." Most of the answers sounded good, but very few, if any, of the

312 respondents had a clear definition of what they meant by "authority of the Bible."

Do you see why this is so important? I mean, these phrases sound right, but what do people mean when they use words like "foundational"? When they say the Bible is a book of "guidelines" are they really saying that it's just a general list of suggestions? When they say that the Bible is "inspired," do they mean it in the same way that Rembrandt or Michelangelo were inspired? Do they simply mean God's Word is "inspirational"?

Our definitions of the key biblical terms must be both clear and practical. When I speak of the authority of the Bible, what I mean is this:

> The Bible is the absolute standard for life and practice and everything it touches upon. It is the foundation for all of my thinking in every area.

A definition like that helps to rule out liberal interpretations that mean something different. It's important to have clear definitions like that for all of the important words we use in Christianity. However, as careful as we can be, this research has found that even the very best of words and definitions can't necessarily be trusted to mean the same things to good Christian people. One will have to go far beyond the words and definitions and delve deeply with very specific and detailed questions to really discern what someone believes and teaches.

Let me give an example to help further explain.

On October 26–28, 1978, the first summit of the International Council on Biblical Inerrancy (ICBI) took place in Chicago. This was "for the purpose of affirming afresh the doctrine of the inerrancy of Scripture, making clear the understanding of it and warning against its denial."

If you have never read this document,[7] I urge you to do so. It covers in detail definitions of inspiration, infallibility, and inerrancy. There were around 300 signers of this document, including Dr. Henry Morris (president and founder of the Institute for Creation Research, and co-author of famed book *The Genesis Flood*), Dr. John Whitcomb (theologian and co-author of *The Genesis Flood*), and Dr. Duane Gish (who was vice president of the *Institute for Creation* Research when Dr. Henry Morris was president). There is no doubt the authors of this current book could sign this document.

However, I want to bring your attention to Article XII from the 1978 document:

> We affirm that Scripture in its entirety is inerrant, being free from all falsehood, fraud, or deceit.

We deny that Biblical infallibility and inerrancy are limited to spiritual, religious, or redemptive themes, exclusive of assertions in the fields of history and science. We further deny that scientific hypotheses about earth history may properly be used to overturn the teaching of Scripture on creation and the flood.

And I would say AMEN to that. Nonetheless, Dr. Henry Morris said this of the document and the ICBI:

The leadership of this group includes many who accept theistic evolution or progressive creation, as well as many who prefer to ignore the creation issue altogether. Consequently, unless the ICBI can somehow become convinced of the foundational importance of strict creationism for maintaining a consistent belief in inerrancy, its efforts will likely prove of only ephemeral effectiveness. The writer and others were able to persuade the ICBI to incorporate a brief article on creation and the flood into its "Chicago Statement on Inerrancy," but the Council leadership felt it could not stand on literal-day creationism and a worldwide flood, so the article was mostly innocuous.[8]

Note that although Dr. Morris (and myself) agree with the definitions of inerrancy, inspiration, and infallibility in this document, Dr. Morris understood that did not stop many who believed in millions of years and even evolution from signing it. Obviously, what a number of these scholars understood by these terms was not how Dr. Morris understood the same terms! This is a major problem in modern Christianity.

Interestingly, the ICBI conducted a second summit in 1982. Dr. Henry Morris, in writing about this summit and the papers presented concerning how to interpret the Genesis record of creation, stated: "Dr. Bradley presented the only full-length paper. The presentations by Dr. Archer and myself were merely discussions of Bradley's paper. The 'stacking' of the ICBI program was evident in that both Dr. Bradley and Dr. Archer were known to be opposed to the literal-day record of Genesis. The statement finally adopted by the council was so innocuous on the subject of origins that it would not even exclude evolution as an acceptable interpretation. *That* was the reason I could not sign their statement on biblical hermeneutics."[9]

Dr. Henry Morris would not sign this second ICBI document called "The Chicago Statement on Biblical Hermeneutics" because he understood it really did not stand on an inerrant, infallible Scripture — even though those signing it would all say they believed such.

Keeping all this in mind, now consider these questions asked as part of our research project:

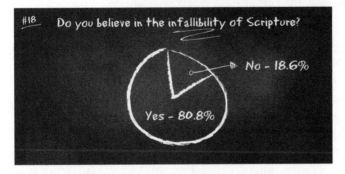

The percentage of no answers is in itself a great concern, but what do those who answered yes really mean? That is one of the major problems our research has once again brought to light.

Clearing Things Up

I began looking at various statements of faith from churches, Christian colleges, etc., on the Internet. I found that most statements of faith had a very general statement (if any) on creation. They were so general, in fact, that they could certainly allow for billions of years and evolution. Such general statements can sadly lead to the door of compromise being opened and eventually lead a college, church, etc., down the liberal path.

One can't just accept what one is told from a college as it may not mean what we think it means (infallible and inerrant mean something different to some of these professors than it would to you). We need to understand that many colleges are actually destructive because of their compromise/liberalism/belief in millions of years.

It was thrilling to read this creation statement from *Appalachian Bible College* (located in Beckley, West Virginia, in the beautiful Appalachian mountains):

> We believe that the first eleven chapters of Genesis are the literal history of the early Earth (Matthew 19:4, 24:37).
>
> We believe that this material universe is the result of a sequence of unique creative acts of God the Son, accomplished with the aid of God the Holy Spirit and directed by God the Father (Genesis 1:1, 2; Colossians 1:16). We believe these creative acts were *ex nihilo*, completed by the mere spoken commands of God (2 Peter 3:5). We further believe that these creative acts were accomplished in six literal twenty-four hour days (Exodus 20:11). Therefore we hold to a young earth view supported by the genealogies and other time information provided in the Word of God. We also believe that the material universe was created in total perfection (Genesis 1:31) but subsequently was sentenced to a slow decay and eventual destruction by the Curse (binding), which was part of the penalty for the disobedience of the parents of all mankind, Adam and Eve, whom we view as real, literal people, created on the sixth day of Creation (Genesis 1:27, 2:7–3:19). We reject all concepts of a pre-Adamic race. We believe that the biblical Noahic Flood (Genesis 6–8) was a real, year-long global event, the result of the judgment of God on the hopelessly rebellious descendants of Adam and Eve (Genesis 6:5, 1 Peter 3:6), and resulted in much of the present geology of the Earth, including most of the fossil graveyards of myriads of plants and animals then living. We believe that only eight human souls, Noah and his family, survived the Flood (Genesis 7:13 and 8:18) and that all mankind now living are descended from this family, dispersed over the face of the Earth by the confusion of tongues described in Genesis 11.

Now that's the type of strong statement we need to have in our Christian institutions. How refreshing to find a Christian college that is prepared to make such a statement with such detail to do their best to not allow the secular religion of this age (humanism, which encompasses millions of years/evolution) to in any way infiltrate the college and undermine the authority of God's Word — and lead young people down the path of doubt to unbelief! I challenge Christian colleges, churches, etc., to begin to reconsider their statements of faith to see how they can be strengthened in this area that has involved so much compromise in today's world.

Just as an encouragement, here is the text of a letter I received from the president of Northland International University (one of the few Christian universities that stands on a literal Genesis):

> Dear Friends at Answers in Genesis,
>
> Thank you for the incredible support you have been to Northland International University. As we prepare this next generation of leaders, we do it in a postmodern era where God has been left out, the idea of absolute truth has been jettisoned, and society has been thrown into a moral free fall.
>
> You have rightly identified this battle as a battle for the authority of the Word of God. If we cannot believe what God has clearly stated in Genesis 1–11, how can we trust the rest of the Bible? We fully concur with your doctrinal statement and in this foundation: God's Word is inspired, infallible, inerrant, and sufficient. It is trustworthy in every way. We also believe that true science confirms what God has said.
>
> Thank you for the investment you have made in our undergraduate and graduate programs, for the exceptional teaching, and abundant resources. We hope to build stronger ties with AIG and give our full support.
>
> Your friend,
> Matt Olson, President, Northland International University,
>   http://www.ni.edu

There are very few well-known Christian leaders who are willing to take a vocal stand on taking the Book of Genesis as literal history. Thankfully, there are some leaders who have the boldness to make such an uncompromising stand, such as Pastor Johnny Hunt, Reverend Brian Edwards (UK), Dr. John MacArthur, and Dr. Albert Mohler, as well as a number of others.

Dr. Mohler is president of The Southern Baptist Theological Seminary in Louisville, Kentucky. At the 2010 Ligonier Ministries/Christianity.com conference "Tough Questions Christians Face," Dr. Mohler gave a presentation entitled "Why Does the Universe Look So Old?" In his conclusion, he declared:

> I would suggest to you that in our effort to be most faithful to the Scriptures and most accountable to the grand narrative of the gospel, an understanding of creation in terms of 24-hour calendar days and a young earth entails far fewer complications, far fewer theological problems, and actually is the most straightforward and uncomplicated reading of the text as we come to understand God telling us how the universe came to be and what it means and why it matters."[10]

"Truth"

President Greg Hall was recently teaching a class at Warner University on the topic of the authority of Scripture. During the discussion, he posed the question, "Do you believe the Bible is true?" Almost everyone in the class agreed that it is true but not everyone. A few found the question impossible to deal with. One student said, "It depends what you mean by 'truth.'"

Greg said, "Truth is that which corresponds to reality."

The students brought up the so-called errors and contradictions in the Bible — and the need to be able to interpret the text given the cultural setting, etc. They said the Scripture is "true in what it affirms" (a statement that is, in and of itself, almost completely meaningless). Greg publicly defended the Scripture in front of the whole class, affirming that the Bible does correspond to objective reality, that it is a book that accurately describes life as we experience it, that it tells the truth about historical events, and is reliable in every issue that it speaks to.

Then Greg pulled the students aside privately into his office for deeper discussion. He took a stand, being concerned not only for the students' well-being but for the possible compromise that their influence would have on the class and the school. The compromise that we're seeing in Christian colleges always centers on this: what we believe about the inspiration, inerrancy, and infallibility of Scripture. *This is the issue.* The authority of Scripture is a central point of faith. If you don't get the first two chapters of the sacred text right, you cannot get the rest right either.

Unfortunately, the survey revealed little consistency in these issues, showing the great number of people in Christian institutions who are conflicted about what they truly mean by what they say.

#8 Do you believe that the Bible is literally true?

No 5.3%

Yes - 93.9%

Young Earth

No 19.0%

Yes - 79.1%

Old Earth

What is the truth? That depends on who you ask and their particular viewpoint or interpretation of the Scripture. In the above table, note virtually all young-earth believers, 93.9%, believe the Bible is literally true. It is surprising this number is not higher. Also, nearly four in five who adhere to an old-earth theory believe the Bible is literally true. Keep in mind these two concepts are polar opposites. These findings quickly reveal the large number of Christian leaders who are mistaken and hold a biblical position contrary to the literal interpretation of God's Holy Word. This is extremely important to understand because once a Christian accepts a non-biblical view, they must then accept other non-biblical ideas to fulfill the logic of their error.

The so-called gap theory is a great example of this. Many great Christian leaders of the past 200 years have been gap theorists. They thought fitting the millions of years into a supposed gap in Genesis 1 was a way of dealing with the issue. In that sense, I have a much greater respect for such people than I do for those proposing theistic evolution or other old-earth views that reinterpret much of the Bible to mean something other than what it says. Theistic evolutionists, day-agers, advocates of the framework hypothesis, etc., are reinterpreting the clear teaching of Scripture to fit millions of years, and often Darwinian-type evolution, into the Bible (be it geological, astronomical, or biological evolution).

I say that the gap theory does (in spite of contrary intentions of godly men) "unlock a door" to allow a "crack" to undermine Scripture, and thus even great men (who were head and shoulders above people like me theologically) were inconsistent in this area. If one allows a crack in the door (as we would see the gap theory doing), then the next generation will open it further. It usually doesn't get shut by the next generation.

In chapters 3 and 5, we will look more closely at the results of this survey. The news does not get better. As we look into the issues more deeply, you'll see reasons to become more and more concerned about what is happening — and it's not just about secular campuses but about the infiltration that is taking place in Christian institutions. We have nearly 100 percent agreement on New Testament issues, but when we get back to Genesis, we can clearly see that changes. They don't typically discuss different "theories" about the virgin birth or the Resurrection, but they definitely discuss different "theories" about how things came into being in Genesis!

Overall, we found that only 24 percent of the 312 people surveyed answered every question correctly . . . and these are the "good guys"! These are the institutions that require testimonies of faith from their professors or have strong religious affiliations. Please understand this: if you send your students to a Christian college or institution, three out of four times they will stand in front of teachers who have a degraded view and interpretation of Scripture.

We do understand the "world" is the enemy and what those in the world say doesn't surprise us. But we should be dismayed and shocked at what is happening in the Church. A trumpet is making an uncertain sound — and our children are increasingly becoming the casualties.

Like it or not, we are at war — "a war of worldviews," as Greg Hall will describe in the next chapter. We've been fairly aware of our fight with the secularists who deny God and adhere to humanism where man's thinking rules. What most families are not aware of, however, is the depths to which these influences have infiltrated Christian institutions.

And most parents aren't finding out until it's too late.

Endnotes
1. For a full list of the colleges that took part in the survey, go to creationcolleges.org.
2. For a full list of the colleges that took part in the survey, go to creationcolleges.org.
3. A young earth is a corollary for trusting the Bible as the authority — having six normal days of Genesis 1 (which are almost negligible), about 2,000 years from Adam to Abraham (Genesis 5 and 11), about 2,000 years from Abraham to Christ (genealogies and scholars generally agree on this), and about 2,000 years from Christ until today.
4. Larry E. Dahl and Donald Q. Cannon, editors, *The Teachings of Joseph Smith* (Salt Lake City, UT: Bookcraft, 1997), p. 345–347.
5. William Dembski, *The End of Christianity: Finding a Good God in an Evil World* (Nashville, TN: Broadman & Holman Academic, 2009), p. 159.
6. Bruce Waltke, "Why Must the Church Come to Accept Evolution?" http://biologos.org/blog/why-must-the-church-come-to-accept-evolution/, posted March 24, 2010; accessed and downloaded March 29, 2010; pulled from the website on about April 2, 2010.

7. *The Chicago Statement on Biblical Inerrancy,* International Council of Biblical Inerrancy, Dallas Theological Seminary Archives, 1978.
8. Henry M. Morris, *King of Creation* (San Diego, CA: Creation Life Publishers, 1980), p. 45–46.
9. Henry M. Morris, "The Days Do Matter," *Back to Genesis*, No. 190 (October 2004).
10. http://www.christianity.com/ligonier/?speaker=mohler2.

Chapter 2

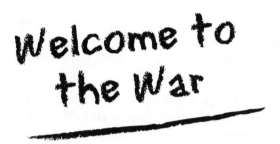

Welcome to the War

Greg Hall
President of Warner University

The fool has said in his heart, "There is no God" (Ps. 14:1).

We are at war. We are at war with weapons far greater than any bomb, missile, or gun. And these weapons are aimed at targets far more strategic than any building, land mass, or army, because "our struggle is not against flesh and blood, but against the rulers, against the authorities, against the powers of this dark world" (Eph. 6:12; NIV). We are at war against thoughts, thoughts raised up *against* the knowledge of God. And these thoughts are aimed at the minds of our children.

In the secular arena, the battle is often blatant, where the best the Christian can hope for are the condescending glances of those in power. In the Christian arena, however, the battle is often much more subtle. If the survey taught us anything, it's that the battle has now come home again, where many — if not almost all — of our Christian institutions of higher learning are turning out to be "already compromised" to one degree or another.

It is spiritual warfare. There is a great deal at stake: our culture, our well-being, our way of life . . . but most importantly, the hearts and minds of our youth. It has been said that (from a human perspective) the Church is always only one generation away from extinction. Here in the 21st century, we have come face to face with that reality. We live in a time when we must "demolish arguments and every pretension that sets itself up against the knowledge of God, and we take captive every thought to make it obedient to Christ" (2 Cor. 10:5; NIV).

One national publication recently proclaimed that the United States is no longer a Christian nation.[1] This has been a long time coming, but it has not come by accident. Yet we also know that the gates of hell themselves cannot stand against the Church as she takes the light of truth into enemy territory (Matt. 16:18). The anti-Christian, atheistic segment of our culture has become very militant.[2] What were once skirmishes between the two sides is now open warfare. The prominent players in this anti-Christian movement and the books they have written include Dr. Richard Dawkins, *The God Delusion*; Dr. Sam Harris, *The End of Faith*; Dr. Victor Stenger, *God: The Failed Hypothesis*; Christopher Hitchens, *God Is Not Great*; and Dr. Michael Onfray, *The Atheist Manifesto*. They all talk about the final battle being against Christianity.

Nobel laureate Dr. Steven Weinberg writes: "Anything that we scientists can do to weaken the hold of religion should be done and may in the end be our greatest contribution to civilization."[3] At the core of all these so-called scientists and educators is the commitment to Darwinism (with its tenets of evolution and millions of years) — and unless you think I am talking about a few militant educators/writers, consider that a recent poll of the National Academy of Science shows only 7 percent of this group consider themselves believers.

Virtually every student in America who goes through public education is required to read text books written by this group. Thank God that a remnant of committed Christian educators exists in grade school, high schools, and colleges and universities. They are among those who understand the deception that can happen at all levels of education — those who take a daily stand for truth, who believe and teach that the best explanation for the existence of the universe is stated in the Bible beginning with "In the beginning God created the heavens and the earth" (Gen. 1:1).

This creation versus evolution/millions of years debate is as current as this morning's newspaper. All over this land, school boards now debate with teachers and townspeople whether their schools should teach only evolution and keep creation only in the realm of what they define as religion. It is such a hot topic that during the presidential campaign season, candidates from both parties were asked their position on the topic.

The following militant atheists are the people our secular college and university students and faculty are paying attention to. What are they saying? Listen to a brief compendium of thoughts directly from their literature and you will get an idea of what we are up against:

- Dr. Francisco Ayala: "Life is the result of a natural process, without any need to resort to a Creator."[4]
- Dr. William Provine: "Modern science directly implies that there are no inherent moral or ethical laws and, when we die, we die."[5]
- Dr. Steven Pinker: "Religion taught men to believe in an immortal soul, modern science has destroyed that belief."[6]
- Christopher Hitchens writes "of the moral superiority of atheism."[7]
- Dr. Douglas Futuyma: "By coupling undirected, purposeless variation to the blind, uncaring process of natural selection, Darwin made theological or spiritual explanations of the life processes superfluous."[8]
- The National Association of Biology Teachers (NABT) asserted that all life is the outcome of "an unsupervised, impersonal, unpredictable, and natural process."[9]

These people consider themselves brave pioneers, teaching the *truth* about man's origin and facing death and extinction with valor. They worship at the altar of Darwinian evolution. They are, I am convinced, more interested in promoting their philosophic anti-Christian agenda than a scientific one. Their agenda is very simple: get the biblical God out of the picture and replace it with a humanistic worldview (i.e., man is the ultimate authority to determine truth apart from God; Darwinism is arguably the most popular form of humanism). And they have figured out exactly how to do it. This was stated nearly 30 years ago in a magazine called *The Humanist*:

> I am convinced that the battle for humankind's future must be waged and won in the public school classroom by teachers who correctly perceive their role as the proselytizers of a new faith: a religion of humanity that recognizes and respects the spark of what theologians call divinity in every human being. These teachers must embody the same selfless dedication as the most rabid fundamentalist preachers, for they will be ministers of another sort, utilizing a classroom instead of a pulpit to convey humanist values in whatever subject they teach, regardless of the educational level — preschool day care or large state university. The classroom must and will become an arena of conflict between the old and the new — the rotting corpse of Christianity, together with all its adjacent evils and misery, and the new faith of humanism.[10]

They have made the battleground public education where they have a captive audience. They represent the ideas of a secular culture that is determined to eliminate any reference to the God of the Bible as the sovereign

Creator of the universe. They know they can easily change these concepts in the culture by implanting them daily into the minds of impressionable youth — our children. And they have sadly, in large measure, succeeded.

The Body Count

Steve Henderson, president of *Christian Consulting for Colleges*, has researched the faith commitments of college students at evangelical and secular colleges. Read what he says:

> A few years ago, George Fox University professor Gary Railsback, a fellow researcher, prepared an interesting study. Using his data, I determined that more than 52 percent of incoming freshmen who identify themselves as born-again upon entering a public university will either no longer identify themselves as born-again four years later or, even if they do still claim that identification, will not have attended any religious service in over a year. This means over half of our kids are reporting a rejection of family religious values if they attend a public university.[11]

A recent press release on the ongoing *National Study of College Students' Search for Meaning and Purpose* offered some interesting information on students who are beginning their college years. While 79 percent of all freshmen believe in God, 69 percent pray, and 81 percent attend religious services at least occasionally, 57 percent question their religious beliefs, 52 percent disagree with their parents about religious matters, and 65 percent feel distant from God.[12]

In a revealing study, UCLA Higher Education Research Institute tracked 16,000 high school seniors from freshman days to graduation, demonstrating the impact of college choice on spiritual commitment. The 16,000 kids identified themselves as "born-again" in high school. Upon graduation, 52 percent no longer considered themselves Christian.[13]

College students are asking deep questions about their faith. Unless they are at a solidly biblical Christian college, they may find themselves in an environment that is not conducive to providing supportive answers. Even if they are at a Christian college, our research has proven that they may be getting hit with "friendly fire," as professors they consider to be allies attack the foundations of their faith with liberal, compromising ideas that undermine biblical authority, create doubt, and can lead to unbelief.

A March 29, 2005, *Washington Post* article by Howard Kurtz titled "Study Finds College Faculties a Most Liberal Lot" reports that most faculty at non-Christian colleges disdain Christianity, with 72 percent indicating they are liberal, 84 percent favoring abortion, and 67 percent indicating homosexuality is acceptable. In most cases, students reflect the values of college faculty they encounter in their upper division coursework. These faculty members are typically the advisors and mentors of students. Certainly the above findings indicate that the answers and directions students receive from most faculty at these institutions will not be supportive of traditional morality and religious values.

After sharing this study in a message in an evangelical church, I had a woman call me the following morning. She was very polite and asked if she could comment on my Sunday sermon. I had shared this study and attempted a strong advocacy for Christian higher education.

She politely suggested I might want to change my sermon. She explained I had offended her daughter by my remarks, home from a semester at a major public university. She felt I had been too hard and unreasonable in my comments about secular public education. I apologized for creating this offense but told her I honestly believed in what I said. She still suggested I moderate my comments but added as we ended our conversation, "In all honesty, I must tell you, my daughter was in church yesterday for the first time in a year."

According to the research, this woman's daughter is not alone. Scores of parents are spending a significant amount of their savings to pay for an education that is undercutting the foundations of Christian faith! Scores of parents are unwittingly paying the way for educators to destroy the beliefs of their children (Prov. 22:6). You have to admit, that's pretty clever on secularists' part — and pretty foolish on the parents' part.

Infiltration in the Ranks

I do find, however, that students have little problem understanding that the enemies of God will stop at nothing to discredit the Scripture. What they don't understand, though, are the numbers of Christian institutions, ministries, churches, pastors, and Christian educators who are doing the same. But in many ways, these influences are more dangerous: they are a lurking and growing enemy within our own camp. In the worst of cases, these people are wolves in sheep's clothing, many times very intentionally leading students away from the authority of the Scriptures while posing as our friends (Matt. 7:15).

My point is this: I cannot take the position I have on secular education and not be honest about the issues related to Christian education, too. I find folks want simple explanations of what is really taught at Christian schools, and they have a right to know. I believe in the significance, importance, and eternal value of a Christ-centered education. Yet it is only honest to say that it is very, very important to be discerning when choosing Christian schools, too.

My life in Christian higher education has been amazingly fulfilling. I have met some wonderful and committed believers. I have had association with numerous outstanding Christian institutions making a difference in countless lives in expanding the kingdom. I will remain an outspoken advocate for Christian education as a tool God uses to raise up new generations of competent and caring individuals.

There is, however, an issue that persists — one that needs to be addressed or some Christian institutions will find their influence diminished or, in the future, nonexistent. The issue is this: the spiritual well-being for many students is hindered and not enhanced while attending Christian schools. The church knows this and is miffed by it. Some people find it unacceptable and will encourage some of their youth to attend secular institutions as a result. Over the course of 35 years in ministry (nearly 20 as a college/university president), I have heard this issue raised over and over again, sometimes with deep contempt.

I am sure the loss of spiritual vitality of some students is a matter of personal discontent that is no fault of any institution. But some of the stories deal directly with who we are and what we do. In those cases, we must own the problem and deal with it. The Church wants and needs to be strong. It does not want to hear stories about young people whose lives are hurt by our schools instead of helped. They do not want to hear their faith was disassembled in the classroom by those who discredit the Scripture or have a view of the Christian faith that is far afield from orthodox Christian belief.

However, I do acknowledge there are still a number of faithful people, terrific scholars among them, who believe the Bible to be true in every way (these people should be encouraged and prayed for; we need more of them). I have heard other scholars say that "the Bible is true in all it affirms" (whatever that means), but they go on to say that it was never intended to be an academic text and should be trusted only in matters of faith, not matters of science. That equivocation is heresy to me, considering that *all* the treasures of wisdom and knowledge are hidden in Christ (Col. 2:3, and "*all* Scripture is given by inspiration of God, and is profitable for doctrine, for reproof, for correction, for instruction in righteousness" (2 Tim. 3:16; NKJV, emphasis added).

Based on research, we find that many of today's young people are being contaminated by the very people parents trust with their children's spiritual training. In most cases, the students are not being prepared for the spiritual battle we observe daily in our culture.[14] Sadly, they are becoming casualties of this battle — but casualties caused from those supposedly on their side of the battle. If this was a matter of a few select personal instances that would be one thing — yet still a cause for concern. However, there are far too many instances and far too many testimonies of what went spiritually wrong. This is a matter of spiritual concern for Christian institutions everywhere. The *Grand Rapids Press* ran a survey of colleges in Michigan recently and stated:

> In a recent survey of area colleges and universities, *The Press* found all of the institutions that teach biology teach Darwinian evolution. Only one, Cornerstone University, questions the theory's validity and spends significant time teaching alternative explanations. Even most of the Christian schools — Calvin, Hope, and Aquinas colleges — base their curricula on Darwin's theory.
>
> "Evolution is the paradigm out of which we teach biology," said David Warners, a biology professor at Calvin. "We're not trying to hide things; it's just that we're not looking for a fight."

Notice that they say they are "not looking for a fight"; this helps reveal that they realize that what they are teaching *is in opposition* to the Church's teachings! Even at the one university where evolution is questioned, some professors base their teaching on Darwin. The article continues:

> Bultman notices many students enter Hope with a "creationist/ intelligent design" worldview, he said, and are frustrated by the biology curriculum. Warners said there is a similar trend at Calvin, as many students begin college as strong opponents of evolutionary theory.
>
> "It's a challenge," Warners said of teaching evolution, "and it needs to be done very sensitively."[15]

In other words, these Christian colleges strategically take students who believe the Bible and systematically destroy that belief and teach them to believe in evolution. This is the sad state of the Church in America. No wonder we are losing the coming generations! Dr. R.C. Sproul recently sent out this warning:

> The classroom is not a place where open debate is usually encouraged. To the contrary, on the campuses of many universities and even seminaries, open season has been declared on Christian students. For some reason, it seems that professors in such settings take delight in trying to undermine the faith of their students. . . . In most cases, it is easy for a man or woman with a doctorate in years of experience in higher education to humiliate a student, no matter how strong the student's faith is or how articulate the student may be.

If you're looking to send your children to an institution that has a Christian history or a Christian relationship, do not assume that the current faculty is fully persuaded of the truth claims of Christianity. You may indeed be throwing your children into the fire of crucible they are not expecting and are not really prepared to withstand. I am not for educating people in a sheltered environment where there is no interaction with the secular mindset and with pagan worldviews, but we need to be fully prepared to understand when and where those worldviews come into collision with Christianity and how to avoid collisions that may be disastrous.[16]

Is my institution free from this problem and do we exhibit perfect fidelity to all matters of Christian teaching? Frankly, no; we've had our issues. As with all schools, some of the criticism is fair and some of it is not. But no matter what, it's time for all of us to do some self-evaluation, even as we do our best to discern the content and intent of others (Luke 6:41–42).

There are probably still a good number of people who think that the time-honored foundation of the Christian tradition is at the core of our educational system today. Not so. To believe this system is undergirded by biblical principles is entirely false. Not only is our educational system not based on Christian principles, but there is a growing hostility in educational circles, especially in higher education, toward all things Christian. And it all has to do with worldview. If you are not familiar with this raging battle for the minds of humanity, please turn to appendix B. It is simply imperative that you understand what is happening and how it affects our education system at all levels. For example, biologist Dr. Richard Lewontin says of science education:

> The objective . . . is not to provide the public with knowledge of how far it is to the nearest star, and what genes are made of. The problem is to get them to reject irrational and supernatural explanations of the world.[17]

The anti-God perspective has obviously gained a foothold in our public education system. That comes as no surprise when you consider who is behind this and how militant they have become toward Christianity. Christopher Hitchens writes:

> How can we ever know how many children had their psychological and physical lives irreparably maimed by the compulsory inculcation of faith? If religious instruction were not allowed until the child had attained the age of reason, we would be living in a quite different world.[18]

Again, Dr. Lewontin writes:

The objective . . . is to get them to reject irrational and super-natural explanations of the world, the demons that exist only in their imaginations, and to accept a social and intellectual apparatus, science as the only begetter of truth.[19]

Or, how about this quote from Dr. Richard Dawkins:

How much do we regard children as being the property of their parents? It's one thing to say people should be free to believe whatever they like, but should they be free to impose their beliefs on their children? Is there something to be said for society stepping in? What about bringing up children to believe manifest falsehoods? Isn't it always a form of child abuse to label children as possessors of beliefs that they are too young to have thought out?[20]

These ideas and philosophies are the foundation of the curriculum of public education and *have infiltrated* Christian education at almost all levels. Your children may be captive in a system intent on discrediting Christianity. It is not surprising that this is the intent of the secularist educators. What is surprising is that so many Christian parents seem to not care.

The central issue is this: as Christian leaders it is time to face the issue of just how committed we will be to the authority of Scripture. It is also time to answer to the Church for this problem. It is time to realize that it is possible to hurt young minds. With vigilance we must work to put our young people in classes taught by professors who are committed believers, who even though they might require students to think and develop their own faith, will not compromise Christian truth and exchange it for a liberalism or unbelief that breaks faith instead of building it.

I pray that the tone of this book will, if needed, castigate and challenge, but also build unity and nurture the Body of Christ. I am absolutely for "hammering" both secular and Christian institutions — but doing so in a way that asks the Church to "wake up" and be the "jury" in this matter of taking responsibility for the education of our youth. We must teach both parents and students to discriminate and do so in a way that builds the Kingdom of God, not breaks it.

Where England is today spiritually (it is all but dead), the USA will be tomorrow if we keep heading in this direction. In the research we saw that our kids were *already gone* from the Church. Now we see it in the Christian colleges and the universities that are following in the footsteps of the Ivy

League — those that are *already compromised*. In order to protect ourselves and our children, we must be prepared to fight in the battle of the world-views. But in order to do that, we must be aware of where the attacks are coming from. And as you will see in the next chapter, the source of compromise is coming from a very unexpected place.

Endnotes

1. *Newsweek,* February 2009
2. Interestingly, this is without warrant by their worldview. In an atheistic worldview, nothing matters, so why care enough to oppose Christianity? The fact that they oppose Christianity reveals they really don't believe what they profess to believe.
3. Remarks by Steven Weinberg at the Freedom from Religion Foundation, San Antonio, November 1999.
4. Francisco Ayala, "Darwin's Revolution," in John Campbell and J. W. Schoff, eds., *Creative Evolution* (New York: James & Bartlett Publishers, 1994), p. 4–5.
5. Cited by Kenneth R. Miller, *Finding Darwin's God: A Scientist's Search for Common Ground Between God and Evolution* (New York: Harper Perennial, 1999), p. 171.
6. Steven Pinker, "Is Science Killing the Soul?" A dialogue with Richard Dawkins and Steven Pinker (London, February 10, 1999).
7. Christopher Hitchens, "The Future of an Illusion," in *Love, Poverty and War: Journeys and Essays* (New York: Nation Books, 2004), p. 334.
8. Douglas Futuyma, *Evolutionary Biology* (Sunderland, MA: Sinauer, 1986).
9. "NABT Unveils New Statement on Teaching Evolution," *The American Biology Teacher* 68, no. 1 (January 1996): 61. The NABT statement created such an uproar that the organization subsequently dropped the words "unsupervised" and "impersonal." The change was largely cosmetic, however, since the remaining words "unpredictable" and "natural" were understood to mean essentially the same thing.
10. J. Dunphy, "A Religion for a New Age," *The Humanist* (Jan.–Feb. 1983): p. 23, 26.
11. "A Question of Price Versus Cost," *Christianity Today,* March 2006.
12. *Christianity Today,* March 2006, p. 86.
13. *Christianity Today,* March 2006, p. 87.
14. One way to start getting prepared is by reading the New Answers Book Series, by Master Books, that answers around 95 of the top questions surrounding the creation/evolution and biblical authority debate.
15. "150th Birthday of 'On the Origin of Species' Prompts Area Colleges to Assess Darwin's Impact," *Grand Rapids, Michigan, Press* (September 26, 2009).
16. R.C. Sproul, "Be Prepared," *Tabletalk Magazine* (November 1, 2010).
17. Richard Lewontin, "Billions and Billions of Demons," *New York Review of Books,* January 9, 1997.
18. Christopher Hitchens, *God Is Not Great: How Religion Poisons Everything* (New York: Twelve Books, 2007), p. 217, 220.
19. Richard Lewontin, "Billions and Billions of Demons," *New York Review of Books,* January 9, 1997.
20. Cited by Gary Wolf, "The Church of the Non-Believers," *Wired,* November 2006; Richard Dawkins, *The God Delusion* (Boston, MA: Houghton-Mifflin, 2006, 2008), p. 315.

Chapter 3

Conflict between the Classrooms

Ken Ham

> But now there are many members, but one body. And the eye cannot say to the hand, "I have no need of you"; or again the head to the feet, "I have no need of you" (1 Cor. 12:20–21).

I was having lunch with a highly educated man some time ago when he turned and asked with a slight air of cynicism, "Do you take a religious view of Genesis or the scientific view?"

I responded this way, "Let me ask you a question. Can you define for me in the context of this conversation what you mean by the term 'scientific'?"

There was a long silence. "Hmmm, I don't really know. I haven't really thought about that," he admitted.

Part of the problem we see in Christian colleges that are already compromised is that *most* people haven't thought about that! Most people think that the battle over creation and evolution is being fought between "science" and "religion." But there are two problems with this thinking:

1. Most people can't define the word "science," and thus they end up misunderstanding how the word is used in our modern world.
2. Most people have an incorrect understanding of the word "religion" and, as a result, falsely think in terms of neutrality and nonreligion versus religion.

The primary dictionary definition of the word *science* is basically "knowledge." We need to understand that one can have knowledge concerning what happened in the past (e.g., the origins issue). This is called "historical science." However, this knowledge is based on certain assumptions about the past. If the assumptions are wrong, the conclusions reached will likely be wrong and we will misunderstand history. Understanding the assumptions used to build historical knowledge is extremely important.

But knowledge gained by observation (five senses) and based on the repeatable test (empiricism) is called "observational" or "operational science." This is the knowledge that enables us to build our technology, understand how a cell works, and develop medicines.

When most people use the word science today, they are usually thinking in terms of "operational science." This becomes very confusing when secularists use the word science when talking about aspects of genetics that can be examined in a lab, and then turn around and use the word science when discussing the topic of nonobservable aspects of evolutionary ideas (e.g., life from nonlife, reptiles evolving into birds, etc.). Knowing that mutations in DNA can occur and be measured is not the same as asserting that we know how those mutations occurred in various populations over millions of years.

Because most people (including most students — and most professors) do not understand the distinction between historical (origins) and operational science, they wrongly think that the battle of origins is one of science versus the Bible. That is simply not true. It is a battle between two totally different accounts of the past — a battle between people holding to different accounts of the past based on the conclusions of historical science.

The role of operational (or observational/repeatable) science is that it can be used to confirm which historical science best explains the evidence. Operational science can be used to help confirm or deny which account of historical science is true. Historical science uses certain assumptions to arrive at conclusions about the past. If these assumptions are incorrect, they will lead to a false knowledge of the past.

Actually, creationists and evolutionists both have the same operational science but different accounts of origins based on the assumptions in their methods of historical science. This needs to be clearly understood so people don't incorrectly believe that creationists are against science! Creationists love science; we praise God for making a universe where operational science is possible and for the benefits it has brought to mankind through technology and understanding.[1] We also love historical science, but only when the assumptions used to understand the past are firmly rooted in what God has revealed to us in the Bible.

We wanted to detail the above for you so that as we continue this discussion aimed at understanding what is happening in our Christian colleges, we will be using the same definition of the word science. Unless otherwise stated, when we speak of *science* from this point on, we will be referring to observational or operational science — not historical science.

Also, when we use the word *religion* in our discussion, it will be used mostly in the context of Christianity. People need to understand that there is no nonreligious position. A religion is basically a system of belief held to with ardor and faith. Atheism is a religion, Islam is a religion, Secular Humanism is a religion, and so on. Although scientists will use operational science when discussing evolutionary ideas, there are also many aspects of belief (or religion) in embracing evolution as the explanation for the life we see on this planet (such as the belief that life arose by only natural processes from matter over time). This can be called a naturalistic worldview since it rejects supernatural explanations of the origin of the universe and the life that we find on this planet.

The same can be said for biblical creationists. We use operational science to help us understand the past. However, there is a major difference: we accept the supernatural account of origins revealed in Genesis as a core belief and use operational science to confirm those ideas. What anyone believes about origins is ultimately based in a faith about the past.

Most people falsely assume that the "facts of science" *support* evolution and millions of years, while biblical creation is supposedly a matter of "religious faith." We hear this type of rhetoric in the media all the time when both the secularists and the theists draw distinctions between the supposed scientific "fact of evolution" and an old earth, and the religious "faith of creation" and a young earth.

In other words, people, even in our churches, have been led to believe that real scientists will adhere to evolution while it is religious people who believe in creation. In fact, the numbers from the survey of Christian colleges prove the exact opposite: in many cases, it tends to be the scientists who believe in the Bible's account of origins and accordingly a young earth, while the majority of those in the religion departments embrace evolution and undermine the authority of Scripture!

When we look at the history of science, we see a remarkable list of amazing achievements (because of operational science) that have made life better in our world. Man's ability to think, critically analyze, experiment, and imagine have resulted in these remarkable achievements. Space shuttles, instant worldwide communications, satellites . . . operational science is propelling us forward at light speed. It's been a long time since Copernicus, Kepler, Galileo, and Einstein, but our knowledge in physics still continues to grow. Scholars research relativity to quantum physics to string theory in pursuit of an increasing knowledge of how our universe works.

Or consider the astounding advances in medical technologies and practices made possible by science. Greg was attending the University of Pittsburgh during the days the School of Medicine was developing transplantation technology. What was once almost science fiction is now commonplace surgery. Many lives have been saved as a result of this science. And this is just one example of how medical science has amazingly advanced. The growth in medical science has made it possible to understand the intricate workings of the human body. It has made it possible to diagnose an illness and develop cures for diseases once thought impossible to deal with. Formerly high-risk procedures such as heart surgery or organ transplantation have become routine.

Consider the science behind computer technology. Some of us can remember the days before the computer. Some can remember the first computers as massive instruments that could only do simple computations. Today, the average cell phone has far more computational power than the computer that sent the first man to the moon.

Yes, mankind has accomplished incredible things using science. But does a proper understanding of science really support the beliefs of the evolutionist? That was the assumption of the man I was having lunch with when he asked, "Do you take a religious view of Genesis or the scientific view?" His question opened up a really good discussion about historical science, operational science, and so forth. He had never even heard of it before. He (like most professors at these colleges) did not understand the distinction between beliefs about the past (historical science) and knowledge gained by repeatability and observation (operational science) that is used to build our technology. He was actually mixing a naturalistic view of origins (i.e., no supernatural/no God) with operational science.

Many a scientist has become a creationist when he is willing to look beyond the closed-minded presuppositions of the naturalistic worldview and when he opens his mind to using the historical science rooted in the Bible to build his way of thinking about the evidence. Then he can often clearly see that what he observes confirms the Bible's account of history.

We also have a growing number of people from the naturalist community who are looking at current evolutionary belief and saying, "We have some real problems here!" Many secularists don't want to discuss the problems, as they don't want people given even a hint that there could be problems with evolution and millions of years. They want naturalistic evolutionary explanations presented as fact, regardless.

Of course, those who already believe in the authority of Scripture are not surprised to find the scientific evidences confirm what they already know to be true from God's infallible Word.

Now, surprisingly, when it comes to Christian colleges, the creation/evolution/age-of-the-earth debate takes an interesting twist. The one department that you might think would be the most conservative in their beliefs, the religion department, turns out to be the most liberal — having dismissed what the Bible clearly teaches concerning certain events in Genesis in favor of the interpretation of evidence emanating from the naturalistic worldview.

The Science Department Versus the Religion Department

As was noted in earlier chapters, our survey was taken by 312 people at 200 Christian colleges and universities. The 312 were categorized into four different groups: college presidents, vice presidents, members of the religion department, and members of the science department. We will talk about the presidents and vice presidents in chapter 5, but for now, let's take a look at the responses of those who are actually in charge of teaching your kids in the classrooms of the religion and science departments.

First off, the heads of the science (teaching biology, physics, geology, etc.) and religion (teaching theology, Bible, etc.) departments showed unanimous agreement with important issues about Christ. With very little fluctuation, both the religion and science departments believe in the truthfulness of the New Testament. Both groups strongly affirmed the virgin birth of Christ, His substitutionary death on the Cross, heaven and hell, Christ's Second Coming, and the bodily Resurrection of Jesus Christ.

Second, their responses (even though we will later show serious issues with how these professors use language to suit their own ideas) to views about the nature of Scripture did not vary with glaring significance either.

Inspiration
Q19: Do you believe in the inspiration of Scripture?

	Religion Department	Science Department
Yes	100.0%	93.0%

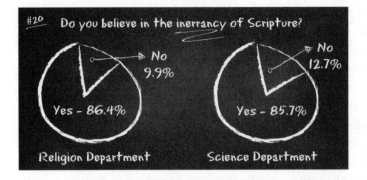

Q18: Do you believe in the infallibility of Scripture?

	Religion Department	Science Department
Yes	92.6%	88.9%
No	6.2%	11.1%

As you can see, the responses are fairly close, with the religion departments claiming a slightly higher view of Scripture than the science departments. But are the rest of their answers consistent with this claim of a high view of the Bible, or is this just more "newspeak"? Answers to more probing questions show the fuller picture:

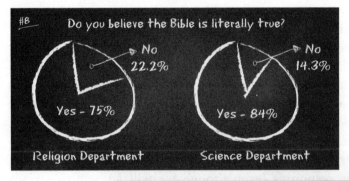

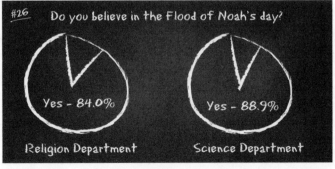

Q27: Do you believe the Flood was worldwide, local, or nonliteral?

	Religion Department	Science Department
Worldwide	56.8%	55.6%
Local	30.9%	41.3%
Nonliteral	12.3%	3.2%

Notice that while 75 percent and 84 percent said they believe the Bible is literally true, only slightly more than half of people from each department believe in a literal worldwide flood! Approximately 25 percent are being inconsistent in their answers. If they really believed the Bible is literally true, they would also believe in a literal interpretation of Genesis that clearly says the Flood was worldwide. But they don't.

How did they answer when we asked questions about creation and evolution?

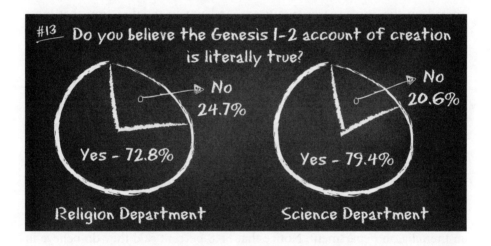

#13 Do you believe the Genesis 1–2 account of creation is literally true?

No 24.7%
Yes – 72.8%
Religion Department

No 20.6%
Yes – 79.4%
Science Department

Q15: Do you believe in the Genesis account of creation as written?

	Religion Department	Science Department
Yes	90.1%	84.1%
No	7.4 %	15.9%

Again, we see relatively high numbers regarding what they say they believe about creation, though the no answers by a significant percentage should greatly concern us in regard to what some professors at these Christian colleges are teaching our kids. But when we ask more specific questions, we begin to see stunning differences.

Q16: Do you believe in God creating the earth in six literal 24-hour days?

	Religion Department	Science Department
Yes	56.8%	71.4%
No	42.0%	27.0%

Q17: Do you believe in God creating the earth, but not in six literal days?

	Religion Department	Science Department
Yes	55.6%	27.0%
No	44.4%	71.4%

This question was so important that we asked it both ways. We first asked if they believed that the earth was created in six 24-hour days. Then we asked if they believed that the earth was created, but *not* in six literal days. The spread on the answers was significant, and not in the direction that most people would think. *It turns out that the science department is much more biblical in their beliefs than the religion department!* Notice in question 17 that only 27 percent of people in the science department believe in nonliteral creation days. Yet 55.6 percent of the people in the religion department believe in nonliteral creation days.

This question also revealed one of the more graphic examples of the "newspeak" that concerns us in regard to Christian colleges today. In the religion department, 72 percent said they do believe in a literal interpretation of Genesis 1–2, but then 55.6 percent turn around and say, "I do not believe in six literal days"!

Since we asked this question both ways, it also revealed further confusion in the religion department. Notice that 56.8 percent said they do believe in six literal days, and 55.6 percent do not believe in six literal days. Several people say they both believe and don't believe!

The survey confirmed what I have been seeing on Christian campuses for years. In general, the science department is more likely to hold to the more conservative point of view. The scientists are the ones that I think understand the difference between operational and historical science. Oftentimes the science department is trying to tell the religion department that they are in error. But the Bible professors often point to secular scientists (whose starting point is usually naturalism) to justify their beliefs.

The religion chairs and the Bible departments are choosing to be influenced by worldly philosophy rather than what the Bible clearly teaches concerning historical science and the facts of observational science that confirm the biblical record. This isn't surprising, considering most of them attended seminaries that adhere to compromise views such as the "documentary hypothesis," a theory that denies that Moses wrote a cohesive historical account of history in the first five books of the Bible. This theory became popular in the late 1800s and claims that the first five chapters of the Bible came from a variety of sources, that the compilers of the Bible borrowed from pagan creation accounts, and that Genesis was written using Babylonian myths and legends. Virtually every seminary, with very few exceptions, liberal or conservative, will teach this "documentary hypothesis" as truth, and nearly everyone teaching in religion departments today came out of that system. They are the ones who are discrediting the Scriptures, they are the ones who capitulate to naturalistic science textbooks, and they are the ones trying to compromise with the world rather than standing to defend the Word of God. Even some of the most historically conservative universities in the country struggle with this issue.

The division between the science and religion departments was most obvious in the question about the age of the earth.

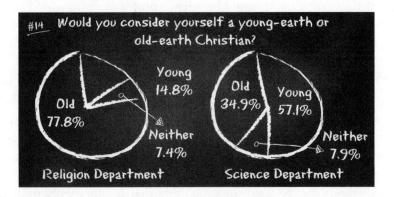

I find this result intriguing and very disturbing. Those who understand how things work on an operational scientific level are some of the strongest advocates for a biblical worldview. In our opinion, based on years of experience, even in the real conservative Christian colleges in America, the science professors, by and large, are the ones who often aggressively support and defend the biblical worldview . . . much more so than those in the religion (or Bible) departments!

Beyond that, the survey also showed that the science department is more aware of these differences than the religion department is. The religion department thinks everyone has the same view, but the science department tends to know better.

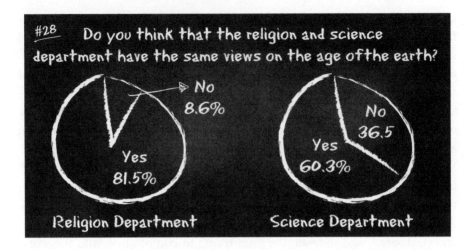

Because I have talked to so many professors at so many schools over the years, I wasn't surprised by this result. But what I am finding is that most Christian parents and students are stunned by this discrepancy. They still expect that, if anything, it would be science professors who would be more likely to lean toward evolution/millions of years and that religion professors would be more likely to lean toward a literal creation. But that's not the case — as the survey clearly shows.

When I engage liberals from the religion departments on these issues, most of them repeat the familiar mantra: "Science has proven that evolution/millions of years is true." But when I ask them for specifics, they often don't have much of a clue, as they are depending on some other authority. If I ask them why they believe in an old earth, they invariably answer, "Because of radiocarbon dating." But any scientist should know that the radiocarbon dating method can't be used for something that is supposedly millions of years old. It can only be used to go back 100,000 years at the most. And the presence of radiocarbon in fossils/deposits/diamonds claimed to be millions of years old contradicts such an old age, as after 100,000 years there would be no detectable radiocarbon.[2]

Can the religion department explain the existence of coal deposits and how they were formed? Can they explain the actual structure of the fossil record? Can they explain the assumptions behind radiometric dating methods? No, they can't. They just say, "Because science has proven . . ." when in reality, science has done no such thing. What they are really accepting is not operational science; they have simply given in to the worldly pressures from those in power who boldly and blindly hold to a naturalistic worldview.

I was recently at a campus where the leaders of the science department wanted me to get together with the religion department so that I could explain this to them. It can be very frustrating for the scientists because the Bible and religion departments of their own schools often won't listen to them. Instead, they listen to scholars who believe in ideas such as the documentary hypothesis and hold to a naturalistic worldview. This unwillingness to listen to creation scientists who trust the Bible can cause considerable consternation between the departments, leading to conflict for the students in regard to what they hear in the various classrooms.

It is surely worse than an eye saying to a hand, "I have no need of you." What is really happening is that many religion professors are, in reality, saying to their science colleagues, "I disagree with you!" It's worse because of the consequences of such compromise with the world: they are causing division that is impacting the souls of the students by undermining biblical authority and creating a doubt of God's Word that can lead to unbelief (Rom. 16:17).

There's no question that this problem is bigger than just colleges and universities. It's a problem at all levels of Christianity. Recently, even the Assemblies of God denomination has rewritten their theological belief statements in order to accommodate evolution and millions of years because they believe "science has shown" it to be true. Again, nothing could be further from the truth.

Science in Perspective

While we celebrate the mind-boggling advances in numerous fields of study made possible through scientific inquiry, it is important for students today to put science in proper perspective. To explain that perspective, let me ask you a question. Choose either comment A or B based on your understanding of science:

A. Science gives us objective knowledge of an independently existing reality.
B. Scientific knowledge is always provisional and tells us nothing that is universal, necessary, or completely certain about the world.

The reason this is an important question is that science education in our schools is solidly based on proposition A. This is exactly what you would expect from the science being driven by naturalistic philosophy. Many scientists have become very dogmatic, almost religiously so, about living up to proposition A. Most people believe that the knowledge scientists provide is objective and exists as an independent reality. The scientific method does work and it provides a knowledge of sorts. It is just not the absolute knowledge that secular scientists have claimed it to be.

Some, like Dr. Thomas Kuhn in *The Structure of Scientific Revolutions*,[3] have shown how scientific knowledge is developed. First, the scientist begins with a set of beliefs. These assumptions form the scientific educational process. At the center of the science education literature promoted in the majority of this nation's schools is the Darwinian concept of evolution. Naturalism, the philosophy at the center of most historical science, promotes the idea (in fact, works hard to sell it as truth) that the general laws and forces of nature are enough to explain the existence of the universe and everything in it. The naturalists have no use for a Creator; that concept is unnecessary for them.

This naturalistic science has a tendency to be less than honorable. It has a tendency to be less than academic. Students need to know these flaws and be able to explore them and discuss them and should be able to offer the explanation of the origin of life from Scripture free from the typical scorn and ridicule they receive from naturalistic scientists.

Why is it that scientists are so fearful of the debate with believers about the origin of life? Why cannot both beliefs of origin — creation and evolution — be discussed with students? Why do evolutionists attempt to control this conversation; is there something to hide? What is the real problem?

Astronomer and physicist Dr. Lee Smolin gives us the needed insight. He admits that if science concedes that the universe began at a point in time (some call it the big bang; I call it the moment of creation) then, he says, "It leaves the door open for a return of religion."[4] And that is a problem of biblical proposition for the naturalistic scientist, who, first and foremost, must get God out of the picture.

At the very heart of the science our students have been raised on is the assumption that there is absolutely no room for the supernatural or miracles in the explanation of the origin of life. The point must be made that this is a religious belief — the religious belief of naturalism or atheism. It is all about worldview. There was a time when the Christian faith promoted study and exploration because it was an "act of worship." Science began as the religious pursuit of knowing the mind of God, of learning to "think our thoughts after Him." In other words, the worldview used to understand the evidence in the present was built on God's Word.

Then came the presupposition that the Bible should be left out of the discussion. With this came the suggestion of an earth that had aged millions of years (geological evolution), followed by Darwin and his speculations (biological evolution). A scientific revolution followed that presented a natural explanation for all that exists with no further need for what was called religion as an explanation for anything (such as astronomical evolution like steady state or big bang and chemical evolution for the origin of life). As the famous evolutionary scientist Ernst Mayr writes, "The Darwinism revolution was not merely the replacement of one scientific theory by another, but rather the replacement of a worldview in which the supernatural was accepted as a normal and relevant explanatory principle by a new worldview in which there was no room for supernatural forces."[5]

This is how science became dishonest. How can anyone who claims to be a scientist turn aside categorically from anything that may be a useful or truthful understanding of the world around us? Yet, when it comes to investigating or promoting — even as a possibility — the creation of our universe and life by a sovereign Creator, they cast it aside. This is intellectual suicide and these scientists should know it . . . and so should the teachers in religion departments at Christian colleges that support and propagate such closed-mindedness.

The extreme some scientists and philosophers have gone to in order to maintain their naturalistic philosophy and keep God out of the picture is astounding. Dr. Francis Crick, in his book *Life Itself*,[6] seems to at least recognize that the origin of life has miraculous features and offers this theory: space aliens brought life to earth from some other planet. Dr. Crick is on the one hand a very serious scientist — the co-discoverer of DNA! On the other hand, perhaps he hopes this theory of his will be picked up by the *National Enquirer*.

Thankfully, there are many scholarly and intellectual scientists who are believers (such as those at organizations like Answers in Genesis and the Institute for Creation Research — and there are many who do leading research in the secular world). Today's student needs to turn to them for perspective and help.

Our survey clearly showed that some scientists and many professors of religion at Christian colleges seem closed to any way of inquiry other than science based in a naturalistic, materialistic philosophy — even though they would claim they believe God's Word as written. If there is a discrepancy between what the atheists say and what God's Word says about the natural world, they tend to defer to those who do not believe in God at all.

The Conflict in Perspective

Another open-ended question shed a great deal of light on these issues.

Q7: *What does your institution teach about science and faith?*

- We compare and contrast: 43.0%
- We teach science and God are one: 20.5%
- We teach science is valid: 17.6%
- We teach that there is no real conflict: 7.7%

In light of all the things we have discussed in this chapter, these answers are difficult to interpret because we have to ask, What do they mean by science? What is the worldview behind the "science" they are talking about? In *general*, science is usually defined as a worldview and philosophy that includes millions of years of evolution and anything that secular scientists say is true. It is built upon man's fallible ideas. If your science is based on assumptions that have already ruled out the possibility of God, then attempting to add God or the Bible to this requires one to change God's Word to fit with man's word. But if you approach the evidence from the starting point of God's Word, then the facts will have a very different interpretation: observational science will be shown to overwhelmingly confirm the interpretation as God's world agrees with what is recorded in God's Word.

What do these people mean when they say that they "compare and contrast science and faith"? Does that mean that they are teaching secular science alongside of the Bible and trying to get them to fit together? How about those who say that "science and God are one"? A scientist who believes in God could make this statement in good conscience, knowing that the results of operational science reflect the truth about the Creator who designed and brought everything into being. Others might say that "God and science are one" in an attempt to make the creation account in the Bible conform to the ideas of secular scientists who have a godless worldview. See the problem here?

When they say "science and God are one," do they really mean that evolution/millions of years and the Bible are one? When they say that science is valid, are they claiming that secular dating methods for the age of the earth are valid? We can't say so for sure, but this all has to do with how you define the word *science*.

If you define it in the way that it is commonly used today (that science cannot allow the supernatural, only explaining things from a perspective of naturalism), then this is a real mess. As we have stated, the word *science* means knowledge. Are they gaining knowledge by starting their thinking from God's Word or man's word? As the Bible teaches in several places, "The fear of the Lord is the beginning of knowledge" (and wisdom).

Certainly the other parts of the survey showed that the mess indeed exists. There is a strong movement in evangelicalism that is trying to make the facts of the Bible conform to the naturalistic worldview. But we must remember: the starting point determines your worldview, and therefore your interpretation. If you start with man's ideas (humanism) to develop your worldview, there's no question about where your conclusions will end up.

In the end, it's actually very difficult to determine what these people mean by what they say. Therefore, it is absolutely imperative that you ask clarifying and probing questions when you're evaluating a school, listening to a lecture, or even reading a written statement of faith. As we discovered in this survey, compromise can come at you from every direction. And in many cases, it will come from those who you might expect it the least — the religion and Bible teachers in Christian colleges and universities.

Let me again make an important distinction here: the battle is not between religion and science but between a biblical and a naturalistic worldview. Please understand this: the scientific method is an absolutely brilliant research paradigm (developed by a creationist, no less). The things that have been discovered and confirmed by using the scientific method have been an indispensable part of advancement in the modern world. The scientific method is perhaps the most beneficial tool, next to the Bible, for investigating the physical world in the history of mankind. Science is not the enemy. The enemy is a naturalistic worldview that is closed off to the possibility of the existence of God and that His Word is true and the only starting point to understand the universe that He created. It's not a matter of "science" versus "faith." The problem is that the naturalistic worldview has hijacked science in a way that has supposedly disproved the existence of God (because they started with that assumption, which is self-refuting anyway). Nothing could be further from the truth.

Christian leaders representing the Church need to stand up in this nation and condemn the compromise with the pagan religion of the age (millions of years/evolution — the pagan religion of the age to explain life without God) and stand for God's authoritative Word. Only then will we see God's blessing on the Church and the resulting change in the culture that is so needed.

I don't question whether such scholars are Christians, but we still need to point out their compromise of accepting man's opinions over God's Word. The problem with many Christian colleges is they will believe the science text written from a naturalistic worldview *first*, and the sacred text *later*. My heart is also taken by those, like many of my friends and colleagues, who love the Word, love God, love the Church, and, even if in some ways they may need to be "trained" in the truth, serve God out of sincere, heartfelt devotion.

Let there be no mistake: as believers committed to the authority of God's Word, we are facing an epic battle — a "collision of worldviews" in our churches, in the marketplace, and in the secular and Christian colleges and universities. And as you will see in the next chapter, the stakes could not be higher. At stake are our kids and how they will respond to the life-transforming truths of the gospel of Jesus Christ, who is the Way and the Truth and the Life.

Endnotes

1. In fact, few realize that committed Christians were often the ones who developed most fields of operational science (Mendel, Pasteur, Faraday, Newton, Galileo, and others).
2. L. Vardiman, A.A. Snelling, and E.F. Chaffin, editors, *Radioisotopes and the Age of the Earth: Results of a Young-Earth Creationist Research Initiative* (Santee, CA: Institute for Creation Research and Chino Valley, AZ: Creation Research Society, 2005).
3. Thomas S. Kuhn, *The Structure of Scientific Revolution,* Third Edition (Chicago, IL: University of Chicago Press, 1996).
4. Lee Smolin, *The Life of the Cosmos* (New York: Oxford University Press, 1997), p. 183, 264.
5. Ernst Mayr, "Evolution and God," *Nature* (March 1974): 285.
6. Francis Crick, *Life Itself* (New York: Simon & Schuster, 1981).

Want to know which colleges were contacted as part of the ARG study? Visit www.creationcolleges.org and also find a growing list of Christian colleges we recommend you search out.

Chapter 4

Worth Fighting For

Greg Hall

For what do righteousness and wickedness have in common?
Or what fellowship can light have with darkness? (2 Cor. 6:14; NIV).

When I was a student studying German, I was given an assignment to read an essay by the title *"Welche Religion ist die wehre?"* The translation: "Which Religion Is the True Religion?" The message of the essay was simply this: they are all true. Every person has their own religion and it is as true as the next person's religion.

This essay would fit well into our culture today. The spirit of our time is tolerance. There is no such thing as "truth." What is true for you may or may not be true for the next person . . . and who is to judge? Consequently, with tolerance and relativism as the prevailing way of thinking, Christianity is not in any sense unique. It is like all other religions of the world, and Jesus is one among many gods.

This is why the issue of the authority of Scripture is so paramount. When we see the compromise of the religion departments and (to a lesser degree) the science departments and the conflict that arises because they don't adhere to a unified worldview, we see the potential for relativism to find its way into the institution — just as it has time and time again in the

Ivy League and other schools that started strong and then lost the focus on the authority of Scripture.

And that's tragic, because the Bible carries the most precious and important of all messages.

The Uniqueness of Christianity

In some ways the religions of the world *seem* similar. All *seem* to advocate various ways to reach "god" or some form of greater "truth." Each religion generally has a commanding personality as a leader. The religions of the world each teach a system of belief that serves as some sort of moral basis for humankind. Most religions have ways of helping human beings relate to each other. If men and women seek peace and harmony and understanding of the world around them, each of the religions has something to say.

However, eventually each of the religions makes certain claims about things like the nature and character of God, how exactly man reaches this God, the prospects of life after death, etc. There we find the subtle and sometimes not-so-subtle distinctions among the religions. And then we must remember the concept of the law of noncontradiction and admit, as it suggests, that two contradictory ideas cannot both be true.

If you are interested in any religion for the express purpose of reaching God (which is religion's main purpose) I would like to point you to the main distinction between Christianity and other religions (and remember — ultimately there are only two religions: God's Word or man's word) because the significance of this distinction is eternal . . . and it's worth fighting for.

> *1. Christianity does not teach you how to reach for God. It teaches you how God has reached for us.*

This concept changes everything. It puts into perspective how religions function with considerations of a moral code and patterns of required behaviors and beliefs. This is how Christianity is unique. The emphasis is not on how or what you do but what's been done for you. What's been done is that God the Father, in His Son, Jesus, reconciled the world to Himself by the work of atonement (Col. 1:20), Jesus dying on the Cross for the sins of all who believe in His name (1 John 2:2; Rom. 10:9). It is not what we have done but what He did (Eph. 2:8). This points us in the direction of the most amazingly unique thing about Christianity when compared to all other religions — *the person of Jesus Christ.* Anyone seeking religious truth will be blown away by Jesus. He is so unique that Christians know Him to be both fully man and fully God. Christians call this the incarnation "God with us," Immanuel. Jesus has no rival in any aspect of His life:

- No one ever loved like He did.
- No one ever treated a person with dignity or respect like He could.
- No one ever taught what He taught or modeled a way of life like He did.
- No one ever was a better mentor.
- No one ever spoke like He did or commanded respect like He did.
- There is not one person in history who could approximate His wisdom or virtue.
- There has never been a healer like Him.
- No one ever prayed like He prayed.
- No man or woman has ever had a better friend.
- There is no scholar with His intelligence.
- No scientist has ever understood the physics of the universe like Him.
- There has been no other human who had His power — over the created order or over the human heart.
- No psychologist has ever understood the human mind like Him.
- No sociologist ever understood how cultures and societies function with the exception of Him.

He is not an icon representing a deity we do not know, understand, or relate to. No, He remains actively involved with His subjects, offering on a moment's notice help, support, guidance, wisdom, power, mercy, and love. He literally wrote the book on human existence and the history of the universe. As the author of life, He holds the keys for unlocking the mysteries of this life and the life to come.

He is Jesus, our Lord and God, and there is no other. "Salvation is found in no one else, for there is no other name under heaven given to mankind by which we must be saved" (Acts 4:12; NIV). There is no one as glorious as He.

The really glorious part of the uniqueness of the Christ of Christianity is that He solves a problem that, in our very honest moments, we all recognize we share in common.

2. Christianity teaches that mankind is born with a sinful nature since the Fall that wreaks havoc with virtually everything about life in this world.

This human nature is responsible for the vast evil and innumerable problems we face in every facet of life. As a group, humanity is broken. There is unimaginable empirical evidence that helps verify this, so we all know it. In our inner being, we know this problem requires a cure. No one has ever been able to cure themselves.

And so, while the other religions try to reach for God, Christianity teaches it is the other way around: He, through Jesus, reaches for us, a notion unique among all of the religions. In our hearts, we know it's true because God puts the evidence of the rightness of the cure of Christ deep in the human spirit. And "since the creation of the world God's invisible qualities — his eternal power and divine nature — have been clearly seen, being understood from what has been made, so that people are without excuse" (Rom. 1:20; NIV). The unchanging truth of the living, written Word of God attests to this. That is the primary and final testament to Jesus. That is why when people ask for evidence that Christianity is true, I say, "Look in your own heart and find the answer; it is there. There is a place in every human heart that only God can fill."

Who can you possibly compare to Jesus? He has no equal and no rival. When we are honest in our innermost being, we know that who He is and what He does is the truth for all humankind.

3. Christianity proclaims a unique urgency to believe.

In the other religions of the world, there is not the sense of urgency to believe the message of the religion like there is in Christianity. In most religions, man operates in his own strength, making every effort at self-improvement. Hinduism and Buddhism use techniques of meditation to deal with problematic issues of the "self." Judaism and Islam use rituals. They use these rituals to cope with the expectations of the law.

The God of Christianity does not ask for endless efforts of self-improvement. When it comes to measuring the condition of the human nature, He demands perfection. That is right. The standard for Christians is perfection; He settles for nothing less. *The Christian only receives this perfection by believing in the only real perfect man who ever lived, Jesus.* It is only by believing in the atoning, sacrificial death of Jesus upon the Cross as the payment for our sinful condition that the righteousness (perfection) of Jesus is imputed to everyone who believes. This is a response never conceived by any other religion. It is unique in every way.

Do you need evidence of the truthfulness of this message? Consider again your own heart. I really do believe most people in the inner sanctum of their own spirit know and comprehend the reality of this message (Romans 1 makes it clear there are no atheists — people suppress the truth in unrighteousness): we are sinners, unable to save ourselves, facing a holy God to whom we will give an account of our lives, a God who settles for nothing less than perfection. We also know in this inner place that it is Jesus — uniquely demonstrated to be God's Son and the only sacrifice He accepts that makes for peace with Him. The Creator has created the human heart with the capacity to know this truth.

And here, Christianity differs from other religions in the most profound way imaginable:

> *4. When it comes to the claims of Christ, you can reject them but you cannot ignore them.*

With the truth about Christianity as revealed in Scripture, you cannot pick and choose what you will accept (that is humanism, having yourself as the ultimate authority over God). You take it all or not at all. Many have attempted this, trying to select certain aspects of the truth while ignoring others. A good example of this strategy of trying to eliminate Scriptures that do not seem to apply to our case is Thomas Jefferson. He seemed drawn to Christ but did not buy His claim to be divine, to perform miracles, and to serve as the only way to reach heaven. So Jefferson devised his own version of the Scripture, *The Jefferson Bible*, where he literally cut out the parts of Scripture he did not want included. Don't be too hard on Mr. Jefferson; this is an oft-repeated phenomenon. People may not go to the extreme of actually dismantling the book, the Bible; they just do so in the confines of their hearts and minds. The problem is, we do not get to experience Christianity on our own terms, only His.

If Jesus is not one among many gods, and the message of Christianity is uniquely true, it would stand to reason that there is a sense of urgency about believing this truth. In a culture so relativistic, where tolerance is key and all ideas considered equally valid, it is a challenge to get even earnest believers to catch a vision of how urgent it is to get this message out. At the very least, it is so clear to see that the worldview of naturalism and the worldview of the Bible are absolutely at odds — oil and water that truly cannot be mixed.

How Christianity Got Marginalized

America has become an increasingly diverse nation, and that includes religious diversity. We are growing, and as a nation full of people from different faiths it stands to reason that their influences are going to be felt. If America has become a non-Christian nation due to this trend, it is a demographic issue. It also becomes a wonderful opportunity for those of us who are Christian to enter the marketplace of ideas and engage this diversity with a message we believe to be for all people, cultures, and religious backgrounds.

But, there is another reason we are not a Christian nation (or really "Christianized nation," as no nation has ever been truly a "Christian" one) any longer. Unfortunately, this reason doesn't have much to do with demographics. While there is reason to celebrate the changing diversity of America, there is reason to fear what is really happening. It is not that our Christian message suffers from diversity, it is suffering because, in the marketplace of ideas, it has been marginalized. It has been moved to the edges of society.

Through the ages, Christians have been among the greatest thinkers and influencers of life in this world. How many scientific innovations and inventions have been forged in the minds of godly men and women? How many great works of literature have been written by devoted followers of Christ? How many of the world's greatest institutions of service and learning were developed by Christian leaders and servants? How many humanitarians, public servants, community activists, and inspiring religious leaders are Christ followers? The list is amazingly impressive.

So what happened? Why are Christians not the major shapers and influencers of our culture like they once were? Why has the Christian faith been marginalized in recent times?

1. We Christians have abdicated our positions in the battle for the mind.

We lack talent, critical thinking skills, and a willingness to engage with intellectual vigor and rigor the ideas that compete for attention. Where is it today that Christians go to prepare themselves intellectually? Does the mind have a chance to grow in Sunday school? If you think Sunday school is intellectual and spiritual training for Christian youth, read *Already Gone*[1] and you will find out it is clearly not there. How about in our church worship services? Is this where we gain enough knowledge and wisdom to stand against the intellectual tide raging against us? It is not likely in a typical, consumer-driven church where worship is driven by personal preference and followed by the mind-numbing therapeutic pulpit. How about in our colleges, universities, and seminaries? Is this where Christian intellectual virtues are developed? Unfortunately, the answer to these questions is too often no. Where did we go? Answer: we went to the world. We sent ourselves to be among the liberal bastions of our culture that break faith instead of building it.

The current disposition of Christians seems to be anti-intellectualism. Faith, in many circles, has been trivialized or marginalized because we have lost the desire for critical thinking and sound scholarship. Dr. Os Guinness, in his book *Fit Bodies, Fat Minds*, says:

> Anti-intellectualism is a disposition to discount the importance of truth and the life of the mind. Living in a sensuous culture and an increasingly emotional democracy, American evangelicals in the last generation have simultaneously toned up their bodies and dumbed down their minds. . . . Evangelical anti-intellectualism is both a scandal and a sin. It is a scandal in the sense of being an offense and a stumbling block that needlessly hinders serious people from considering the Christian faith and coming to Christ. It is a sin because it is a refusal, contrary to the first of Jesus' two great commandments, to love the Lord our God with our minds.[2]

Feelings seem to be the dominant concern in the Church today. These concerns for the issues of the heart are completely legitimate. But it is only half the story. Christianity is a heartfelt experience, but it is an experience of the head as well. We are similar to the Tin Woodman in L. Frank Baum's *The Wonderful Wizard of Oz*, who chooses a heart rather than a head:

> "Why didn't you walk around the hole?" asked the Tin Woodman.
>
> "I don't know enough," replied the Scarecrow cheerfully. "My head is stuffed with straw, you know, and that is why I am going to Oz to ask him for some brains."
>
> "Oh, I see," said the Tin Woodman. "But, after all, brains are not the best thing in the world."
>
> "Have you any?" enquired the Scarecrow.
>
> "No, my head is quite empty," answered the Woodman; "but once I had brains, and a heart also; so having tried them both, I should much rather have a heart. . . ."
>
> "All the same," said the Scarecrow, "I shall ask for brains instead of a heart; for a fool would not know what to do with a heart if he had one."
>
> "I shall take the heart," returned the Tin Woodman; "for brains do not make one happy, and happiness is the best thing in the world."[3]

Too many Christians today have gone missing in action in the battle for the mind. Many have opted for the therapeutic happiness of the Christian subculture instead. Again, to quote Dr. Guinness:

Never mind that "heart" in the Bible is more a matter of understanding than sentiment — so "heart" versus "head" is a false choice. ... Ever since the mid-eighteenth century we evangelicals have had a natural bias toward the Tin Woodman's choice — empty brains and happy hearts.[4]

2. Christians have twisted the message of the gospel of Christ to the point that we repel men and women who are "unchristian," instead of attract them.

In his book *Unchristian*, David Kinnaman surveyed the new generation to find out what they really think about Christianity. The negative perceptions of Christians are striking. The secular world thinks Christians are hypocritical, too focused on getting converts, anti-homosexual, sheltered, too political, and judgmental.[5]

There are exceptions, of course. We all know genuine, authentic Christians who live much like Jesus before us; we are compelled by the overwhelming evidence of Christ in their lives. They are probably, in large measure, the reason many of us are Christians. But even if this research angers you or makes you cry "foul," can't you see its truthfulness, too?

The research of *Unchristian* rings true, and we have to admit that as Christians, we need to take responsibility for this dilemma. We can change this perception, one attitude at a time. We do so by presenting our faith winsomely, as a proposal of truth, not in the ways of putting others down or combativeness.

Recently I listened to a debate that happened several years ago on the subject of the origins of life between creationist Dr. Phillip Johnson of Berkeley and Dr. Will Provine of Cornell. These two great intellects really went at it. The intellectual interchange was magnificent. They pulled no punches and gave each other no slack. They were straightforward in their criticism and analysis of the other's argumentation.

This Stanford University debate, however, was not characterized by acrimony; quite the contrary. At one point in the proceedings, Dr. Will Provine explained to the students that even though they debate sharply, they have the utmost respect for each other as men; in fact, they will have dinner together when the debate is over. Our relationship with the world, as Christians, should be the same. We should be able to tell the opposition the truth, but do so in a way that's winsome and seen as a proposal to be considered for what we know to be true. We should be connected to and sincerely engaging with those who may vehemently disagree.

There is one final reason I feel that Christianity has been marginalized:

3. As we bought into our anti-intellectual Christianity geared toward personal preference and happiness, and as we have failed to produce a winsome intellectual approach to belief, the opposition seized the moment and monopolized the debate.

In the Stanford University debate between Dr. Phillip Johnson and Dr. Will Provine, a student asked a very perceptive question. She asked evolutionist Dr. Provine why in the debate of creation versus evolution it's so one-sided. Why is it so, she wanted to know, that across America only evolution is taught in public schools? Why is there such an uproar when a group of Christians here or there have tried to get creation science in schools and it is categorically denied? Dr. Provine said, "The answer is simple: evolutionists monopolize the debate."

They monopolize the debate and control the information. They teach in the colleges and universities of our nation. They write the textbooks our students read. These schools graduate the political leaders and school board members who make policy decisions on curriculum. We have eliminated ourselves from serious intellectual debate on this and other prominent social, political, or philosophical issues and have forfeited our right of influence.

A Call to Christian Soldiers

So what do we do about all this? We are in a war where subtle and militant attacks on the Bible continually bombard us. We have been marginalized and our voice has been largely muted in the marketplace and in the classroom. What do we do? How do we find our voice again and begin to speak the truth in love once more?

First, we clearly need to be continually developing our own biblically based worldview. If we understand the authentic truth, we will be unlikely to be fooled by the counterfeits. The biblical worldview, like Jesus Himself, is unique in its explanation of life and existence. The biblical worldview remains the only authentic explanation of the origin of life. The Scripture teaches humankind what we need to know about life's beginning and ending. It is a credible historical document with a perfect understanding of human nature and our place in the grand scheme of creation.

We need to understand that as Christians, all our thinking should begin with the revelation of God's Word. We need to know what it means to build a consistent Christian worldview and be able to correctly understand and interpret the facts of the present. We need to know what we believe and why we believe as we do.

We also need to understand that those who don't start with the Bible start with the fallible ideas of man. On this they build their worldview. Both Christians and non-Christians have starting points. The reason they interpret the same evidence in regard to origins differently is because of those different starting points. I highly recommend the book *The Ultimate Proof of Creation*, by Dr. Jason Lisle, to further understand how a person can learn to think logically and understand how to argue consistently in these matters.

Second, I think we need to become experts in evolution and the "millions of years" mindset. That's right. There is nothing to be afraid of. In fact, once students become familiar with what Darwinism is, how the age of the earth is interpreted from data, how these ideas gained notoriety, and an understanding of the numerous flaws in the thinking, it becomes clear that even many scientists know that evolution is an idea in serious trouble and millions of years is not proven fact. If students will research the issue, they will find many problems with the interpretations crucial to the foundation of evolution, the big bang, and the various dating methods. There is the myth of absolute dates from radiometric dating; the myth of strict uniformitarian geology; the myth of a gradualistic fossil record; the myth of beneficial information-adding mutations; the myth of natural selection as a mechanism for molecules-to-man evolution; the myth of evolution not contradicting the bio-genetic law; the myth of homology supposedly supporting evolution; the myth of the so-called missing links.

It is the case that biblical creation cannot be taught in the public schools today — something that clearly reflects a one-sided, closed-minded approach to education (closed-minded to any supernatural aspects). As believers, we should not want it said of us that we do not want our students to be exposed to such ideas. The Bible doesn't hide error from us, but it clearly speaks to us concerning the nature of the error and teaches us what we should believe. All of us need to know how to defend our faith, and as part of that, we need to understand how secularists think and how to combat their false religious ideas, including evolution and millions of years.

Third, we need to understand the basic tenets of naturalism. Most people are totally unaware that they live under the control of this worldview. It is up to us to explain it to them, show its consequences, and offer the biblical worldview as an alternative. (Again, I recommend the book *Ultimate Proof of Creation*.)

We consider the concept of a sovereign, all-powerful God who created the universe *ex nihilo* (out of nothing) to be the only logical position to take as an explanation for the origin of life. After all, why would there be laws of logic, the uniformity of nature, and the laws of nature if there were no God? These only make logical sense in the context of the infinite Creator God of the Bible. There is nothing philosophically or intellectually invalid about such a position. Unless, that is, someone comes into the discussion with a mind closed off to the possibility of God altogether (and they would no longer have a basis for uniformity, morality, or logic either!). If someone starts off closed-minded, "suppressing the truth" as Romans 1:20 states, they will not believe, no matter what evidence is presented to them. They first need to change their starting point. And only the Holy Spirit in a person's heart and mind can start that process.

A sovereign, all-powerful God can create what He desires out of nothing and, as our Scripture says, hold it all together. He can also decide to reveal Himself in meaningful ways to those who will believe, be it in nature around us, in the Word (Scripture) He gave, in the Son (Jesus) He sent us as His exact representation, or in the Spirit He left to live in His children.

Christian students need to be confident and assured that these Christian worldview tenets are philosophically, intellectually, and spiritually valid if by no other reason than that of the definition of God, let alone by the personal experience of believers. Your personal experience of God matters in this discussion!

But this will require a new kind of thinking for a new generation of Christians. Romans 12:2 is an often-cited Scripture on this subject: "Don't copy the behavior and customs of this world, but let God transform you into a new person by changing the way you think" (NLT).

David Kinnaman puts it like this:

> We are learning that one of the primary reasons that ministry to teenagers fails to produce a lasting faith is because they are not being taught to think. This gets to the core of the get-saved perception: young people experience a one-size-fits-all message that fails to connect with their unique sensibilities, personality, or intellectual capabilities. Young people desperately need to be taught to process the rich complexities of life, to probe and test and stretch their faith from the perspective of a Christ follower.[6]

And this new kind of thinking needs to begin *now*. There is no time to waste. Today is the day of action for soldiers of truth to take up the Bible, the sword of truth, and run toward the battle. As our research has clearly illustrated, we have generations of our youth going to Christian colleges where God's written revelation (which is foundational to a proper Christian worldview) is being undermined. As generations of students begin to doubt God's Word as written (particularly in Genesis), and as they are encouraged to accept many of the fallible ideas of man (e.g., millions of years and evolution), they are being conformed to the world's thinking instead of thinking as a Christian needs to (Rom. 12:2).

Many in the Christian academic community point the finger at those who take a literal interpretation of Genesis and accuse them of being the cause of the anti-intellectualism discussed earlier. These same professors who compromise Genesis are the ones who themselves have actually helped bring on this seeming anti-intellectualism.

Because so much of the Church has been confused on the issues of origins and because so many Christian leaders have taught people to accept millions of years and even evolution, many Christians basically ignored the whole issue and concentrated on spiritual, relationship, and doctrinal matters. They avoided the historical science of Genesis, and gradually their "faith" shifted toward more emotionalism and experientialism in the Church, along with watered-down teaching. Yes, one can see what seems to be anti-intellectualism, but it is because the Church has not taken a stand on God's Word from the very beginning! What hope is there for the right sort of Christian leadership when so many of those training our leaders have already embraced the world's philosophies in many areas?

A story is told about Satan calling his emissaries of hell together because he wanted to send them to earth to aid men and women in the ruination of their souls. He asked, "Who would go first, and what would be the strategy?" One said, "I will go." "And what will you tell them?" Satan asked. "I will tell them there is no heaven." And Satan said, "They will not believe you, for there is a bit of heaven in every human heart. In the end everyone knows that good will triumph over evil. You may not go."

Then another came forward, darker and fouler than the first. "If I send you," Satan said, "what will you tell them?" "I will tell them there is no hell." Satan looked at him and said, "No, they will not believe you, for in every human heart there is a thing called conscience, an inner voice which testifies to the truth that not only will good triumph but evil will be defeated. You are not to go."

The last creature that came forward was more diabolical than them all. Satan said to him, "If I send you what will you say to men and women that will lead to the destruction of their souls?" And he said, "I will tell them there is no hurry." Satan said, "GO. You are the one."

And that seems to be the place we are today; the strategy seems to be working. As Christians we are certainly in no hurry; there is no sense of urgency. But there is urgency. The Church has been marginalized. What is at stake is the very heart and soul of our faith, particularly of our youth. It is essential that this generation of young people be confronted with this astounding truth, again from the pen of C.S. Lewis in his essay "A Slip of the Tongue": "In the end, if you have not chosen the Kingdom of God, it will not matter what you have chosen instead."[7]

The survey confirmed our hunch that compromise *is* taking place in Christian higher education. We know that the natural tendency of fallen man gravitates toward naturalism, liberalism, and an eroding of the authority of the Bible. We have grave concerns that this great compromise is marginalizing the central, life-giving message about Jesus Christ.

Christianity is in desperate need of leadership right now. Gone are the strong voices of the past that spoke out with confidence about the authority of Scripture. Parents and students would like to believe that the leadership of Christian colleges is focused, unified, and standing on God's Word. But as you will see in the next chapter, the survey suggests otherwise. Floundering leaders are part of the widespread confusion we see in all levels of campus life and learning. While the leaders stumble, the battle rages. At stake is the truth about Jesus Christ and the gospel of His grace — and that is worth fighting for.

Endnotes

1. Ken Ham, *Already Gone* (Green Forest, AR: Master Books, May 2009).
2. Os Guinness, *Fit Bodies, Fat Minds* (Grand Rapids, MI: Baker Books, 1994), p. 9–11.
3. Ibid., p. 30.
4. Ibid., p. 31.
5. David Kinnaman, *Unchristian* (Grand Rapids, MI: Baker Books, 2007), p. 29–30.
6. Ibid., p. 81.
7. C.S. Lewis, "A Slip of the Tongue," *The Weight of Glory* (San Francisco, CA: HarperSanFrancisco, a division of HarperCollins, 2001), p. 190–191.

Want to know which colleges were contacted as part of the ARG study? Visit www.creationcolleges.org and also find a growing list of Christian colleges we recommend you search out.

Chapter 5

Confusion across the Campus

Ken Ham

God is not a God of confusion but of peace (1 Cor. 14:33).

The uniqueness of Christianity, as Greg Hall shared with us in the last chapter, must always be at the forefront of our minds. Yes, a war over worldviews is being waged across the globe. The battles are intensely fierce on the campuses of both secular and Christian colleges and universities. Sometimes it is so easy to get wrapped up in the fight that we forget the cause. We are not fighting for some obscure ideology, for some sort of social morality, or even for political integrity. What we're fighting for is truth.

Jesus said, "You shall know the truth and the truth shall make you free" (John 8:32; NKJV). Why do we fight for the authority of Scripture? Because the message Scripture proclaims has the power to set captives free and to liberate those who are living in the shackles of lies that bind them to the world system. When Jesus said, "I am the way and the truth and the life" in John 14:6, He claimed to be the one and only way to the Father, to a life of liberty, peace, grace, mercy, and forgiveness. Truly the Bible contains the most valuable and precious message on earth and for all eternity. God has placed it in our care to share it, protect it, defend it, and live it. Jude 1:3 boldly calls us to this stance:

I felt compelled to write and urge you to contend for the faith that was once for all entrusted to the God's holy people (NIV).

The words that Peter wrote nearly 2,000 years ago are as true today as they ever have been:

Who is there to harm you if you prove zealous for what is good? But even if you should suffer for the sake of righteousness, you are blessed AND DO NOT FEAR THEIR INTIMIDATION, AND DO NOT BE TROUBLED, but sanctify Christ as Lord in your hearts, always being ready to make a defense to everyone who asks you to give an account for the hope that is in you, yet with gentleness and reverence (1 Pet. 3:13–15).

Are Christian colleges and universities living up to this verse today? Are we?

Confusion in the Cockpit

When someone buys an expensive airline ticket and steps onto an airplane, they do so trusting that the pilot and the copilot are working together to ensure the direction and the safety of the aircraft and everyone on board. Recently we've seen heroic cooperation in the midst of life-threatening emergencies, where the leadership of the aircraft works together, saving all onboard.

When Christian parents begin writing substantial checks and send their children into the care of Christian colleges, it is usually accompanied with similar expectations. They believe that they are putting their children into a safe spiritual environment where their faith will be nurtured and where they will learn to defend and stand strong in their faith as they enter into adulthood. Parents do this in good faith, believing that those who are in leadership over the institution share their values and concerns, and are working together with the parents to provide the best environment possible for their children to grow mentally and spiritually.

Are these expectations reasonable? Or are they simply hope in an illusion? When we looked at how presidents and vice presidents of Christian colleges and universities answered our survey, the answers became profoundly clear.

Q11: What makes education different at Christian compared to secular schools?

The number-one answers given were grouped as follows:

#11

What makes education different at Christian compared to secular schools?

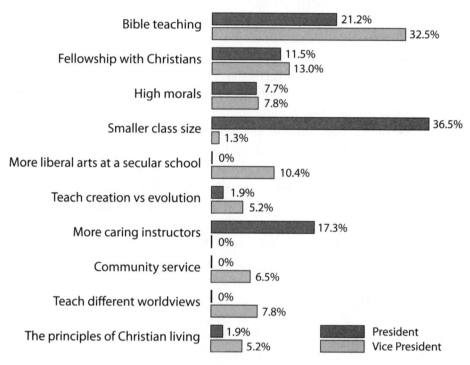

Bible teaching	21.2% / 32.5%
Fellowship with Christians	11.5% / 13.0%
High morals	7.7% / 7.8%
Smaller class size	36.5% / 1.3%
More liberal arts at a secular school	0% / 10.4%
Teach creation vs evolution	1.9% / 5.2%
More caring instructors	17.3% / 0%
Community service	0% / 6.5%
Teach different worldviews	0% / 7.8%
The principles of Christian living	1.9% / 5.2%

President
Vice President

Important observations can be made here, about both what the presidents and vice presidents said and what they didn't say. One of our immediate concerns is that no one mentioned apologetics and defending their faith! In fact, throughout the whole survey of 312 people, only one person mentioned the importance of apologetics and defending the Bible. I am wondering if one of the most blaring issues here is that none of them mention "the gospel" as a differentiating factor. I think this too would floor people in considering that "Christian" colleges don't even differentiate themselves in terms of gospel when compared to the world. And there's nothing about teaching them to have a comprehensive Christian worldview and little about preparing them for interacting in the secular world.

We have found from our own personal experiences that most Bible colleges, Christian colleges, and seminaries do not teach apologetics. Apologetics is basically missing from our churches and Sunday schools, youth ministries included. (Which is not surprising, given that most pastors were not trained in apologetics at their colleges/seminaries!)

Second, 25 percent of the answers had nothing to do with Christianity at all! Smaller class sizes, fewer liberal arts classes, and caring instructors? Are those the most important things that distinguish a Christian school from a secular school? We would hope for something different than that! Yet these responses are consistent with other things we see in the study. Christian schools are reluctant to differentiate themselves from the world. There are plenty of liberal arts schools that would distinguish themselves by class size, the care of their professors, etc. The most critical analysis of the situation might lead someone to conclude the Christian schools are really just like secular schools, except with some stricter rules, a few Bible classes added in, and a chapel service that may or may not be mandatory to attend. We hear story after story from students who go to Christian colleges hoping for a refreshing and distinctive Christian environment, only to be confronted with behavior and activities such as drunkenness and promiscuity, which they were hoping to avoid. Are some Christian colleges basically secular institutions in disguise?

The third concern we gather from the data shows a drastic lack of agreement between the president and the vice president on important issues. (As we will show, this lack of agreement extends to other areas.) There should have been one answer that stood out for each school — a rallying cause, belief, or vision that distinguishes them from the world. But other than saying they "teach the Bible" in some of their classes, we couldn't find any clear vision among these leaders of Christian education. In some circumstances it seems like they may be upholding a handful of Christian "traditions" rather than equipping the next generation of believers. Now it may be that the school has some sort of mission statement, but regardless, the survey shows clearly what was on the minds of the leaders of these institutions.

Skim the numbers in the following graphs once again, and you'll find great disagreement between the president and the vice president. If the pilot and copilot of an airliner functioned in the same way, we know that the flight would be headed for disaster. This "confusion in the cockpit" appears to be the reality at most Christian colleges and universities. No wonder so many students' experiences end in disaster.

We were encouraged, however, to find that presidents and vice presidents, like those in the religion and science departments, have a strong belief in issues regarding the New Testament. But as usual, once we started asking questions about Old Testament — particularly detailed questions — the answers became much more concerning. In many cases, the division between the president and the vice president was striking.

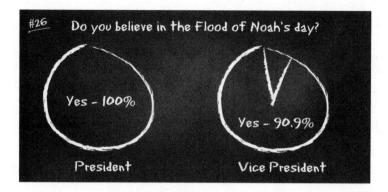

Both of these percentages were higher than were the religion and science departments (84.0 percent and 88.9 percent, respectively), so we're pleased to see at least a general belief in this historic event.

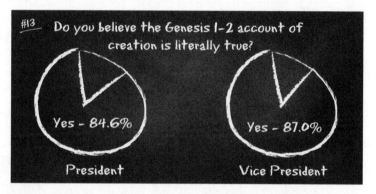

Again, the president and the vice president showed slightly higher levels of belief than the religion and science departments, and we see only a minimal amount of discrepancy between these two offices. They gave similar responses and compatible numbers when asked if they believed the Genesis account "as written."

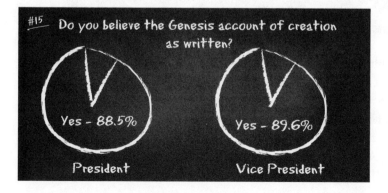

So in the general questions everything appears (and as you will understand as we go on, we have to emphasize "appears") to be fairly solid and headed in the right direction. But then again, we haven't gotten to any of the details yet. When we asked specific questions that show what they mean by what they say, the numbers are quite different.

Q14: Would you consider yourself to be a young-earth or old-earth Christian?

	President	Vice President
Old earth	48.1%	37.7%
Young earth	51.9%	50.6%
Neither	0.0%	10.4%

There is some indecision on the parts of the vice presidents; other than that there's a fair amount of unity here, even though the leaders, like the rest of the faculty, are almost evenly split in their beliefs about a young and old earth. This issue draws the line in the sand time and time again and helps us to discern between what people say and what they actually mean. As we have seen, it's much easier to agree on general statements than on the specifics. As the questions become more detailed, a very unusual "disconnect" begins to appear between the presidents and the VPs of the schools.

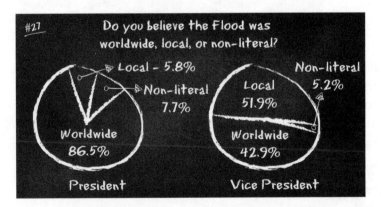

The presidents' responses are somewhat encouraging, but it is disheartening to see that well over half of the vice presidents of Christian universities believe in a local or nonliteral flood. And we are really giving them the benefit of the doubt about what they mean by "worldwide." This is yet another area where "newspeak" shows up. Many times when someone says "worldwide" what they really mean is "the whole world as it was known to exist then." Many people think that Noah's Flood covered only the known world at that time

— meaning that it was simply a regional flood. Hugh Ross (from the biblically compromising ministry *Reasons to Believe*), for example, says he believes in a "universal" flood, but it's only part of the world that was covered. Some people say they believe in a global flood, but they only believe it was on part of the globe. So even those words don't necessarily mean to these academics what they mean to us. I'm not saying that they're necessarily being deceptive; they're just not being descriptive. If you want to find out what they really mean, you have to ask very specific questions. In fact, the more we considered the results of this research, the more this problem became apparent. It is really an epidemic. You can't really assume that what these professors and presidents are saying to you is equivalent to your plain understanding of the words and phrases.

Several years ago I got a supporter to write to a number of colleges to get in writing what they believed about the Flood. The responses were mind-boggling. Most colleges won't even give you a statement anymore. They don't want to be held accountable in black and white, and even if they did, what would they say? When the president and vice president believe such radically different things, what could they write that would represent the school? They couldn't write anything specific, because there is no consensus on the details.

Q16: Do you believe in God creating the earth in six literal 24-hour days?

	President	Vice President
Yes	78.8%	40.3%

Again, notice that nearly twice as many presidents say that they believe in a six-day creation compared to vice presidents. Not only is this result telling, but it also calls for the question, "Why is that?!" Why in the world would there be such a huge difference in belief between these two positions?

Q17: Do you believe in God creating the earth, but not in six literal days?

	President	Vice President
Yes	42.3%	58.4%

The vice presidents answered this follow-up question consistently, though the majority did so incorrectly. But the presidents? Notice that 78 percent said they do believe in six literal days, but 42 percent said they do NOT believe in six literal days. If you add that up, it means that 20 percent of the presidents answer yes to both questions!

So much of this hinges on their views of the authority of Scripture. Notice how they answered these key yes/no questions:

Q19: Do you believe in the inspiration of Scripture?

	President	Vice President
Yes	98.1%	98.7%

Q20: Do you believe in the inerrancy of Scripture?

	President	Vice President
Yes	21.2%	77.9%
No	78.8%	5.6%
Don't know	0.0%	6.5%

Q18: Do you believe in the infallibility of Scripture?

	President	Vice President
Yes	17.3%	94.8%
No	82.7%	3.9%

Take a look at that again. Both offices strongly believe in the "inspiration" of Scripture (98%+). But when asked about inerrancy and infallibility, the presidents answered with an apparently low level of belief. Only 21 percent believe in inerrancy and only 17.3 percent believe in infallibility! And let me remind you that these are the presidents of religiously affiliated colleges and universities that are members of the CCCU (Council for Christian Colleges and Universities). These are the men and women in the big office, with the big desks, who are charting the direction of the school. They are the representatives, the guardians, and the voice of the school. These are the *leaders*. And this is their level of belief in the authority of Scripture? Does that concern you as one possibly entrusting your children to them?

Interestingly, the vice presidents seem to have a much higher view of Scripture than the presidents do, though this doesn't really line up with their answers to questions about the days of creation and the Flood as outlined above. The vice presidents are the ones who are usually approving the hiring of faculty. They are the ones that are in the middle of the division between the science and religion departments, and they appear to show a relatively higher view of Scripture.

One huge part of the concern, however, is this huge gap of belief that exists between the president and the vice president. You look at these kinds of numbers (21.2%–77.9%, 17.3%–94.8%) on central issues regarding the authority of Scripture, and you have to wonder what is going on.

We can only speculate on why these huge gaps exist between presidents and vice presidents. Do they *really* believe this differently? If not, why would they skew their answers? How could they ever really work together in a unified way for the institution?

Unfortunately, other questions only lead to more head scratching.

The differences between the president and the vice president are less pronounced on this issue, but we should still be concerned about the 25 percent of the presidents who do not believe the Bible is literally true. Yet again, when we correlate this question with one that we already looked at, the results are not consistent:

The vice presidents say they believe the Bible is literally true, but far less than half believe in six literal 24-hour days. More presidents believe in six literal 24-hour days than claim that the Bible is literally true. It is tempting to try to get inside their heads and figure out where these discrepancies and inconsistencies come from. For example, the vice presidents said that they have a higher view of Scripture than the presidents, yet on important issues such as the Flood, they show a much lower belief level in historical biblical events.

In all honesty, it's tough to interpret such inconsistent data. Perhaps the only logical conclusion is that their belief systems/worldviews are highly inconsistent as well. What we can conclude from this data, however, is that some presidents of Christian colleges answered regrettably on key issues regarding the authority of Scripture, and we find very, very little unity between the presidents and the vice presidents who are in the cockpit of these institutions.

Detached from the Classroom

The interesting finding about this question is that there is virtually *no* agreement between the leadership about the educational background of their faculty. In most institutions the president does not hire the faculty. Generally, the chairs of the individual departments recommend faculty to

#3   Do you know if your faculty and administrators received their degree from a Christian institution?

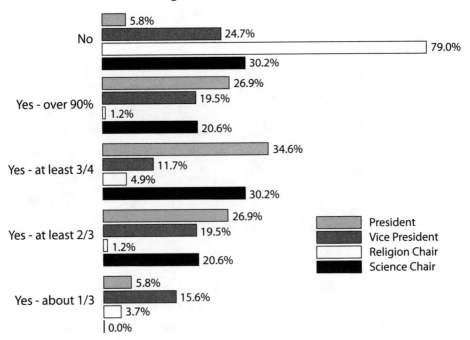

the vice president, who makes the decision. But even so, 24.7 percent of vice presidents didn't know.

One of the big reasons you have evolution/millions of years (and other compromises in regard to Genesis/Old Testament) being taught in Christian colleges is because so many of the faculty come from secular institutions. They don't know any other way of thinking than what they heard in their own personal education. Yet if the educational background of the faculty is an important issue for you when you start choosing schools, we don't know who to tell you to ask. Unless you actually see a piece of paper listing the faculty's educational background, it will be very difficult to determine how many people actually did get their degree from Christian institutions (and it depends on which Christian institutions anyway, because some are no different than the secular ones!). The mixed data did reveal one thing, however: for the leaders, unbelievably, this does not seem to be an important question at all . . . but even if it is, nobody really knows the answer.

A further concern is that presidents seem to be very detached and unaware of what is actually being taught in their classrooms on key issues regarding the evolution/creation debate.

#6 What does your institution teach about evolution?

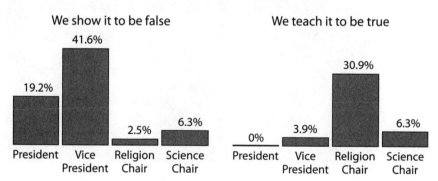

You can see problems all through this data, but the most obvious one is this: 0.0 percent of college presidents think that their institution is teaching evolution to be true. Yet 30.9 percent of the religion departments are clearly doing so. (If you remember our analysis of this data in an earlier chapter, you will recall that this number might be significantly higher depending on what the "teach and dissect" category means.) Only slightly more of the vice presidents (3.9 percent) are aware that the religion department is teaching evolution to be true.

There is a huge disconnect going on here. And on issues as critical as this one, the disconnect is scary.

Unaware of the Conflict

Not only are some of these presidents apparently unaware of what is being taught in the classrooms, but because of this they are also unaware of the conflict that exists between the departments they oversee.

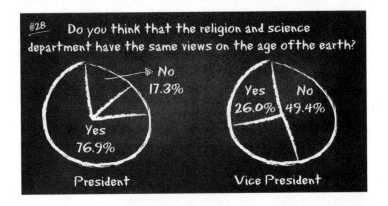

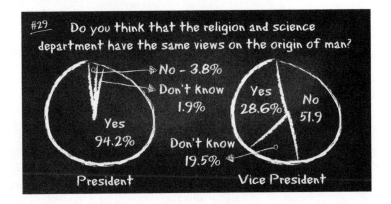

Note that the presidents have significantly higher impressions on unity of curriculum across the campus than the vice presidents do. We already know from the data whose perception is more accurate. The vice president knows about the conflict. While the president is out shaking hands at luncheons, raising money, and promoting the school to potential students and their parents, the vice president is getting all the calls from the parents and is in the crossfire of the squabbles between the departments.

This lack of perception is not exclusive to Christian colleges and universities, however. America's Research Group recently did a survey for a mattress company where the same questions were asked to the president, to the head of merchandising, to the mattress buyer, and to the salespeople. What the owners thought and what the salesperson did coincided only 6 percent of the time. What the merchandising manager thought and what the buyer said coincided only 45 percent of the time. But the buyer and the salespeople were fifty-fifty, so they had four different people in four different positions all believing four different things about what was going on in the organization. Christian colleges are no exception — but they should be!

The leadership at most of the Christian colleges doesn't know what is being taught in the classroom, and it's very difficult for them to find out. The leaders have dozens or hundreds of professors in the classrooms for many hours every week . . . and the president is supposed to monitor that? Sure, maybe a few professors will sign off on a doctrinal statement that they maybe don't fully believe in — or even disagree with — to get the job. And, as we have already shown and discussed, they can agree to words and phrases in the statement that may mean something different to them than what it meant to those who formulated the statement for the institution. Some might just skim it and sign it without serious consideration — and when they get to the classroom they can teach whatever they want. We hate to say that, but it's true. There is a strong emphasis on "academic freedom," as they have been taught and have experienced in the secular world. Many professors consider it an insult to be told what they should be teaching.

Indifferent to Consequences

Again, we see a significant difference here between what the president thinks is happening and what the vice president thinks is happening. The presidents think that there are definite consequences when someone teaches contrary to the Bible; only about half of the vice presidents believe that this is taking place. That's a huge spread again.

Several factors could be contributing to this. As we saw above, the presidents are largely unaware of what is being taught in their classrooms, and they probably think that everyone is teaching in accordance with the Bible. The vice presidents know that this isn't true, yet only half of them are aware of any consequences to unbiblical teaching. From the survey, we know that there are a lot of things being taught contrary to the Bible, and nobody seems to be doing anything about it.

As usual, the questions we asked brought up even more questions. What did most of the people we interviewed think when they heard the phrase "contrary to the Bible"? My guess is that they may have only thought about blatant issues, such as teaching that Hinduism and or Islam is true and Christianity is false. When they heard this phrase, did they even think evolution? Did they think millions of years? Did they think of a historical Adam? Those are things that some of them don't consider to be contrary to the Bible anyway!

And what did they think of when we said "consequences"? Did they think we're talking about social consequences? Professional censorship? Perhaps we should have asked the question this way: if someone teaches something contrary to the Bible, do you have the will to fire them or publicly correct them?

We have seen very few instances where faculty were fired for compromise teachings. In those cases it usually has to be something really outlandish. But worrying about the details of "inerrancy," "infallibility," or even evolution/creation/millions of years? There's no consequence for that — and many times it is even encouraged.

In many situations, there is really only a "consequence" if the word gets out to the public and parents become involved. Once it becomes public and the parents become concerned, then there is action. The action is not necessarily because of what is being taught (because others are probably teaching the same things and haven't been highlighted) but because of public relations damage and possible loss of donors and support.

A Disconcerting Conclusion

The analysis of this data unfortunately confirmed the hunches that we had about what was happening and what is happening at the highest levels of leadership at many Christian colleges and universities. These numbers show such Christian institutions and those that are "religiously affiliated" may have a disconnect from the reason the college should exist. There is great disunity among the leadership, and compromise teachings have infiltrated the classrooms. Many schools struggle to differentiate themselves from secular institutions, and clear conflict exists between departments.

Equally concerning are the inconsistencies that we find in people's answers. As a group, these respondents are highly educated and amazingly confused. Many of us have *felt* this was true, but now we have the statistics, drawn from their own words, to show it. President Greg Hall summarized the situation this way:

> There is no idea or concept that more accurately describes my 20 years of experience in "Christian" higher education than the periodic, but continual, evidence of equivocation, capitulation, and compromise among those of us who lead and teach in these institutions when it comes to whether or not we will stand on the truth of biblical authority. In the equivocation we cause massive confusion among students, who are far more discerning than we realize at times, and see it for what it is. I have observed this phenomenon among other Christian colleges and my own. If we are not willing to stand upon the truth and veracity of Scripture, we have no choice but to capitulate and compromise in the classroom. In more than just the disciplines related to science we will find secular philosophies and ideologies in direct conflict with the clear instruction of the Word of God. In most cases there are some very strange intellectual "gymnastics" going on to try to reconcile these worldly philosophies with the eternal truth of God's Word. It is a fool's errand in the worst sense of the word. To cause confusion among students because we can't decide on the place to stand as our first priority, that being the Word of God, is to render ourselves incompetent as Christian educators.

Professing to be institutions of truth, many schools have become the propagators of confusion. They are the authors of confusion. "If the trumpet does not sound a clear call, who will get ready for battle?" (1 Cor. 14:8; NIV). The reason young Christians are not prepared for the battle is that they don't take a firm stand on the authority of the Bible. This generation does not know there is a battle, does not care if there is a battle, does not know the enemy, does not know what is at stake, and does not care. You would hope that the Christian colleges would have been preparing "warriors" for the ensuing conflict. But they have not. They have bought into the enemy's strategy to divide and conquer. As President Hall notes, "While we should have been equipping students, we have been confusing them." And of course all this flows over into the pulpit, Christian schools, other Christian institutions, and so on down the line to the Christian public.

The Leadership Vacuum

Let's take another look at the question that asks about what differentiates a Christian school from a secular one. As we probe deeper to find explanations for the division and difficulties we see emerging from Christian schools, two of the answers might offer us some helpful insight.

#11

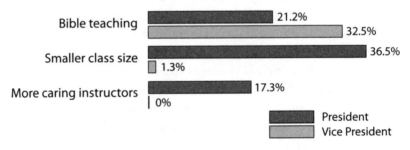

What makes education different at Christian compared to secular schools?

	President	Vice President
Bible teaching	21.2%	32.5%
Smaller class size	36.5%	1.3%
More caring instructors	17.3%	0%

Again, notice that there is striking contrast between what the president and vice president prioritize. Is it possible that these responses reflect the different priorities of their specific positions? As we broke up these answers, an interesting profile of the presidency emerged. It appears that the presidents, rather than being the defenders and leaders of a spiritual institution, give answers that make them sound more like salesmen. But these responses certainly reflect financial and social realities facing many college presidents and would be consistent with what are otherwise unexplainable responses.

Let's take the most obvious one: when asked what makes a Christian school different from a secular school, the presidents' number-one answer was "smaller class size." At 36.5 percent, no other category of answers was close. Is this what should distinguish a Christian school from a secular school? This is a typical mantra for *any* private school — one of their big marketing angles that helps them justify higher tuition (because most people believe that smaller classes equate with a better education). But what does that have to do with being Christian?

The same can be asked of the high response "caring instructors" the presidents gave. None of the other three positions of leadership gave this any sort of statistical significance. Not only is the president's view on this completely different than the rest of his faculty, but we must also question why.

In many situations, it appears that the president is giving answers that put their schools in the best light for Christian parents. They gave the highest numbers when asked how many in their faculty were trained in Christian institutions. But is this number objective? Do they really know? Or is this another situation where the president is trying to sell the institution to Christian parents? In all honesty, we simply couldn't tell.

Presidents believe in the highest levels of unity between their departments, they don't see conflict in the curriculum, and none of them believe that evolution is being taught as truth in their school. Smaller class sizes and caring instructors could be just another pitch for enrollment.

If this is the situation, it's not unique to Christian colleges and universities. In bigger churches, the lead pastor is often more detached. It's the associate pastor who is in the trenches, aware of the division between the committees, and more concerned about what is being taught in the Sunday school classrooms. The senior pastors tend to be more concerned about how they are coming across to the congregation, how the church is being branded, and how the church's image affects the offering plate. I think it's the same in these colleges. The president tends to be more political and the vice president and the chairs tend to be more personal.

Particularly in the wake of the recession, many of these schools are struggling financially. Many institutions are sitting on a time bomb of debt. In this economy, the temptation certainly exists to tell the parents what they want to hear in order to keep the classrooms filled. The pressure to meet enrollment could also be driving these fuzzy answers. We know that's a horrible accusation to make, but it's at least one possibility that must be considered and addressed.

Dr. John Maxwell said, "Everything rises and falls on leadership."[1] The survey found that leadership is in a questionable and chaotic state on Christian colleges and campuses. The tone and precedents set at the highest levels of leadership will, and are, having an effect on the rest of the campus and ultimately the Church in general.

Someone must take ownership and responsibility for the situation and step out with clear leadership in the midst of this crisis. So far, it seems like we just don't see the type of leadership we have known in the past: the men and women who held the authority of Scripture in highest regard, above all things, and then taught and lived and learned accordingly. Where are those leaders today? It's only a matter of time before an institution falls to the level of its leadership. We saw this time and time again with the Ivy League schools, which started with such high and bold principles and eventually descended into compromise with the world.

Somehow, someway, we must regain the certain sound of our trumpet so that the next generation will take up their weapons of faith and join us in the battle for life-changing truth.

Endnotes
1. John C. Maxwell, *The 21 Indispensable Qualities of a Leader* (Nashville, TN: Thomas Nelson, Inc., 2007).

PART 2

The Battle for the Mind

For our struggle is not against
flesh and blood, but against the
rulers, against the powers, against
the world forces of this darkness,
against the spiritual forces of
wickedness in the heavenly places.

— Ephesians 6:12

Chapter 6

The High Call of Taking Action

Greg Hall

All that is necessary for evil to triumph is for good men to do nothing. — Edmund Burke

December 7, 1941, Pearl Harbor. It is yet another stunningly beautiful morning in "paradise." As the sun rises over the Pacific Ocean and spreads its golden rays across the small community, the island slowly comes to life — oblivious to the "day of infamy" that lies ahead. There is an interesting book on the history of what happened that day entitled *At Dawn We Slept*. While the attack that morning was a "surprise" to those who were stationed on this beautiful little piece of volcanic rock in the middle of a vast ocean, the reader learns that in reality there were plenty of "signals." In fact, there were several who had a very good inkling that such an attack was imminent, but they either said nothing, or their warnings fell on deaf ears. The majority of Americans and most of America's leadership were in fact taken by surprise.[1]

This is an interesting comparison to the current battle raging for the hearts and minds of our youth who face daily the onslaught of anti-Christian, atheistic philosophy. When I talk about this in messages around the country, I find Christian parents surprised and shocked at what has happened to public education and particularly how militant the fight against Christianity has become.

And now we find out that as we have slept, compromise has infiltrated Christian institutions as well, creating possibly an even more dangerous situation in colleges and universities that appeared to be our allies. They are, in fact, minimizing the authority of Scripture. It is as though the title of the book *At Dawn We Slept* describes those of us who have just not been paying enough attention to this collapse within the Church.

Yet in the midst of the raging battle, there is something that is happening that gives great hope. The open militancy of those opposed to Christianity will awaken a sleeping giant. It is possible to envision a generation of believers who will rise up and say, "No more!" It is time to join the battle for the hearts and minds of generations to come. I am hoping and praying for a day of renewed influence upon our public educators by Christians who understand this battle and will equip themselves for the fight. I am hoping and praying for the day when compromising Christian colleges and universities humbly confess and repent. I look forward to the day when we will see a strengthening and expanding of a biblical worldview across the Western world. Specifically I pray for:

- The Church to capture a vision of the importance of starting Christian schools.
- The Church to capture a vision for connecting with students in secular schools.
- A strengthening of the home school movement.
- Support for Christian teachers in the public schools. They are strategic in influencing students in a biblical worldview.
- The support of Christian colleges and universities that are committed to a biblical worldview. They are the alternative to secular education.
- The support of committed believers who work on secular college and university campuses making the biblical worldview known to students who may never otherwise hear the message.

Mostly, I pray for the resurgence of commitment to the Word of God as the authentic explanation of all issues of human existence. In the end, the entire discussion of which worldview will gain prominence in our culture is one of *authority*. We believe God's Word to be the authority upon which we are expected to build our lives, and we are fighting back to regain recognition of that authority in our churches, our schools, and our families. Yes, it is time to recapture a generation. We may have lost some important battles; but the war we can still win (Matt. 28:18–20).

The attack of December 7, 1941, catapulted a nation into war — a war we ultimately won. Maybe God is calling us to spiritual warfare, too. It is the war being waged to determine what ideas will gain prominence in the coming generations. It is a war that ultimately we win, too (Isa. 11:9). But we get the clear message now that it is time for believers to stand, fight, and advance. It is time to be honest and forthright about what is at stake — the minds and souls of our youth. It is time for a clear "call to battle." We must not forget the admonition of Scripture. If the trumpet gives an uncertain sound, who will prepare for the battle? It is time for a clear call to arms; a time to join the battle. From the bottom of my heart, I'd like to make that call to the local church, educators at all levels, and parents.

Action for the Church

Frankly, a portion of the local church has abandoned one of its first priorities: to educate its youth in the truth of God's Word as the first order of business in any educational pursuit. Furthermore, we need to convince the Body of Christ that our youth should be highly encouraged to education in a biblical worldview as the foundation of all life-long learning. The education of the churches' youth is a situation that needs to be redeemed.

The Church must get involved early in educating our youth in Christian biblical worldview and apologetics. This is a foreign topic in many congregations, but its implications are profound. Our worldview is the way we look at life. A Christian biblical worldview is learning to look at all aspects of life through the eyes of God. The problem is that Christians have developed a worldview that includes influences from a variety of sources, many expressly unchristian, and this destroys the ability to do good apologetics.

Consequently, it becomes possible to raise kids in church and subsequently turn them over to secular institutions for education without having thought through the potential outcomes of them losing faith in the process. The issue for us is this: if we are going to be Christian, then it requires surrender in every area of life. It makes a claim on every area of our lives and is very important in how we educate our young. If we are going to reclaim the ground lost in this battle, we are going to have to develop strategies for the Church to move *forward* and not into further retreat.

We must be willing to sound the trumpet and let the Church know just how serious the problem is. The enemies of Christian faith learned a long time ago where to wage the war — in the education of our youth. They understood the influence they could gain by this daily captive audience. We Christians played right into their hands by leaving the battle behind and simply joining in. We have lost the concept of what is at stake, *the hearts and minds of our youth.*

Second, the Church needs to support and encourage the Christian teachers whose calling has led them into the center of this battle in the public school setting. These individuals are God's instruments of influence in enemy territory. Thankfully, there are still good numbers of them, and they *are* making a difference day by day, child by child, school by school. The Church and Christian colleges and universities should continue to educate those who will continue to enter the public schools and be sure they are adequately prepared to represent the Christian worldview in a hostile environment. It can and is being done. It happens only intentionally, not by default.

The teachers at the private Christian schools of our nation need encouragement, too. They do their work at a fraction of the pay of public education and do it well. Even at that, due to economic hard times, Christian schools all over the nation are closing — precisely the opposite of what needs to be done in these times. Christians who are committed to the authority of Scripture in all areas of life need to be affirmed and recognized, because as we have seen, many times they are in the minority, even on a "Christian" campus.

Finally, instead of looking at the world and lamenting how corrupt it has become, we need to focus our attention on the Church — on God's people — especially on those to whom the sheep look for leadership. Attention needs to be given to the shepherds of our day who lead us congregation by congregation, and also to the presidents, vice presidents, and professors at our Christian institutions who influence and train the sheep in a campus environment. The nurture and care of souls and minds of the youth of our nation is our duty and opportunity. It is time for the Church to rise to this occasion.

Action for Parents

As we survey the landscape of education in America, do we really realize the philosophy being promoted by these atheistic educators as it relates to child rearing? Dr. Richard Dawkins asks:

> How much do we regard children as being property of their parents? It's one thing to say people should be free to believe whatever they like, but should they be free to impose their beliefs on their children? Is there something to be said for society stepping in?[2]

It's interesting that Dr. Dawkins wants his views imposed on children, all the while arguing that those of parents shouldn't be! And further, society has, in fact, stepped in. These atheist educators are plenty clever enough to know where and how to enjoin the battle for whose ideas shall have mastery and control. They know to make the battleground education — especially the higher education classroom. And so, it should come as no surprise when someone like evolutionary biologist Kenneth Miller admits:

> A presumption of atheism or agnosticism is universal in academic life. . . . The conventions of academic life, almost universally, revolve around the assumption that religious belief is something that people grow out of as they become educated.[3]

If you think this is over-stating the case, you have not spent time enough on a secular campus, listened to a lecture from a secular professor, or read from his or her books. For the most part, well-intentioned Christian parents have directed their children to secular public institutions with big football stadiums and housing with all the expected amenities, and have considered it a great bargain compared to the cost of private Christian higher education. Yet others write checks to compromising colleges and then "check out," unaware (or unconcerned) about liberal, secular influences that are driving curriculum in the classroom.

Parents, it is time to engage again. The battle is raging. Don't give over authority. Don't assume. You need to get educated on this matter. You need to understand the nature of our current education system. When you are choosing a college for your student, whether it is grade school, high school, or college/university, we know that you are making many of these decisions based on cost. But when you consider the spiritual cost, as we have tried to show throughout this book, the cost is too high.

For those who are concerned about the loss of Christian values in our culture, we must face the fact that, in large measure, we have been party to our own undoing almost without a fight. We have turned over generation after generation of young men and women to be fully inculcated with the thoughts, ideas, and precepts that are absolutely contrary to our Christian faith. And we wonder why this nation is in the shape it is in? The Church systematically, seemingly without guilt, turns one generation after another of children over to a pagan, godless, secular education system that turns them from the faith. We do it in public elementary and high schools and colleges and universities. And we pay the enemy to steal their souls. It is time to wake up.

I wish I could tell you all of the stories of how, when I have preached on this subject, parents have come to me in tears. One parent said, "I sent my lovely Christian daughter to the state university, and she came home an atheist." Story after story. *But*, does that mean all will? No, it does not. Parents, I encourage you to redeem the situation. Particularly in the vacuum of leadership from the Church on this issue, your efforts must be intelligent, proactive, and pastoral.

Then, in all honesty, we must address the situation at "Christian" schools. It is possible to go to a Christian school and have the same result — a broken, devastated faith — as with secular schools. This is true. The research shows it to be true, and we must hit it hard. As the research discussed in this book illustrates clearly, one has to be extremely discerning when considering a Christian institution. Just because it is said to be "Christian" does not mean it will teach a Christian worldview as it should. And just because the professors claim they believe in the "infallible" Word of God and in "inerrancy," that does not necessarily mean they are using those terms in the same way as you. If the intent of higher education is to place your students in a godly environment, you need to get as far away as possible from the secular and compromising institutions. Ken uses a biblical analogy to make this point:

> When Moses went before Pharaoh in Exodus chapter 8, one of his responses was to allow the Israelites to go and sacrifice to their God, but they were told, "only you shall not go very far away" (Exod. 8:28). Pharaoh didn't want them to go too far from Egypt. As we know, Egypt can be used as symbolic of the world and its pagan philosophies. Pharaoh wanted to keep them close — not too far from the world.
>
> As you begin to consider the results of the research conducted by America's Research Group (headed up by renowned researcher Britt Beemer) into what the Christian colleges of our age teach, you will find that many of them have tried to stay close to "Egypt." Sadly, so many have not wanted to go very far from what the world teaches in certain areas, and this can (and has) lead to generations being put on a slippery slide of unbelief — the opposite of what their parents were hoping (and paying) for.
>
> Yes, we are advocating that Christian parents need to go far from "Egypt." We should not entrust our children to the Philistines to be trained. But at the same time, this research will awaken us to understand the great need to deeply research, using the right terminology and asking the right questions of the right people (as we will outline for you later on), when considering a Christian institution for the education of our children.
>
> We do need to be far away from those of "Egypt" and those who have stayed close to "Egypt." We so need generations of young people

who are not defeated before they even begin to make their place in this world.

We need to be reminded of what God said to the Israelites in 2 Chronicles 7:13–14: "If . . . My people who are called by My name humble themselves, and pray and seek My face and turn from their wicked ways, then I will hear from heaven, will forgive their sin and will heal their land." Just as the Israelites needed to repent of their compromise with the world's teaching (the pagan religions of the day), we, God's people today, beginning with many of the leaders in our academic Institutions, need to repent of compromise and humble ourselves before the Lord and his Word.

For Educators

I say this again to those of you who are believers and work in the public/state schools: You are God's chosen instruments to do something about this. At the very least, remain faithful and do not fear making your Christian ideas known.[4] You have rights, too! There is no reason to cower or fear. You are able to stand up to this attack. Just like the Christian students intermixed with your unbelieving students, you are the salt and light to the public education world. You are a remnant of truth and grace and mercy in the midst of a compromised culture that desperately needs your influence and your love.

If you don't go to them, who will? How will they experience and know the truth if there's no one there to share it with them and to show it to them? You are that light. You are the salt. By the power of God's Spirit working through you, may Jesus use you as vessels of hope, of forgiveness, and of mercy in the midst of this needy generation. May He use you as a beacon of courage and dedication to the other Christian students in your classes and on your campus. And may God bless and protect you and your families as you execute this vitally important mission. We salute you and affirm you. Godspeed!

Responding to the Attack

December 7, 1941, was not the end. It was just the beginning. The brash and blatant attack of the enemy was a wake-up call to a sleeping nation that rose to the challenge. In this book, we have shared with you many sets of statistics and painted one of the first objective pictures of what is really happening on both secular and Christian campuses. Does this in any way discourage you? Not me. I see the greatest opportunity the Church has ever had to change the coming generations. Many people feel like there is nothing we can do about the decline of our culture. They have become not only inconsolable, but inactive.

On the one hand it is understandable. People, even if once engaged in the cultural struggle, look around and see only defeat and despair. There is probably no one who cannot recite a litany of disaster in our nation: a decline in morals, violence in our streets and schools, corruption at high levels of leadership, loss of integrity in our greatest institutions — the list is endless. And so on that one hand, the despair we sense about the future is understandable. But on the other hand, if we really do believe in a sovereign Creator who is all about the business of reclaiming His lost creation, then not only is this despair not justified, it is inexcusable! It is absolutely time to wake up.

It will take recognition of the issues we face in education. It will take parents making a commitment to send their children to committed Christian educational institutions. It will take a new generation of qualified Christian educators who know worldview matters — and who believe that the war of the worldviews can be won. We may be currently losing, but God is still in control. It will take a new dedication in the local church to make sure its own teaching mission is solid. In general, believers have failed to bring Christian truth to bear in society. As a result, we have a culture that has moved far away from God. We have a culture that does not consult the Word of God. We as Christians are not salt and light to our world and we have lost our influence — for the time being.

It is not time for despair; it is time for hope. It is time to reclaim this generation for Christ. But we have all the resources needed to once again influence our culture for Christ. It is time for the situation to be transformed. God's Word tells us clearly how this transformation takes place, "By the renewing of your mind" (Rom. 12:2). Our day of infamy has arrived. Now we must learn to contend for the authority of Scripture, as a Church, as parents, as educators, and as never before. Are you ready to be equipped to contend for the biblical worldview and the authority of Scripture from Genesis to Revelation?

Endnotes

1. Gordon William Prange, *At Dawn We Slept,* various publishers.
2. Richard Dawkins, *The God Delusion* (Boston, MA: Houghton Mifflin), p. 315, cited by Gary Wolf, "The Church of the Non-Believers," *Wired* (November 2006).
3. Kenneth R. Miller, *Finding Darwin's God: A Scientist's Search for Common Ground Between God and Evolution* (New York: Harper Perennial, 1999), p. 19, 184.
4. Some options are to offer a free class after school hours once or twice a month to refute an evolutionary worldview and build good apologetic teachings, so the school is not liable. Other options are to be available to students after school or point out that certain things come from a Christian worldview and they are often borrowed (wearing clothes, good and bad exist, morality, a basis for logic, uniformity in nature, etc.).

Chapter 7

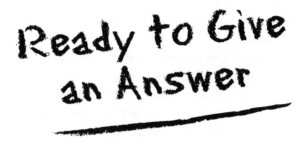

Ready to Give an Answer

Greg Hall

Sanctify Christ as Lord in your hearts, always being ready to make a defense to everyone who asks you to give an account for the hope that is in you, yet with gentleness and reverence (1 Pet. 3:15).

When I was a graduate student at the University of Pittsburgh, I attended classes with a number of Islamic students, most of whom were from the nation of Saudi Arabia. They were very good students, highly motivated, very devoted to one another, and especially zealous for their Islamic beliefs. At the graduate level, students are continually making presentations of one kind or another. It was always striking to me that along with the presentation, the Islamic students invariably talked about their religion.

For instance, if a student was giving a presentation on some kind of educational policy in his country, he would likely begin like this: "Before I speak of the educational policies of my nation, it is first important for me to talk about the tenets of Islam with you. The reason is, you cannot understand the educational policy of my country without understanding Islam. They go together." And so the student had a captive audience, and they always, courageously and forthrightly, told us first about the basic tenets of Islamic religion.

I can remember being impressed with their zeal and their sincerity. One night I said a prayer during the break of a class, asking God to give me the courage and opportunity to share openly about my faith in Christ. At the end of class one of the students from Saudi Arabia came to me and said, "Mr. Greg, do I understand correctly that you are a Christian minister?"

"Yes," I said, "I am."

He then asked me if I had time to spend with him and teach him about the Christian Scriptures.

We made plans to meet a few days later in one of the empty classrooms before class so I could teach him about the Christian Scriptures. Prior to that scheduled meeting, I thought he probably did not even have a copy of the Bible. When I gave him one the next day, I could tell that I had done something very, very wrong. He quickly took the Bible, shoved it into a book bag and took off very abruptly. I honestly thought I would never see him again.

But he did show up for our appointed meeting, and he explained what happened when I gave him the Bible. "Mr. Greg, it is a capital offense for me to have a copy of the Christian Bible. I could be killed for this. We must not let my colleagues know what we are doing. We must meet in secret." And meet in secret we did, for many weeks as I taught him about the Scriptures.

I began by having a discussion with him about our common ancestor in the faith, Father Abraham. The connections between Abraham, Sarah, Hagar, Ishmael, and Isaac were fascinating to him and he would take copious notes on everything I said. I will never forget the lessons we had on the Gospel of John. One night he opened that Gospel and read these words to me: "And the Word became flesh, and dwelt among us, and we saw His glory, glory of the only begotten from the Father, full of grace and truth" (John 1:14).

"What, Mr. Greg, is the meaning of this?" I can honestly say, even after 20 years, that when I recall the enthusiasm he had for learning and his desire for truth, a feeling comes over me that I cannot explain. When I realize that God has put the desire to know His truth in every human heart no matter what our background or faith, I am awed at how God works to make His truth known.

"What you are reading about is the 'incarnation,'" I told him. "Christians believe that Jesus is God incarnate. God in human flesh. We believe He is fully God and fully man. Jesus is Immanuel, 'God with us.'"

Then he questioned me about the phrase "the glory of the One and Only," and I talked to him about the Christian conviction of the uniqueness of Jesus, that we believe that He is the only way any of us ever get to God. He alone is the payment God accepts for sin. He alone has the plan for the salvation of all who believe in Him.

At that, my friend got angry. *Very* angry. And he said to me, raising his voice, "Do you mean to tell me that Jesus is the only way we can get to God?" I said that was exactly what I meant. And I tell you honestly, I was scared. But then, all of a sudden a calm and peace came over him and he said to me, "Thanks, for telling me the truth."

Over the course of many weeks we continued to meet. I would talk and he would take notes. I would write on the board and he would take more notes. He asked question after question. I thought, *I have never encountered anyone with more enthusiasm and energy for God's Word.* He could not get enough. I had in fact, never had a student like him. And have not since.

Then one day, he asked "the" question. He began with these remarks. "I thank you for spending time with me. I have enjoyed our discussions. And I am impressed with your command of the topic and especially your knowledge of your Bible, *but* . . . do you have any evidence that it is the truth?"

The Question

"Do you have any evidence that it is the truth?" That is a fair question. In the marketplace of philosophies, ideologies, or worldviews, it is a question anyone must answer before putting their faith in any one particular system or pattern of thought. Now, I understood that we all have the same evidence and that how one interprets it depends on one's starting point. However, from his perspective he obviously wanted me to defend the Christian faith. As Christians we are commanded to give a reason for the faith that is within us. As a matter of intellectual honesty and practicality, what possible good is a worldview for which you cannot give a defense? If we cannot give a defense, we probably don't know enough about our alleged worldview for it to be of much value to us either!

Having an answer to this question is far more important than most people realize. The main issue is this: ideas have consequences. Truth is at the heart of what has become nothing less than warfare in the marketplace of competing worldviews as to which ideas will get your attention and gain prominence in your mind. Once those ideas are firmly embedded in your thinking, your mind will devise the ways for you to act in accordance with what you "know."

What we believe about the world around us and developing a framework for thinking and acting starting with the Bible is the single most important thing we do as humans. When we see that these "ideas" have serious personal consequences, we will naturally want to see the evidence that confirms they are true. I have been in the ministry of the Church for over 30 years as a pastor and university president and there has never been a time in those years when Christians have not had to learn to contend for the truth of God's Word, the Bible.

It has always been the case that the enemies of God have tried to dishonor and discredit the Scripture. In fact, the original sin of humankind was a moment of an attempt to pervert the very Word of God. From Genesis 3 we read:

> The serpent . . . . said to the woman, "Did God really say, 'You must not eat from any tree in the garden'?" The woman said to the serpent, "We may eat fruit from the trees in the garden, but God did say, 'You must not eat fruit from the tree that is in the middle of the garden, and you must not touch it, or you will die.'"

Then, in an attempt to pervert the truth again, the serpent responded:

> "You will not certainly die. . . . For God knows that when you eat from it your eyes will be opened, and you will be like God, knowing good and evil" (Gen. 3:1–4; NIV).

Note that the very first attack was on the Word of God. Eve believed the tantalizing lie of the deceiver rather than the truth of God's Word. This encounter brought sin into a perfect world — it was an "act of cosmic treason"[1] as Dr. R.C. Sproul put it — and it was a result of a successful attempt to discredit God and His Word. That has always been the case, and it always will be. Today, both secular and Christian colleges are filled and infiltrated with people who seek to discredit God's Word in the same way. Thankfully, there are a number of highly skilled, highly credentialed scholars and pastor/teachers who have a very high view of Scripture and teach it as the truth.

- They understand the Bible to be God's written revelation to man and that the 66 books of the Bible have been given to us by the Holy Spirit as the plenary (inspired equally in all parts) Word of God.
- They believe the Bible to be an objective propositional revelation, verbally inspired in every word, absolutely inerrant in the original documents. As such, it is "God breathed" and infallible as a rule of faith and practice and on everything it touches upon (biology, geology, etc.).
- They teach that God spoke in this Word through the Holy Spirit, who superintended the human authors so that by using their own personalities and varying styles of writing still composed and recorded God's words to man without error.

- They show that while there are many applications of Scripture to the issues of life, there is one true interpretation. Through the Holy Spirit who guides us into truth, it is possible for believers to ascertain the absolute intent and meaning of Scripture.

But it must be recognized at all times and in all ways, the truth of the Bible stands in judgment of man, and not the other way around. As Dr. R.C. Sproul says in the introduction to the *New Geneva Study Bible*:

> It is a sacred book because it transcends and stands apart from, above, every other book. It is holy because its ultimate author is holy. It is holy because its message is holy. . . . The Bible is an inspired book that is "breathed out" by God . . . it offers more than brilliant insight, more than human sagacity. It is called "inspired" not because of its supernatural mode of transmission via human authors, but because of its origin. It is not merely a book about God; it is a book from God. Therefore, the church confesses its trust and confidence that the Bible is Vox Dei, the veritable "voice of God."[2]

At stake in the battle for the Bible is the very nature and character of God. And at stake in the greatest issues, questions, and debates about the meaning and purpose of life around us is the authority of Scripture. You must remember and be willing to be discriminating and discerning, because there are plenty of persons who think what I have just described for you is crazy and they will do anything possible to discredit this position and the Scripture itself.

The Bible is true in all it says, equally inspired in all parts. When it describes the origin of life in the Book of Genesis there are actually those of us who believe it actually happened just that way — just as the writers of the New Testament believed. And contrary to what naturalistic philosophers try to teach our students, operational science has in no way proved this to be false — it is the other way around. Observational science today has strengthened the case for understanding the creation account in Genesis 1, not undermined it.

You *must* "get it right" when it comes to Scripture. That is of utmost importance, because the debate of the origin of life is not Darwinism versus creationism, the debate is really over the very authority of Scripture itself. It is an issue of authority. Where do you stand and what do you believe? And do you realize how your thinking will likely be affected by the educational environment you place yourself in? Are you prepared to answer "the question" of "evidence" when you are confronted with personal doubts and attacks from militant naturalists and compromising Christian institutions? Your life and mind are literally at stake in this whole discussion.

Some will agree with me that this book, the Bible, is glorious. Some detest it. Some ignore it. Some professing to be believers will argue with me, preferring that I would eliminate words like "inerrant" and "infallible" when describing it. They will consider me a fool. And all I can say is, "Guilty as charged. I would be honored to be a fool for Christ's sake" (see Matt. 5:11).

But I have a question for believers who undermine the authority of Scripture. Why, if you are a believer, do you spend so much effort on teaching a different position? Some think it is a matter of intellectual honesty. I just have a hard time understanding the energy I see expended on making the Bible look like any other religious text rather than the supernatural work of God that it claims itself to be. In other words, why call yourself a believer if you do not trust the Bible, which is the source of why you claim to believe?

In an age where "tolerance" is the spirit of the day, people (non-Christians and Christians alike) do not want anyone telling them what is truth and what is not. People want to decide for themselves (i.e., elevate themselves to level of God); picking and choosing from the options according to their momentary desires. Some say, "What is true for you may not be true for me." And so they say, "We discover truth by deciding what it means to us." Fewer and fewer people today believe in objective truth. It's all "relative." So why can't we handle the truth?

Suppose two men were standing at the top of a very high building. One man says to the other, "I am going to jump."

The other man says, "You cannot jump; you will die in the process because of the law of gravity. It is a fact you will die if you jump."

So the man replies, "I do not believe the law of gravity is true. I do not think it will happen like you say. The law of gravity might be true for you, but it is not true for me."

Will such a belief change reality? Of course not. However, we accept the jumper's rationale every day in the spiritual dimensions of life. We do so every time we deny objective truth and think truth is only personal preference. We readily agree that physical laws remain true no matter what we may think about them. But sadly, we, as a whole, believe spiritual laws and moral laws are anything we want to make them.

What is at stake in that silly illustration? Authority. And it is why each of us must draw the battle line for what spiritual authority will dominate our lives. I implore you to trust the Bible and the God who gave it. At the center of the believability of Christianity is the question of the reliability and validity of the sacred text — our Scripture, the Bible. And sadly, it is doubt with regard to this sacred text that is being promulgated by many of those entrusted to teach our children — as our survey sadly shows.

Evidences of Truth: Historical and Prophetic Tests

At the same time I was meeting with my Muslim friend, I had been studying Paul's sermon from 1 Corinthians 15. When he asked if I had evidence for the truth, part of the answer to his question was in those verses.[3]

First, we talked about *historical* evidence for faith. In verse 3, Paul said, "For what I received I passed on to you as of first importance: that Christ died for our sins according to the Scriptures, that he was buried, that he was raised the third day according to the Scriptures" (NIV). And we talked about the historical reliability of the Bible. This is evidence that is important in seeking the truth of Christian faith.

As he came from an Islamic background, I understood that he already believed in a creator — in one god. So I didn't in essence have to deal with that issue at that time. The Koran, though, does not give a history as Genesis does. So he did not understand the origin of sin and death and his need for a Savior. I asked a question: Would you believe in Jesus if it was determined some or all of Scripture could not be considered to have actually happened in history? The fact is, if you put the Bible to the test any other document must be put to, through the academic discipline of historiography, you will find out the New Testament alone is one of the most, if not the most, historically reliable documents in human history.

Next, we talked about the *prophetic* evidence for the truthfulness of the Christian message. I asked him if the Koran had prophecy and his answer was no. The Bible however, in the Old Testament, foretold events that came true in the New Testament with phenomenal accuracy. I can remember telling him about the dozens of prophecies of Jesus that were made hundreds of years before they were fulfilled in His life.

We talked about Josh McDowell's book, *Evidence That Demands a Verdict*. The prophetic evidence presented in this book includes a mathematical calculation of the odds of prophecy coming true — overwhelming odds! As a scholar, my Muslim friend identified with the historic and prophetic evidence. We already had some "common ground," if you like. Thank God that many, many volumes of material are readily available to anyone who wishes to strengthen their faith by being able to explain the evidence and use the correct interpretation of that evidence (based on

God's Word) to give a gentle, reverent answer to others who are asking the question.

The final evidence I want to share with you is far more powerful than the first two combined, they actually pale in comparison. First Corinthians 15:10 reads, "But by the grace of God I am what I am, and His grace to me was not without effect" (NIV). *The dynamic evidence for the truth of the Christian message is the power of Christ to change and transform the human heart and experience, now and forever.*

But further, the Bible is true because only it satisfies the preconditions of intelligibility. Only the Bible has the basis for knowledge, logic, uniformity, morality, and so on. In other words, if the Bible is not true, nothing would make sense. Other worldviews, including Islam, must borrow from the Bible to make sense of reality. For example, why we wear clothes comes from Genesis 3; why does logic exist and why can we use it, because God is logical and we are made in the image of a logical God. (Logic, which is not material but abstract, has always been a problem for a naturalistic/materialistic worldview where only material things are said to exist.)

Evidences of Truth: The Personal Test

We need to know if the Bible is true. We need to know if it can be trusted. We need to determine if the Scripture should in fact be considered as any kind of authority for the issues of our lives. Does Scripture make claims or demands upon the human family with which we must contend?

The Bible has for all time been a source of contention for those inclined not to believe it and for those who gladly base their lives upon it. The most powerful thing about the Bible is that it is not neutral — in fact, there is no such position as a "neutral" one. One way or another, we must all contend with its claims. To not make a decision about whether or not it will serve as the authority for your life is, in fact, to decide against it.

There is no way out of this dilemma. And so you can see why its message can be so contentious for so many. Is there any other literature in human history that has caused such a situation? The Bible stands alone in its claim to be a written revelation of the sovereign God, its author. Its authority carries the weight of its author — authority and author share a common root word for an especially good reason when it comes to Scripture.

Now, when you consider the Scripture's claims upon your own life, you can do so in different ways. One, you can approach it like a scholar might. You can contend with the historicity of the document, or its several literary styles and genres. You may want to approach it in a more scientific way, trying to determine if the scientific evidence related to such physical events as the origin of life in the creation account or the events of the Flood are consistent with operational science. Today, doubts in regards to these accounts are where the slippery slide of unbelief has really begun for many.

But I suggest at some time in your life you explore it simply by reading it (starting at the beginning — Genesis) in its context and believing that the God who gave it has a message to give to His creation. It's a message that can be understood. It's not a secret; it does not take special talent. It is a message laser-focused for understanding to any human heart trying to comprehend it. You must realize this book was not given to the theologians and scholars in the first place. It was given to common folk who, I believe, were created with a place in their soul to seek the knowledge and apply the wisdom to life in this world and the one to come. Romans 1:20 states that an awareness of God comes from the evidence of creation. I also know that the Scripture itself teaches that "faith comes from hearing, and hearing by the word of Christ" (Rom. 10:17).

You can be sure the scholars and theologians who believe in the Bible as God's Word have clearly helped in our appreciation and understanding of this book. They have verified the historicity of the Bible many times over. In fact, it is not a stretch to say that the Bible is the most historically reliable book in human history. Sadly though, our survey confirms that many scholars today are dismantling belief in the Bible — and it is creating havoc in our churches and culture.

But the real power of the Bible is that those who read it find it to be the most plausible and authentic explanation of human existence. The Bible claims for itself a kind of spiritual power that many are looking for. If you want a glimpse of what is available for you in the Bible, consider the words of Psalm 19:7–9. This is the Scriptures' own testimony of itself. Here is what it says:

The law of the Lord is perfect, restoring the soul. It perfectly tells the truth about every subject included in the sacred text. It is truth that transforms our souls. Do you ever feel empty inside? Are you looking for more out of life? Do you ever wonder what is true in this life? The Bible is for you; it is God's perfect law of life and it will restore your soul.

The testimony of the Lord is sure, making wise the simple. Do you have all the answers you need for life or is there anything you would benefit from knowing? Do you need clarity of mind as you face the pressures and struggles of life? Do you need to face destructive patterns in your life? The Bible is "sure." That means you can believe it and trust it. You find wisdom for life in its pages. The accounts given there are the stories of all of life's questions and the answers given are your answers, too. The Bible is God's guarantee to you of wisdom enough to live a good life — and yet it is so much more.

The precepts of the Lord are right, rejoicing the heart. The Bible sets the right path for you and it is a path of joy. Do you need direction in your life? Are you confused or scared about the track you are currently on? Do you realize you will end up in the direction you are headed right now? Is it really the way you want to go? Have you seen the alternative route? Just because you don't see it yet does not mean it's not there. God delights in showing you the way to go. Jesus said in the Bible, "I am the way" (John 14:6). He is your direction and destination. He gives the direction for your journey in the Bible. It is the path of joy to follow Him.

The commandment of the Lord is pure, enlightening your eyes. Are you able to face the dark, calamitous days of life? Disease, devastation, and death — they are all part of the human experience. You cannot make believe they are not, and all of us must one day face the darkness of this life. In these times the Bible enlightens our eyes. This is so powerful because in the dark world we need light. In dark times, the Bible gives us vision we otherwise would not have. The vision God gives in His Word is the ability to see the tragic side of life through the eyes of God. Once your eyes are enlightened by Scripture you will see a picture of the glorious life God has for you that makes all the darkness go away forever.

The fear of the Lord is clean, enduring forever. The Scripture remains the only thing in our world untouched by the evil of sin. It is pure and clean, devoid of error. Its truth endures forever. The truth of God's Word is timeless and endures for all generations.

The judgments of the Lord are true; they are righteous altogether. God's Word says of itself it is true. We all want to know what is true in life. People do not follow what is fake or purposefully untrue. There is a desire in every human heart to be right and know what is true. All the evidence supports what the Bible itself claims: it is a trustworthy and true description of a sovereign God who created all that exists and who desires to walk with us in a personal relationship full of grace, joy, and forgiveness.

Decision Time

Every time we are confronted with propositional statements (statements that claim to be true) we have a decision we must make: is it true or not? And there is a follow-up: if it is true do I need to do anything about it (1 Thess. 5:21)?

In our relativistic, postmodern culture there is a paucity of those committed to any kind of objective truth. The postmodern mind says language is the only way we construct meaning and any reference to truth is forever hidden. And so we tell our stories and truth becomes what you can get others to agree to.

But above that wasteland of belief and meaninglessness stands a worldview that claims there is, in fact, objective truth with which to contend in this universe. This truth is that which corresponds to reality. It is truth that is non-contradicting, it does not violate laws of logic, it is absolute, it does not depend on time, place, or conditions. This truth is discovered, for it exists independently of our minds. We do not create it. It is inescapable. To deny its existence is to affirm we are bound by it. It is unchanging. It is the only standard upon which any other claim is measured.

This is the kind of truth we find in the sovereign God revealed in nature and in His Word, the Bible. This is the reality of the One who made these claims:

> I am the way, and the truth, and the life (John 14:6).

> No one comes to the Father but through Me. If you had known me, you would have known My Father (John 14:6–7).

> Jesus said to the people who believed in him, "You are truly my disciples if you remain faithful to my teachings. And you will know the truth, and the truth will set you free (John 8:31–32; NLT).

Answers in Genesis and Warner University seek to give glory and honor to God as Creator, and to affirm the truth of the biblical record of the real origin and history of the world and mankind. Part of this real history is the bad news that the rebellion of the first man, Adam, against God's command brought death, suffering, and separation from God into this world. We see the results all around us. All of Adam's descendants are sinful from conception (Ps. 51:5) and have themselves entered into this rebellion (sin). They therefore cannot live with a holy God, but are condemned to separation from God.

The Bible says that "all have sinned and fall short of the glory of God" (Rom. 3:23) and that all are therefore subject to "eternal destruction, away from the presence of the Lord and from the glory of His power" (2 Thess. 1:9). But the good news is that God has done something about it. "For God so loved the world, that He gave his only begotten Son, that whoever believes in Him should not perish, but have eternal life" (John 3:16). Jesus Christ the

Creator, though totally sinless, suffered on behalf of mankind, the penalty of mankind's sin, which is death and separation from God. He did this to satisfy the righteous demands of the holiness and justice of God, His Father.

Jesus was the perfect sacrifice; He died on a Cross, but on the third day He rose again, conquering death, so that all who truly believe in Him, repent of their sin and trust in Him (rather than their own merit) are able to come back to God and live for eternity with their Creator. Therefore, "He who believes in Him is not condemned; but he who does not believe is condemned already, because he has not believed in the name of the only begotten Son of God" (John 3:18; NKJV). What a wonderful Savior and what a wonderful salvation in Christ our Creator!

My friends, this type of thinking is not an option — it is essential both for our salvation, our survival, and for the integrity of our witness in the world. We need to be thinking about what our children are being taught in regard to such matters, and as our survey makes clear, as we consider the college we are entrusting their education to. If we as a Church, parents, and educators are going to have a credible response to the attacks that we have suffered from secular forces, we must understand how high the stakes are in this war, and then learn to think strategically and accurately about God's Word and the world that He created.

And, oh yes, you may be wondering what happened to my friend from Saudi Arabia. Our time together abruptly came to an end the day the first Gulf War started. I never saw him after that. I think he may have been called back home. But I will always remember him as the most intensely interested person in the Scripture I have ever known. And I will always consider it a privilege to have shared with him the Book that is the truth for life and hope for his salvation in Jesus Christ.

Endnotes
1. R.C. Sproul, *The Holiness of God* (Wheaton, IL: Tyndale Publishing, 1998), p. 116.
2. R.C. Sproul, general editor, *New Geneva Study Bible* (Nashville, TN: T. Nelson, 1995).
3. All evidence is God's (Ps. 24:1 and Col. 1:16). What really matters is the proper interpretation of that evidence.

Chapter 8

The High Stakes of Good Thinking:
The Age of the Earth

Greg Hall and Ken Ham

Love the Lord your God with all your heart and with all your soul and with all your strength and with all your mind (Luke 10:27; NIV).

Greg Hall

When the Psalmist declared, "I am fearfully and wonderfully made," it was never more true than as it relates to the functioning of the human mind. Our cognitive abilities are an endowment from our Creator. Over the course of a lifetime, these abilities are squandered or developed. In fact, the greatest change and development in your life comes from your personal attention to your ability to grow in your power to think and reason. The Apostle Paul put it like this in Romans 12:2:

Do not be conformed to this world, but be transformed by the renewing of your mind.

Here again is the importance of worldview. It will be the framework for human thinking. Worldview is all about making decisions about what ideas you will think about, embrace, and apply to your life. Christian worldview is about discovering the ideas, thoughts, values, and perspectives of Jesus Christ. It is applying these concepts to our lives in such a way that Christ can be woven into the fabric of our lives.

If we are going to bear the marks of a Christian mind, it is time to engage with the person and work of Jesus Himself in ways yet unrealized. To "have the mind of Christ" is what the Scripture promises us. But you cannot know it from a distance. You do not see it from a long way off — you must get up close. And you certainly don't see it vicariously, through someone else's experiences. Stop blindly reading and listening to what others say about Christ. Go to Scripture, read, meditate, pray, and find out what He says to you. Others' experiences may bring clarity to understanding the mind of Christ, but it will never bring reality.

We might think we desire the mind of Christ, but every time we seek information, understanding, or wisdom from other sources or other teachers, we betray our so-called belief in the greatest teacher who ever lived. It is time to understand that the reason we have any inclination to have the mind of Christ or think Christianly in the first place is because Jesus is the smartest man who ever lived. His comprehension about every topic of interest in the human condition is impeccable. We should want to know what Jesus "thinks" about any topic first and foremost. The words attributed to Him in Scripture and about Him in Scripture present everything every person who ever lived needs to know to live a meaningful life in this world and in the world to come. It is time to "think Christianly."

To "think Christianly" is to consider ourselves as His students in every moment of time, in every circumstance of our lives. It is in moments like this that we have the potential to be transformed. The transformation comes as a result of being connected to the One whose thoughts are right about everything. This is the environment in which God wants us to function.

Thinking Christianly means we face the reality and amazing possibilities for life when we say it is God in whom, "we live and move and exist" (Acts 17:28). Jesus knew this connection to the Father. He knew it would be our very sustenance to keep our lives going. He knew it would be for us too — it is the design by which the Creator established how we exist. This kind of connectedness has the very power for living. It meets every need of the human being for meaningful existence. It means God is very much at work and available for help and support in every area of life, and it is impossible to miss Him when we first connect to Him in this way. In Him we live and move and have our being. What a way to live — with the Sovereign God of the universe interactively involved in our daily experience.

To think Christianly is to imitate how God Himself thinks. Jesus undoubtedly made this the focus of attention in His earthly life. Even at the most crucial point of Jesus' move toward the Cross, as He prayed in the Garden of

Gethsemane, He labored over the plan of redemption now reaching its crisis moments. He actually prayed that "this cup would pass," that this particular event of crucifixion could somehow be averted;[1] however, He ultimately sought the mind of God on the matter. Nevertheless, He said, "not My will, but Yours be done" (Luke 22:42). In Christ's humbled state (Phil. 2:8), He submitted to the mind of God the Father (see also John 14:28) in the most significant crisis in human history since the Fall of mankind.

The philosophies and ideologies of the world have seemed to eclipse the face of God; we should not be fooled along with the world — this is still His world, His creation, His life. To seek Him as the great mind behind the design of the universe and all living things is the most intelligent work we could ever do. That we seek any number of worldly resources for wisdom, and solutions to dilemmas of our lives is not only an indictment on our faith but our intellect, too.

To think Christianly is to have a relationship with Jesus that is not commonplace. You can't be a typical church member or believer and have Christ involved in your life the way He and the Father intended. It goes way beyond the experience of the "consumer Christianity" of today. Perhaps people don't interact with Him in the way defined by Scripture because:

1. They don't know Scripture — how could they, given the failure of the pulpit to teach God's Word from the beginning without doubt or compromise with the world's teaching, and produce life-changing doctrine.
2. They don't think He's available — how could He be available given the sorry state of our prayer ability?
3. They really don't think it's Jesus' place to do anything about their lives in a personal way or He just won't, it's not how it works today. Or it may be that today's believer suffers from all the above.

To think Christianly is to firmly believe there is not a question being asked in our culture, or any other culture, for which Jesus does not have the answer. Is your Jesus competent enough to do anything about the issues of your life? And does He have the interest to join with you in the struggles of your life? Does what He thinks matter to you or even cross your mind?

We should be thinking like Paul, who proclaimed in Colossians 2:3 that Jesus holds "all the treasures of wisdom and knowledge." But today we do not think Christianly because we do not consider Him competent in the intellectual or academic pursuits of our lives. And we do not have the mind of Christ because we neither desire it nor seek it. And we live like this to our peril.

To think Christianly is to have this steadfast preoccupation of the pursuit of the mind of Christ and His willingness and ability to be intimately involved in the thinking of His followers. It is also about the continued efforts we must make in our minds toward reformation. In our human brokenness and frailty, our minds need constant attention. There is always a need for reformation. This is why the Apostle wants us to be transformed, and knew the way to do it was by the renewal or reformation of our minds. Furthermore, when Jesus asks us to "repent," as His message clearly was, what else can it mean but to change and reform our thinking about the issues of life? We must learn to think differently about every area of life.

This takes a massive effort of humility. There is nothing more contrary to our human condition than to be responsible enough for our thinking to change it. This change does not come easily, but it is not impossible. The change does not come easily because at the center of our sinful humanity is *hubris* — pride. And it is pride that keeps us attempting to be in control of all aspects of our lives, especially our thinking.

The prideful mind does not respond well to the concept that there is an intellectual force that is greater than our self. The prideful mind cannot fathom that this Jesus is a master intellect whom we must turn to for reformation or reclamation. But this is the very essence of conversion, that in our thinking we understand the need to repent and follow the One who alone is the wisdom of all creation.

And here is precisely the place where thinking Christianly is at play in our culture and where the stakes could not be higher. Here is the place where Christians need to stand most firm. Here is the place where the battle of ideas and/or worldview needs to be won; otherwise, the rest of the discussion is fruitless.

The ultimate goal of thinking Christianly is to present God as Creator and Father of everything that He has made and build our entire worldview on the foundation of His written revelation. He is the maker and owner of everything that is made. Here is where humankind is made to realize we owe our very existence to something (someone) other than ourselves. Here is where *hubris* is put in its place. Here is the beginning of knowledge and wisdom. In the beginning God created the heavens and the earth . . . and that is the only foundation for clear thinking ever made available.

When we study Romans 1, we see the significance of God making Himself known in creation. "God's invisible qualities — his eternal power and divine nature — have been clearly seen, being understood from what has been made" (Rom. 1:20; NIV). In our secular, naturalistic culture, people have rejected what God has clearly presented to them. This is precisely why they want to fight and believe they can win the war at this battlefront — the origin of life. In the naturalistic scheme of things, it is impossible to conceive of anything transcendent or supernatural. The study of origins, of creation, is where they want to eliminate God once and for all.

But it will not happen. This is remarkably poor thinking on their part. Evidence for God as Creator abounds for the thinking person. The naturalistic way of thinking of the world is flawed and prejudiced by promotion of a vain philosophy not founded in Christ (Col. 2:8–9), and not based on good science. The truth of life is that the ultimate questions of life — where we come from and where we are going — have not changed since the beginning of time. We can, and should, seek the mind of Jesus on these matters. Jesus, our master teacher and Creator of the universe, has been the one and only to ever know every answer. And He's revealed what we need to know in His written Word to us.

Second only to surrendering to Jesus Christ as your Lord and Savior, I believe that thinking Christianly is the most important thing you will ever do. But please understand, this does not happen by default. As Romans 12 says, by default we are conformed to this world. Transformation comes through commitment to moment by moment intimacy with Jesus, a very practical relationship with His living Word, and a daily walk of obedience that allows the Holy Spirit to move in our lives so that we naturally live according to the truth as He lives through us.

In the next section, Ken will discuss a very important aspect of thinking Christianly, but before you read on, please stop right here and spend some time talking with Jesus. Ask Him to move in your life. Ask Him to be the Lord of your mind. Ask Him to set aside your pride so that you can willingly and joyfully submit to His compassionate authority, and be set free by the truth of His life and the words of the Bible. My friends, this is not a place where you need God's "help." This is something that only He can do (1 Cor. 12:3). Ask that He would begin the supernatural transformation that only comes through the renewing of our minds according to the truth and authority of the Scriptures.

Thinking Christianly about the Age of the Earth
Ken Ham

As Greg mentioned earlier, *the ultimate goal of thinking Christianly is to present God as Creator and Father of everything that He has made.* Certainly, that includes each and every one of us. He is our Creator, and He is our father. He is the provider of everything that we have. He is responsible for everything we are and He is the source of strength for everything that we are going to become.

The pressure to conform to the world is everywhere we turn. It's in the media, in books, in museums, and in zoos. And as we've seen, it's not only in public schools and secular universities, but even Christian colleges have given in to the pressure to conform to the naturalistic worldview. Many are engaging in "newspeak" in order to justify their compromise so they can stand on both sides of the issue. The problem is that this double-mindedness is neither necessary nor consistent with good thought. It is certainly not "thinking Christianly."

The professors and leaders in the education world are highly educated . . . but have they learned the skills of consistent, biblical thinking? When we look at how the presidents, vice presidents, and professors of Christian universities responded to several of the questions regarding the age of the earth in the survey, the answer is obvious.

Q14: *Would you consider yourself a young-earth or old-earth Christian?*

Old earth	49.0%
Young earth	42.3%
Neither	8.3%

Because this issue is so hotly debated, we are not surprised about this nearly even split in belief. What is revealing, however, is the inconsistency between this belief and the other things that they claim about their belief in Scripture.

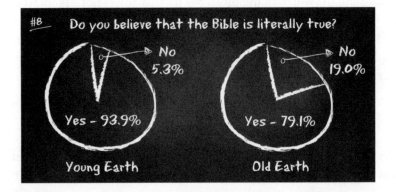

Of those who believe that the earth is young, 93.9 percent believe that the Bible is literally true; and the consistency in these two beliefs is clear. But notice that 79.1 percent of those who believe the earth is old also believe that the Bible is literally true. The word "literally true" apparently means nothing to them. Some may actually believe that the Bible literally teaches that the word "day," as used in Genesis 1, is a long period of time that allows for millions of years. But in order to allow for this interpretation, they must twist the established rules of biblical interpretation to the extreme *and* reinterpret massive numbers of Scriptures throughout the rest of the Bible such as Mark 10:6 and Exodus 20:11. This certainly isn't the intent of "thinking Christianly," and we must ask the question, "Why would they force such an interpretation when it is not the clear and simple reading from Scripture?" It's clear that something besides the truth of God's Word is influencing their thinking here. Obviously, it's the influence of the naturalistic worldview and probably the pressure from their peers who believe in an old earth who may also believe in evolution over millions of years.

Since the 1800s, we've had many scholars say, "We take the Bible as literally written; it says six days." But then they add the word "but." And this is where they begin to become conformed to this world, rather than being transformed by the renewing of their minds according to the truth of Scripture. It usually sounds like this: "Yes, the Bible says six days, *but* because 'science' has proven the earth to be billions and billions of years old, these must not be six literal days." (Remember, "science" has done no such thing. Evidence from operational science does not confirm an old earth. But that's not the main thing I'm trying to emphasize here.)

The point I'm making is that these people are ultimately reinterpreting Scripture through the lens of the secular, godless, naturalistic worldview. It is an *authority* issue. What they are really doing is taking outside ideas from the world and trying to force Scripture to fit with them. They are conforming to the world, rather than being transformed by the renewing of their minds according to the truth of God's Word. Of course, with God's Word as the source of truth, this doesn't work at all, and their explanations come across as weak and inconsistent.

Some will argue that this is really just a matter of different interpretations, similar to the debates that we have about end-times scenarios and eschatology. But I say, "Wait a minute. People who argue different views on eschatology by and large argue *from* Scripture. People who argue against Genesis argue because of secular influences (i.e., from a different religious viewpoint: that of secular humanism)." That is a big difference. Unquestionably, figurative language is used throughout Scripture to make analogies or metaphors (for example: God is our rock and our fortress) but in these passages the figure of speech is obvious. One still interprets it literally, for to do so is to consider the genre. Understanding the symbolic or figurative language enables one to literally interpret what is intended. In Genesis 1, there is no indication for any reason that the Hebrew word for "day" doesn't mean "day" in its ordinary (approximately 24-hour) meaning. Scripture makes this clear as the six days of creation are qualified by a number, evening and morning. This is a matter of authority, and it is a matter of truth — of correct interpretation. Even leading Hebrew lexicons do not leave open Genesis days as long ages:

> *Yom*: "Day of twenty-four hours: Genesis 1:5"[2]
> *Yom*: "Day as defined by evening and morning: Genesis 1:5"[3]

Seriously, those people who leave open long ages are either misinformed or they are consciously engaged in "newspeak." Observe the inconsistencies in the answers to the following questions:

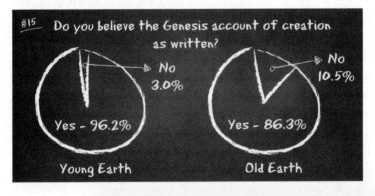

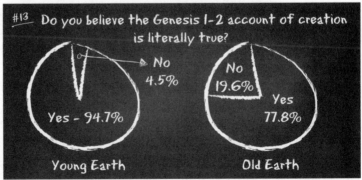

Again, the more specific the question, the more clear the inconsistencies become. We're not just asking if they believe the Bible is literally true in general, we specifically asked if they believe that the *Genesis 1–2 account of creation* is literally true. Of the people who believe in an old earth, 77.8 percent say yes! It's possible that some of these people believe in what is known as the "gap theory" (which teaches that God did create in six literal days, but that each of these days were preceded by millions of years), but I really doubt it. Very few people in the Christian world give much credence to this idea anymore.

Do you see the inconsistency of belief? And a failure to "think Christianly"? Let's not even argue about who's right or who's wrong here. On both sides of the issue, people are talking out of both sides of their mouth. Of people who believe in an old earth, 77.8 percent say that they believe the Genesis 1–2 account of creation is literally true, yet only 52.3 percent of them believe in God creating the earth in six literal 24-hour days?

Clearly, more than 25 percent of them either don't understand that Genesis teaches six literal days, or they just never simply thought this through! More astoundingly, 52.3 percent of people who believe in an old earth believe that God created it in six literal 24-hour days! How can someone be an old earther and say they believe in a six-day creation (unless they do adhere to the gap theory)? I don't know. Believers in a young earth, however, also show inconsistencies: 26 percent of them do not believe that God created in six literal 24-hour days. So if somebody believes in a young earth, but does not believe in six 24-hour days, what do they believe?

Q17: Do you believe in God creating the earth but not in six 24-hour days?

	Young earth	Old earth
Yes	31.1%	59.5%
No	68.2%	37.9%

Again, we see great inconsistencies in these responses. Are there some "hybrids" of belief here that we can't categorize? Do these leaders and professors not understand the issues? Or are they talking out of both sides of their mouth? We saw earlier how Dr. William Dembski says he actually believes in six literal 24-hour days of creation, and yet he believes that the world is billions of years old. His explanation for this is outlandish — that Adam and Eve were made from human-like animals that God gave souls as well as amnesia regarding their former, pre-human existence. But we at least have to give him credit for trying and recognizing there is a problem! I'm concerned that the majority of these people are not only not thinking Christianly, but they're just not thinking at all! Clearly, what they say they believe is not consistent with what they say they also believe. This is again illuminated when we look at their views of Scripture:

This is an interesting claim as well! Wouldn't you think that the young-earth group would have a higher view of Scripture when it comes to infallibility and inspiration than the old-earth group? Basically this is about even, with those believing in an old earth having just a slightly higher view of Scripture than those who believe in a young earth (backward from what we would expect). What can we conclude? There is no correlation between their purported view of Scripture and whether or not they believe in young or old earth at all.

What we appear to have is a basic biblical illiteracy among some of the leaders and professors of Christian colleges. Not only are their responses contradictory to the clear teachings of Scripture, but they are also inconsistent with themselves. This is far, far from "thinking Christianly." Perhaps this is because most of them have never been trained in it, and are therefore stuck in a quagmire of belief, where they claim to believe in Scripture but are really being influenced by the secular worldview. This confusion becomes clear in their responses to questions about the Flood:

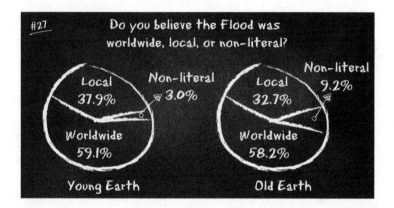

People who believe in an old earth are statistically more likely to believe that the Flood was not a real event at all, but other than that there's not much distinction between whether or not they believe the Flood was worldwide or local. It's intriguing to see that 58.2 percent of those who believe that the earth is old actually believe that the Flood was worldwide. At least they believe the Bible on this point — but it shows another inconsistency: if you believe in an old earth, you really shouldn't believe in a global Flood.

The idea that the earth is millions of years old, in our modern era, first arose in the early 19th century. The supposed evidence for millions of years was considered to be the fossil record, said by secularists to have been laid down gradually over millions of years. But if there had been a worldwide Flood, this would have destroyed this record and re-deposited it, thus destroying the supposed evidence for millions of years! There are so many problems one could consider. If you're going to believe in an old earth and believe in a global Flood, you must either do some amazing mental gymnastics to accommodate the conflicting ideas or allow for inconsistency in your thinking.

Those who believe in a young earth show similar inconsistencies. Of the people who believe in a young earth, 37.9 percent also believe that the Flood was local. That's inconsistent as well. How do they believe that the massive sedimentary strata containing billions of fossils formed if it neither happened during a worldwide Flood nor took place over millions of years? That stance doesn't even make sense. Their understanding of history in light of Scripture is not consistent. I have found that many academics in the Christian world do not have a big picture understanding in geology, biology, astronomy, theology, etc. — and they don't realize the massive inconsistencies and dilemmas they are living with.

Another problem is the issue of death — physical death. The Bible makes it clear that humans and animals were vegetarian before sin (Gen. 1:29–30). Also, the original creation was "very good" (no diseases like cancer, no thorns). Man wasn't told to eat animal flesh until after the Flood (Gen. 9).

However, in the fossil record, said to pre-date humans by millions of years, we find:

1. Thorns said to be millions of years old (but thorns came AFTER sin — after the Curse — Gen. 3:17–19)
2. Animals with evidence they were eating each other — bones in their stomachs/teeth marks on bones (but animals were vegetarian before man sinned)
3. Animal bones with evidence of diseases like cancer, brain tumors, arthritis, etc. (but everything was "very good" before sin)

There is great concern here that people are not thinking Christianly, even though they say they are. If you walked up to the president or vice president or a professor on a Christian campus, and asked them if they believe that the Bible is literally true, almost all of them will give you the same answer. When you ask them specific questions related to the truth of Scripture, however, we again find out that many of them don't believe that at all. So words really don't matter, and many of them have concocted convoluted explanations for their compromised beliefs. They have turned to the secular scientists to tell them about history while still trying to cling to parts of the Bible.

I believe that some of it is just ignorance in the context of Scripture and a consciously thought-out biblical worldview. But I have to be honest. I meet with a lot of these leaders and professors, and many times their attitudes are laced with an arrogance and a condescending attitude that looks down on other Christians in a voice that says, "Don't worry about it, you wouldn't understand anyway. Of course what we teach is true. You don't know what we mean by that, but we do — and that's all that matters." What we're seeing is 1 Corinthians 8:1–3 being lived out:

> We know that we all have knowledge. Knowledge makes arrogant, but love edifies. If anyone supposes that he knows anything, he has not yet known as he ought to know; but if anyone loves God, he is known by Him.

I am sometimes belittled and cut down by professors at "respected" Christian universities because I don't have the academic credentials that some of these people do. They think that because they have the credentials, they have the truth. They say, "How dare Ken Ham question us, because he is not trained in biblical languages; he didn't go to Bible college; he didn't go to seminary; etc." In some ways I'm glad that I don't have those credentials, because I might have ended up like some of them: compromising the truth clearly laid forth by Scripture in the midst of a bunch of academic mumble jumble created to accommodate secular scientific ideas.

Or worse than that, they might actually believe that since *they* teach it, that *makes* it true — that they are the ones who actually determine truth. You might as well not argue with men and women like that. Not only do they think that what they teach is right, but they feel like they *are* right because of their position of authority and their level of education. Once again, it's a matter of authority. Do these people submit to the authority of the Word of God? Or have they submitted themselves to the authority of fallen men, and their own personal knowledge of what they think is truth? Certainly, they have become like the Chaldeans that the minor prophet Habakkuk spoke of in Habakkuk 1:7:

> They are dreaded and feared; their justice and authority originate with themselves.

Unquestionably, we have been "fearfully and wonderfully made." God has given us a mind, and our lives can be transformed by the renewing of that mind. Will we be conformed to the world? Or will the transforming power of God's living word become our final authority?

May God, by His infinite grace and mercy, give us the willingness to bend the knee to the authority of His Word. By the power of His Spirit may we be empowered and willing to "think Christianly" in every aspect of our lives, that we may be willing to receive His love and His forgiveness for our own arrogance and our own personal compromise, so that we can speak the truth in love through our words and through our lives in the midst of this world that so desperately, desperately needs to see Christ in us and being lived through us.

Endnotes

1. And rightly so, for God was about to punish the sinless Christ for the sins of the world. The anguish of this was being torn between punishing Christ who did not deserve it to save mankind, or not doing it that would result in no salvation.
2. Ludwig Koehler and Walter Baumgartner, *Hebrew and Aramaic Lexicon of the Old Testament,* Volume 1 (Leidin; Boston, MA: Brill, 2001), p. 399.
3. Francis Brown, S.R. Driver, and Charles A. Briggs, *Hebrew and English Lexicon of the Old Testament,* 9th printing (Peabody, MA: Hendrickson Publishers, 1906), p. 398.

Want to know which colleges were contacted as part of the ARG study? Visit www.creationcolleges.org and also find a growing list of Christian colleges we recommend you search out.

Chapter 9

Decisions, Decisions, Decisions:
Choosing the University That's Right for You

Greg Hall

I am afraid that schools will prove to be the great gates of Hell unless they diligently labor in explaining the Holy Scriptures, engraving them in the hearts of youth. I advise no one to place his child where the Scriptures do not reign paramount. Every institution in which men are not increasingly occupied with the Word of God must become corrupt. — Martin Luther

was on my way to speak at a church in the Midwest. One of the alumni of our university picked me up at the airport. Accompanying him was a sharp young man from his youth group who was thinking about enrolling in our school. So we talked about the usual: majors, campus life, financial aid, job prospects, etc. Then the young man asked me a question that I had not been asked before, or since, in my 20 years serving as a university president. He asked, "So, if I come to your school, will my faith be built or broken?"

I asked him what he meant by that question, but I already knew exactly what he meant. He clarified the question in exactly the way I thought he would. He told me a number of the young men and women from his youth group had gone to "Christian" colleges. He said he noticed something about several of them that bothered him. In his words, "They were once 'on fire' for God" but having gone to these schools it appeared their faith had been broken. Some of them seemed no longer Christian at all. They did not go to church, or if they did it no longer seemed to occupy the place of importance in their lives it once did. And so, he asked the question again, "If I come to your school, will my faith be built or broken? Will I end up like some of them?"

The young man's question surprised me, but his reason for asking it did not. His question surprised me because for a high school junior it is very astute. He knew his observations of the lives of some who have attended Christian schools were real. At a place where it seemed obvious that Christian faith should be developed, grow, and thrive, for some, it had done just the opposite.

The reason the question didn't surprise me is because I have heard similar stories over and over again. In all honesty, it is not reasonable to criticize the way secular education has tried to eclipse the face of God. But we should be evaluating the experience of some who attend Christian schools whose faith was diminished or even destroyed as a result.

Perhaps you have heard some of the rationalizations. Some say the teaching is misunderstood by these students. It is claimed, "We are simply asking the tough questions, helping students struggle with faith in real and meaningful ways." Sometimes it is claimed these students have been too sheltered and need to be exposed to the deeper questions of life. I have heard some say, "We may break down faith but it is only so we can build it back in a sophisticated and intellectual way."

All this rationalization may have elements of truth, but by and large it is less than compelling. The fact is there are those who teach in Christian schools whose faith is not worth emulating. They teach what they themselves have been taught — much of it at the hands of liberal professors from secular institutions or seminaries well known for naturalism and faithlessness.

A recent press release on the ongoing *National Study of College Students' Search for Meaning and Purpose* offered some interesting information on students who are beginning their college years. While 79 percent of all freshmen believe in God, 69 percent pray, and 81 percent attend religious services at least occasionally, 57 percent question their religious beliefs, 52 percent disagree with their parents about religious matters, and 65 percent feel distant from God. College students are asking deep questions about their faith.

Unquestionably, the college years are a very critical time of life. Older adults look back at those years and can clearly recall how the course of their life was shaped by their time on campus. Parents and students who are looking ahead to college should be humbled by the magnitude of the decision and the implications that it will have on the rest of their life. This is not a time to make a blind decision. We must choose wisely and go in with our eyes wide open, aware of the educational environment that has been chosen. What do we feel are the most important criteria? Dr. R.C. Sproul nailed the issue on the head when he wrote:

> One of the problems we have here is the criteria we use when choosing colleges or university to attend in the first place. So often parents are impressed by the beauty of the campus of the particular institution or by their own remembrance of the commitment of the institution a generation ago, overlooking the reality that the approach to Christianity changes in various institutions as the faculty changes. The most significant barometer for choosing any kind of institution of higher learning is not the beauty of its campus. It is its faculty.[1]

Yes, the type of education you choose is ultimately dependent on who is in front of the classroom teaching your student. When you boil down all the options, first of all you'll have to decide between three general forms:

1. You can choose a secular institution.
2. You can choose a compromising Christian institution.
3. You can do your best to find an institution that is thoroughly committed to the authority of Scripture — understanding that none are perfect! As someone once said, if you find the perfect church, don't join it or you will destroy it!

A Secular Institution

To gain some insight into the decision, we asked the presidents, vice presidents, and professors of Christian universities what *they* thought Christian parents used as criteria when deciding to send their children to secular schools.

#10   **Why do you think Christian parents send children to secular institutions?**

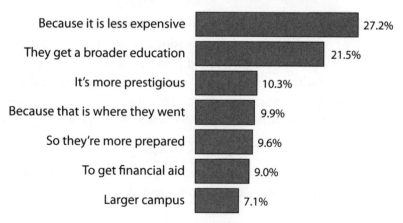

Because it is less expensive	27.2%
They get a broader education	21.5%
It's more prestigious	10.3%
Because that is where they went	9.9%
So they're more prepared	9.6%
To get financial aid	9.0%
Larger campus	7.1%

When we add up some of these categories, it's revealed that the staff of Christian colleges believes that at least 36.5 percent of Christian parents are sending their kids to a secular university for financial reasons. In my opinion, that number is too low. The vast majority of the Christian parents I talk to confess that financial concerns rule out the "possibility" of sending their children to a private Christian institution. They're making decisions because of money, sending kids to a non-private school, leaving them to navigate their way through the debauchery. Along with financial considerations, most parents offer other justifications for this decision:

- Kids need to learn to be in the world. They know that they're going into enemy territory, but we have raised them well. They are young adults now. We believe that they are solid in their faith, able to defend the truth, and will be able to survive.

- As young adults, it is time for them to be in the world, but not of it. Sooner or later they are going to have to learn to navigate through the world on their own. Now is that time.

- There needs to be Christian witness on the campus. Our child is going into this setting as a student and missionary. They are the light of the world. We don't want to put that light under a bushel. It's time to let that light shine to the benefit of those on campus who need to hear and see the truth about Jesus Christ.

- In other cases though, the parents simply do not realize the gravity of the situation. Many years ago, even most secular institutions were still rather Christian in their beliefs. So grandparents and parents may not know what the secular institutions are like in today's culture (even 50 years ago, public high schools still had prayer!).

To be fair, both Ken and I are living proof that surviving secular schools is possible. Both of us attended secular universities, grew through that experience, and, by God's grace, were used as lights to a certain extent in that dark world. However, we admit we had lots of "baggage" to discard along the way — and we grew up when even many secular institutions still held (even though inconsistently) more of a Christianized worldview to one degree or another.

Community College

One prominent Christian financial advisor not only recommends less expensive state schools, but also recommended taking advantage of community colleges near home. There are several advantages to this option. First of all, community colleges create a sort of "buffer zone" where students experience the realities of the secular world while still living at home. It can be something of a transition period, where a student gets their general studies done at a fraction of the price while still being under the guidance, protection, and watchful eye of their parents. Then, after a year or two, they transfer to a different institution that specializes in their area of interest. As finances become more and more of an issue, several families are going this direction.

But let there be no doubt, if you choose the option of a secular public school, know that students are systematically bombarded with the messages of the philosophy of naturalism — the philosophy that is the driving force behind the dominant worldview of public education. The entire premise that your education is being built on is contrary to the truths of Scripture:

- Naturalism assumes that the world you are in today is the only reality — there is nothing beyond this life.

- Naturalism assumes that the origin of life is due to random forces of nature — there is no Creator, no God.

- Naturalism teaches that ethics is a human-based concept — there is no objective truth or reality, only subjective feelings, each with as much merit as the other. All ideas are equally valid and we must be tolerant of all ideas (with the exception of Christianity it seems).

If you choose the secular option, you must go in prepared and with your eyes wide open. You must take with you the weapons you need to defend your faith and take a stand for the authority of Scripture. This can be a faith-building experience — and clearly, there is a need for this type of witness on any campus. But in order to survive, you have to realize that you are going as a defender and a proclaimer, not as a learner and a student. You really have to go in prepared for battle, because the academic atmosphere on a secular university is enemy territory in the battle for your soul and these professors often affect grades if you hold to biblical position (and they are aware of it), especially in science fields like biology and geology. We suggest there are some students more able to cope in a situation than others — and the parents need to be discerning in regard to this matter and understanding where their own children are spiritually.

A March 29, 2005, *Washington Post* article by Howard Kurtz, titled "Study Finds College Faculties a Most Liberal Lot," reports that most faculty at non-Christian colleges disdain Christianity, with 72 percent indicating they are liberal, 84 percent favoring abortion, and 67 percent indicating homosexuality is acceptable. In most cases, students reflect the values of college faculty they encounter in their upper-division coursework. These faculty members are typically the advisors and mentors of students. Certainly the above findings indicate that the answers and directions students receive from most faculty members at these institutions will not be supportive of traditional morality and religious values.

I did my undergraduate degree in philosophy at the State University of New York. I had planned to go to a Christian college to study for the ministry, but for a variety of reasons that did not happen. I know I got a good education as it relates to math, English, social science, etc., at the university — the kind of education that is supposed to prepare you for a life of gainful employment. But there was absolutely *no* evidence of anything Christian or spiritual on that campus. I do not even remember there being any kind of Christian ministry on campus. In classes it was not unusual to hear Christianity mocked.

I stayed spiritually strong during those days because I was very well connected to my home church where my father was the pastor. This is a big key for students who go to secular schools. You must stay connected to a Bible-believing fellowship and, if available, be connected to a Bible-believing campus ministry. This strategy has protected many a student who otherwise would not have withstood the pagan culture of a secular campus.

I had a very negative, fearful experience on that campus when I was a senior preparing to graduate. One day in class, one of my philosophy professors asked me what I was going to do upon graduation. He said he was hopeful I would continue in philosophy and go to graduate school. I told him I was planning to go to seminary and train to become a minister. His reaction is etched in my memory. He was incredulous: "You're going to do *what?*" he said. "You are going to seminary and become a minister?" The ridicule in his voice I still recall. Then he said, "I will do anything I have to do to stop you from such foolishness!"

And what followed was the scariest thought I have ever had. I can remember thinking, *Maybe he is right, maybe seminary and ministry is foolishness and my future should be in philosophy. Maybe I should become like my professor. . . .*

The thoughts did not stick, but in that moment I certainly entertained the possibility — thoughts that would have set my life on a course where I might very well have missed God's calling for me. That story is quite mild compared to many others who have lost their way in the pagan culture of secular education. Some of the most destructive, ungodly, unholy ideas known to mankind have come out of the secular institutions of our nation. That is why I say the secular classroom has the potential of being one of the most dangerous places for Christians in America.

It was tough on a secular campus back then, but I believe it is far more intense today than when I was an undergraduate. And that's just the ideology. There is also the issue of morality. I know what goes on at a lot of secular schools. To be honest, I wouldn't be the least bit comfortable sending my kids into that environment. The reality is that many young persons, once committed Christian young men and women, have gone to secular schools where an anti-Christian, atheistic philosophy has devastated their lives.

At the same time, there are so many exceptions that we can't draw an absolute black-and-white line. I've seen plenty of students flourish spiritually on a secular campus. We've seen many who lose their faith while attending conservative Christian universities. Can we say that this is the one factor that makes a difference in a student's life? We cannot. There is no formula that will guarantee the spiritual safety of the student, but still, the decision must be approached with prayerful wisdom. And a lot of it does come down to how they were trained in the home by their parents.

A Christian College

The vast majority of American young people go through the public schools. Even the vast majority of young people from Christian families also go to public grade schools, high schools, and public institutions of higher education. Only a minority go to private Christian schools and on to Christian institutions of higher learning. In my church, I would estimate that no more than 10 percent of college-bound young men and women go to our church-related institutions. There are undoubtedly more who go to other Christian colleges or universities, but the fact is the numbers are low. When we asked the presidents, vice presidents, and professors of Christian institutions why they felt parents chose a Christian institution, their answers were revealing:

#9   Why do you think Christian parents
send children to Christian institutions?

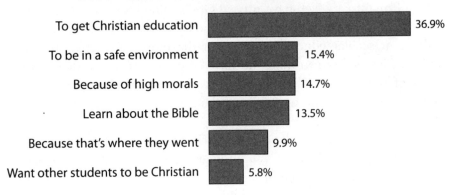

There were other answers, but these accounted for 96.2 percent of all responses. The administration and faculty feel that a safe campus and high morals account for 30 percent of the decisions. We believe that most parents would agree with this, and we also believe that these are very important factors! All you have to do is check out a tailgate party at any college football game and you will understand what we are talking about — tens of thousands of students doing the most unbelievable stuff. There's a reason that parents want a safe campus and high morals for their student. College campuses are notorious for drug use, sexual promiscuity, and alcoholism. Hey, Ken and I saw it firsthand while we were studying at secular colleges. Many other parents have been there as well, and have little desire to see their children submerged in that environment.

For those who feel the college years are still a time of preparation before going out into the "real world," the option of Christian education looks very good indeed. It looks more advantageous, safer, and more morally nurturing. In some cases, that's true. But as we've seen, in far too many cases it's not.

A Compromised Christian College

Both Ken and I feel that perhaps the worst option for a student is going blindly into a so-called "Christian" college that is compromising the authority of the Word of God. As the research has shown, this is far too prevalent. There's a massive amount of confusion across the board. It needs to be called out. We need to deal with it. There *are* good Christian schools out there and we feel they are better than the secular alternatives by far. But these issues of compromise have to be addressed.

Parents are sending their students into the schools assuming that they are going to be faith-nurturing and truth-affirming institutions. In reality, many of them discredit faith, discredit the Bible, and break kids down rather than build them up. That's why both of us are strong advocates for home-schooling, Christian schools, and carefully selected Christian higher education, because kids are dying out there and the Church doesn't seem to care enough to do anything about it. When it comes to colleges and universities, the problem is that the majority of Christian schools seem to be just like the secular — disguised with a few Christian elements.

I have had many parents say to me that they would rather send their kid to a secular school, knowing how blatantly pagan it is, than send them into a Christian school where they are told that they believe in the Bible and its authority, when in fact they really don't. It seems that Christian schools naturally progress from focused conservative faith into compromised secular ideologies.[2] If we learn nothing else from the Ivy League, it should be this: if the salt is contaminated, it's no longer good for anything. If the schools are already compromised, what good are they? Many well-known Christian schools are becoming conformed to the world, rather than to Christ. Jesus says that He would rather we be hot or cold rather than lukewarm. But lukewarmness seems to be the natural trend. Who is the worst enemy? Certainly, the enemy is the world. But doesn't the enemy also include the compromising leaders who lead people astray?

In Jesus' day, He didn't call out the world and the Romans. Jesus called out the Pharisees and the scribes who were hiding behind their religiosity. It was the religious leaders that He called the snakes and the vipers. We should not be surprised at the attacks we get from the world. We should call out those who claim the name "Christian" and yet subtly compromise the authority of Scripture in so many different ways.

Why was Stephen killed? It was because he confronted the religious leaders, calling them stiff necked and pointing out their false teaching. Ken is sometimes rebuked by Christians who don't like the way that he calls out compromising Christian leaders. They say that the real enemy is the world, and we shouldn't be attacking our own brothers and sisters in Christ. But I don't think so. I think the real enemy is the compromise within the Church, and, as we have seen too clearly, in the Christian colleges and universities that are already compromised. We should not be surprised at how the world acts — but we should be appalled at God's people when they compromise God's Word. And for those who are teachers influencing the coming generations — the Scripture has a warning: "Let not many of you become teachers, my brethren, knowing that as such we will incur a stricter judgment" (James 3:1).

So how do we help you decide where to go? I don't want my kids going to a secular institution. But I'd rather have them go to a state institution than send them to the wolves who are dressed in sheep's clothing. Thankfully, there is a third option.

A Committed Christian College

My kids attended the Christian college where I serve. It was a decision of their own choosing. Sure, I gave advice and direction — including telling them my experience in going to a secular undergraduate school. While they could have gone anywhere, they chose a Christian college. I sometimes ask them about their experience at a Christian college and ask what sticks out in their minds as being the most important outcomes of that choice. The answers always center on the same three things:

1. First, they talk about their wonderful friends that they met during college days — friends that they cherish and still are very close to this day, Christian friends.

2. They also talk about the faculty that made a difference in their lives. They will talk about their mentoring, about their kindness, even recalling lectures that meant something to them.

3. Then, they always talk about the importance of the chapel worship services. They describe these as the most important thing about going to a Christian school.

On top of that, they often recall the importance of serving others and being part of a local church. They see the value of finding a Christian mate who shares similar values and similar desires to raise a Christian family. When I added it all up, I realized that this Christian education has helped them to write a biblical Christian worldview with the alphabet of their souls. And I rejoice.

Ken didn't send any of his kids to secular schools, nor did he send them to compromising schools. He and his wife Mally sent them to a couple of the best conservative schools that they could find. Are they perfect? No. On several occasions Ken had to intervene and square off with professors and administrators who were compromising the Word of God. But at least the schools had a clear commitment to the authority of Scripture, rather than a subtle or blatant denial of absolute biblical truth.

So if you want to see what we really recommend, I guess you don't have to look any further than what we did with our children. What we are really saying is that your kids probably shouldn't go to a secular college. Send them to a Christian college, but be very discerning, because there are only a few that are on track in all areas — and even then you have to be careful as they all have "warts."

If your intent is to send your child into a spiritually nurturing environment you must ask the question, "What is the best opportunity for my kid to go and hear the proclamation of true Scripture?" But to get the right answers to that question, you have to ask a lot of other questions.

Asking Questions

Certainly, one of the biggest lessons we learned from this survey is that people don't always say what they mean, and many times even what they mean is in conflict with what they actually believe. So how do you find out what an institution actually believes and teaches? How do you find out what each individual professor believes and teaches? You can look at the official brochures, or you can even ask the president, but does that guarantee that's what the institution and professors believe and teach? Sometimes, but certainly not always.

The survey showed that some presidents seem to be disconnected with what is really happening on campus. Not only that, but we've seen that there is confusion between the departments as well. At the same school, there may be great disagreement on important issues between the religion and the science departments. And within those departments, there can be professors who teach whatever they want without consequence. Even if the school has pinpointed a particular faculty member who is compromising the Word of God, it's very difficult to remove them, particularly if they have tenure. Unfortunately, very few schools have clear doctrinal statements, and even those that do often don't have consequences for those who teach things contrary to the Bible. So it's clear that if you want to find out what a school is really all about, you not only have to ask questions, but you have to know the *right* questions to ask.

Asking the Right Questions

The naturalistic worldview has gained a very powerful foothold on many Christian campuses. This worldview can make it very difficult to get clear answers. Sure, the answers might sound clear at first, but often the answers are coming from a relativistic view of truth that says, "What's true for you may not be true for me." And as we've seen, "newspeak" allows people to say contradictory things as if both are true. People also define words differently, so key concepts might mean something totally different to someone else. So not only do you have to ask questions, but you have to ask the right questions. How do you do this?

First, we would suggest starting with the same kinds of questions that we asked in this survey. These questions are important because they are the questions the average person in the Church is asking Christian colleges to answer. When we were designing this survey, we asked the questions carefully and from several different angles so that we could compare the results. You'll need to do the same thing. They are not the typical "academic" questions. They are the simple, down-to-earth questions that the people ask, and those who ask them have every right to a clear simple answer. They are not "trick" questions. These are the questions the Church wants answers to.

Second, we would suggest asking questions that are both hypothetical and actual. For example, question 12 asks if there are consequences for anti-biblical teaching. The answers you get to this may be vague. You can help clarify that by asking questions like these:

- If someone on your faculty began to teach that literal truths from Scripture were actually figurative, how would their department head respond?

- Do you know of anyone who has recently been disciplined for teaching something contrary to the Bible? Can you tell me more about that?

Figuring out what people mean by what they say is also a challenge. People use words that we are familiar with even though they may mean something different to them. When you are sorting through their catalogs and sitting down to talk to someone, you'll need to ask them what they mean when they say something like "We believe in a literal interpretation of Genesis." But then you'll need to double-check these answers with specific questions that reveal what they really believe, such as, "How much time do you teach it took God to create the world and everything in it?" or "Were Adam and Eve real people that God specially created?" or "Do you teach that the Flood described in Genesis covered the entire surface of the globe?" Hopefully this way you will be able to learn what people really mean when they say things like "infallible" or "worldwide."

Without being deceptive, you might also want to ask questions that play to the liberal mindset, and see if the leaders or professors are willing to take a stand for the truth. For example, you might ask something like this: "If a student presented a speech in class where she professed her sincere belief in evolution and why she thinks it's true, how would you respond?" Or something like this: "If one of your students was struggling with his sexual identity and was truly contemplating whether or not God had created them for same-sex relationships, how would you counsel them?"

From our own experience we have found conservative Christian colleges that have certain professors that teach a compromising message — yet other faculty are either unaware of it or they turn a blind eye to it. Sometimes the administration will say that because of tenure, they can't do anything about a certain professor who is obviously teaching material that undermines the authority of Scripture. And sometimes a conservative Christian college will employ someone who doesn't strictly adhere to the statement of faith — but they are supposedly "okay" in a certain area of expertise the college needs. More and more such professors are employed — and the slippery slide is underway.

You're going to have a challenge finding out from a few individuals what is actually taught across the whole campus. Remember that the survey discovered wide discrepancies between individuals, departments, and positions. So whom do you ask?

Asking the Right Questions of the Right People

You're going to want to talk to as many people in as many different positions as possible. At larger schools it's going to take effort just to get past the admissions department and the students who give you a campus tour. But be persistent. Try to meet with the president or the dean of students. Find out the office hours of professors in various departments and drop in to meet them. The more that parents begin to do this, the more these people will realize they are being held accountable. Eventually, this will cause many colleges to think about these issues — particularly if parents stop supporting them and stop sending their children to them.

Some of the best people to ask are going to be former students or the parents of those students. Experience is a good teacher, and what other people have experienced at a college you're considering can teach you a lot about what things are really like there. Former students will generally be able to tell you the good and the bad about what's really happening on campus and in the classroom. Ken said that he has been on Christian campuses and spent time at lunch with some of the students. He then asks them what they are taught in certain areas — he has been quite shocked at what he heard from students at what he thought were really conservative colleges. This is another way to find out what is being taught — spend time with those who know what their professors are teaching them. These students also hear from their friends about other professors.

At the center of the whole issue is what the teacher teaches, particularly about the Word of God, the Bible. Because of that, we think it's worth it to investigate the educational background of the faculty. Smaller universities should have a complete list of their staff available that lists their experience and educational background. At larger schools, you might have to go to the specific departments to find this information. Oftentimes this is all posted online, and with a few clicks of the mouse you can get a good feel for where the professors were trained. Sometimes it is very tough to stay faithful to a high view of Scripture as God's Word to us when you are part of the secular academy. Many have done so, but it takes strength and discernment to remain faithful. While educational background alone does not determine what someone's worldview actually is, knowing this information will give you a feel for the worldview under which the faculty were formally trained.

Making the Best Choice for Your Family

Unfortunately, choosing a college or university is no longer a clear, black-and-white decision. If we have accomplished nothing else in this book, I pray that we have brought to light important variables that you may have never even considered when selecting a school for yourself or your children. The variables are many, and at the end of your search there will still be a certain number of unknowns. We do believe that by being aware of the issues and asking the right questions of the right people, you can make a much more informed decision than you would have by blindly choosing a college based on more superficial criteria . . . and then naïvely walking into that situation unaware of adversaries that await you. In the next chapter Ken and I are going to share from our hearts a final challenge to students. We believe that by being aware and informed, and by prayerfully trusting in the Lord for wisdom as well as financial provision, you will now be able to make the best choice possible.

Endnotes

1. R.C. Sproul, "Be Prepared," *Tabletalk Magazine* (November 1, 2010).
2. Bodie Hodge, "Harvard, Yale, Princeton, Oxford — Once Christian?" *Answers* magazine, volume 2, number 3 (July–September, 2007).

Chapter 10

For Students Only:
Keys for Surviving and Thriving in College

Ken Ham and Greg Hall

Blessed is the man who finds wisdom, the man who gains understanding, for she is more profitable than silver and yields better returns than gold (Prov. 3:13–15; NIV).

As we wrap up our discussion and analysis of the survey that we did of 200 different Christian colleges, as we put the final comments on our analysis of higher education today, both of us, Ken and Greg, want to share our hearts with you, the students and future leaders of the Church in the world.

In this book we have dissected a lot of numbers, pointed a lot of fingers, and come to some pretty scary conclusions about what's happening on campuses today. But truly, this book isn't about college presidents and professors; this book is really all about you, the college student.

Whether you're headed to college in the next couple of years or are currently enrolled, we want you to know that the reason we have taken up this issue at all is because we believe that you are worth it. Your hearts and minds are worth defending. But in all honesty, we can only do that to a certain extent, and now, even your parents will be limited in their ability and availability for keeping watch over your souls. During the college years, the responsibility for your spiritual well-being rests increasingly with you, not with anyone else.

The college years are tremendously exciting. It's really hard to overestimate the impact that they will have on the rest of your life. During college you are likely to solidify your core beliefs and worldview. It's possible that you will meet and choose a lifelong spouse. And although God will direct you throughout the course of your whole life, it's quite likely that during college you'll also discover your purpose and mission — God's obvious leading in your life for your future. And on top of that, you're probably going to have a blast doing it!

At the same time, as parents and leaders, we need to confess that we are leaving you with a world and a Church that has been seriously compromised. A frightening percentage of your peers are leaving their traditional church. Many are leaving their faith. Many will walk away from Christian devotion no matter what kind of school they go to. The truth is this: you are walking into a spiritual battle. It may not seem like it, but it's true. Satan is strategically using subtle compromise as one of his most powerful weapons to degrade the authority of Scripture and undermine the faith of the next generation.

In other parts of the world, the battle is much more graphic. In China, for example, claiming to be Christian is a life or death decision. The book *The Heavenly Man: The Remarkable True Story of Chinese Christian Brother Yun* shares the remarkable story of Christians in China who have developed home churches and in their devotion and commitment to Christ have watched the power of God explode and thousands become Christian.[1] He and his fellow believers have suffered greatly but remained enthusiastic and faithful in spite of it. They are part of a movement called "Back to Jerusalem." It is a missionary movement, and they are winning thousands to Christ as they retrace the Silk Road from China back to Jerusalem, sharing the gospel as they go. As he says in his book, they are an army of brokenhearted Chinese men and women who have already been through years of hardship and deprivation for the sake of the gospel. In worldly terms, they have nothing and appear unimpressive. But in the spiritual realm they are mighty warriors for Jesus Christ.

They have also started a college where they receive training in the following subjects:

- How to suffer and die for the Lord. We examine what the Bible says about suffering and look at how the Lord's people have laid down their lives throughout history for the advance of the gospel.

- How to witness for the Lord. We teach how to witness under any circumstances . . . on the bus or trains, in the back of a police van or on our way to be executed.

- How to escape for the Lord. Sometimes we need to be in prison to witness and sometimes we know the devil sends us to prison to try to stop our message and it becomes our job to set ourselves free.

This is not exactly the curriculum of a normal or average college or seminary! But then again, there is nothing average or normal about pursuing a life of devotion to God at this level. The point is this: God is calling from our midst a group of students who in days ahead will pursue such a life of uncommon commitment and it will only be by wisdom that the Lord will allow any of us into such a life of significance.

The way we see our Western culture moving away from a Christian perspective before our very eyes (and we believe increasing compromise in churches, colleges, etc., has contributed greatly to this), we may even be in for a time of persecution in countries where there has been much freedom in regard to the proclamation of the gospel. Maybe such persecution will cleanse and strengthen the Church?

No matter where you go to school, we want to finish up this book by sharing with you a handful of principles that we firmly believe will help you to not only survive your college experience, but thrive through it all and maximize this opportunity for all it's worth, that you might become some of those who share such an "uncommon commitment" and experience "such a life of significance."

1. Treasure Christ above all things

If you're going into a Christian college, it's important that you are aware of one of the responses that we *didn't* get to, Q2: "What does it mean to be a Christian institution?" This was an open-ended question; the presidents, vice presidents, and professors said whatever came to their minds first, so this list reflects their priorities:

The Bible guides us:	36.9%
We teach the Bible as literally true:	27.6%
We require Christian behavior:	16.0%
We don't allow secular teaching:	10.6%

Think about this for a minute — 91 percent of the answers were about the Bible and behavior and the teaching — and we are all for that. These are all good answers, but what's missing? Jesus. Hardly anybody mentioned Christ or even the gospel! It seems obvious to us that the most important thing that should distinguish a Christian institution is Jesus Christ Himself — that a college or university that claims the name of Christ should prioritize, above all things, Him and what He has done.

This is just to say that even though you may be going to a Christian college, it's really still just an institution with a Christian name attached. It will be up to you and you alone to prioritize Jesus Christ in your life and in your education and in your future ministry. No one else can do that for you. In order to survive and thrive through the college years, the first and most important thing that we can encourage you to do is to have the same attitude that the Apostle Paul showed in Philippians 3:8–9:

> I count all things to be loss in view of the surpassing value of knowing Christ Jesus my Lord, for whom I have suffered the loss of all things, and count them but rubbish so that I may gain Christ, and may be found in Him, not having a righteousness of my own derived from the Law, but that which is through faith in Christ.

No one can lead you into this level of intimacy with God. The hand-holding is over. It's your choice now. When you make Christ the priority, understanding He *is* the Word, you will then make sure you take His Word as it should be taken — as the revealed Word of the Creator God, who knows everything (Col. 2:3), who never tells a lie (Heb. 6:18), and who has always been there (Rev. 22:13). This will help you to not take the words of fallible man and reinterpret the clear teaching of the Word of God.

The compromising of God's Word at Christian colleges is really an attack on Christ.

Let us explain. When church leaders reinterpret Genesis for instance, we insist this is an undermining of the authority of the Word, in spite of some scholars' sincere intentions to the contrary. It is what we call "The Genesis 3" attack (i.e., creating doubt in regard to God's Word and asking "Did God really say?") and it ultimately undermines the authority of the Scripture. Although such beliefs as those above don't affect the scholars' salvation as such, they do have a great influence on the students and other Christians these professors influence.

Many young people in our churches are already doubting and disbelieving God's Word. The result? At least two-thirds of children raised in theologically conservative churches now walk away from the church (or even the Christian faith altogether).

Do you realize how serious such compromise really is? Consider the following truths:

1. We can only know the Father through the Son (Matt. 11:27).
2. We know the Son (Jesus Christ) through the Word (Rom. 10:14–17).
3. Jesus is the Word (John 1:1–3).

Then consider these verses:

Jesus said to him, "Have I been so long with you, and yet you have not come to know Me, Philip? He who has seen Me has seen the Father; how can you say, 'Show us the Father'?" (John 14:9).

He is the image of the invisible God, the firstborn of all creation (Col. 1:15).

Here are two more verses that help show the connection between the Word and the Son of God:

God, who at various times and in various ways spoke in time past to the fathers by the prophets, has in these last days spoken to us by His Son, whom He has appointed heir of all things, through whom also He made the worlds (Heb. 1:1–2; NKJV).

In the beginning was the Word, and the Word was with God, and the Word was God. He was in the beginning with God. All things were made through Him, and without Him nothing was made that was made (John 1:1–3; NKJV).

Since Jesus is God, then God's Word (the Old and New Testaments of the Bible) is Jesus Christ's Word. Christ said, "Heaven and earth will pass away, but My words will not pass away" (Matt. 24:35). He also declared, "If you abide in My word, you are My disciples indeed" (John 8:31; NKJV; see also John 5:24, 8:37, and Rev. 3:8). And Jesus clearly demonstrated that He accepted Genesis 1–11 as true literal history.

What's the bottom line?

When Christian leaders deliberately reinterpret God's Word on the basis of man's fallible ideas (taken from outside the Bible), not only are they undermining the Word of God, they are actually (though unwittingly) conducting an attack on the Son of God! This is very serious. Yes, when you compromise the Word of God, it is also an attack on the Son of God whose Word it is.

May God help each of us to cling to — and tremble before — His Word (Josh. 1:6–9; Isa. 66:1–2). And may He help us not to follow the teachings that compromise His Word and thereby (even unknowingly) attack His Son.

And this should be a reminder to all of us. We all fall short somewhere (Rom. 3:23) and when we are confronted with the Word of God, we need to humble ourselves, and trust what the Bible teaches in context and correct ourselves (2 Tim. 3:16–17). We need to let go of any pride and be still and know God is God. We need to lay our trust in Him in *every* area — all of us.

For those compromising professors, they have no excuse not to trust the Word of God regarding creation, so the rebuke of this book should be met with wisdom that comes from God:

> Rebuke a wise man, and he will love you (Prov. 9:8; NKJV).

2. Experience the living Word

No matter where you go to school, it is vitally important to have a steady intake of truth from God's Word. Not only this, but it is vital to understand that God's Word is to be the foundation for all of your thinking in every area. Ken's father reminded him of this in many ways — here are a couple of examples he taught:

1. Study Bibles: Always remember when reading a study Bible (or a commentary), that the notes are not inspired like the text (Scripture), but the text (Scripture) is the commentary on the notes!

2. When something in God's Word seems to contradict what fallible man is saying (maybe a scientist or theologian, etc.), then you do two things:

   a. You first of all go to the text and make sure you are taking it according to the genre and context — if you are sure that you are taking it as it is meant to be taken and there is still a conflict, then:

   b. You don't change (reinterpret) God's Word to fit with what fallible man is saying — you stand upon God's Word and continue to research and seek answers. Remember, only God knows everything — always put God's Word first.

But please understand that you must have an intimate personal relationship with God's living Word, and not just take it second hand through other people's teaching, or through daily chapel services. We are all called as students of His Word and way. Proverbs 3:13–15 says:

> Blessed is the man who finds wisdom, the man who gains understanding, for she is more profitable than silver and yields better returns than gold. She is more precious than rubies; nothing you desire can compare with her (NIV).

Of this you can be sure. If you do not want to do your own thinking, there are plenty of people who will do it for you. In fact, that characterizes more people than not who are so undiscriminating about what they allow into their minds. Thinking Christianly is hard work. The easy way out is to let others inform you about how you should think. That's when it could really be said, "A mind is a terrible thing to waste." We have found over the years that so many students will just believe what the professor says because he or she is such a nice person. This should not be the case. As the Scripture states in 2 Timothy 2:15, you should "Be diligent to present yourself approved to God as a workman who does not need to be ashamed, accurately handling the word of truth."

The very meaning and quality of your life is at stake when it comes to what worldview you will use to consider the truth claims you will be exposed to. The only way to be a consistent Christian and build a consistent Christian worldview is to build all your thinking on God's Word — beginning in Genesis. Never take man's fallible ideas and add them to God's Word — never reinterpret the clear teaching of God's Word to fit with man's fallible word.

The purpose and meaning of Christian higher education has never been any better described than in these verses from Proverbs 1:1–7:

> The proverbs of Solomon son of David, king of Israel: for attaining wisdom and discipline; for understanding words of insight; for acquiring a disciplined and prudent life, doing what is right and just and fair; for giving prudence to the simple, knowledge and discretion to the young — let the wise listen and add to their learning, and let the discerning get guidance — for understanding proverbs and parables, the sayings and riddles of the wise. The fear of the LORD is the beginning of knowledge, but fools despise wisdom and discipline (NIV).

And, Proverbs 9:10: "The fear of the LORD is the beginning of wisdom."

That is an important perspective because it is biblical, but important, too, for living in what is called the information age. Knowledge is increasing and we are being offered more and more information. You would think people would be getting smarter. In fact, if knowledge is doubling every three years, as some say, you would think it would not be too long before we, as very smart human beings, would be able to possess the virtues and qualities that would make our world a much better place. You would think by now there would be fewer wars than in the past, and that humankind would, at the very least, be able to see the futility of wars waged. You would think there would be less crime, less hunger, less suffering, stronger families, more integrity, responsible governments, more peace and tranquility, and less disease. Yet, on the contrary, the opposite is clearly the case and it seems to be going from bad to worse — at least here in the United States.

Don't be surprised when this happens — we need to learn the lesson God teaches in His Word. Romans 1:18 says that "the wrath of God is revealed from heaven against all ungodliness and unrighteousness of men who suppress the truth in unrighteousness." The reason so many atheist bloggers and secular media reporters react so negatively and write so furiously against Bible-upholding ministries like Answers in Genesis is because they know in their hearts that there is a God — and they actively suppress that. What we are observing is the outworking of this active suppression. God's Word is being illustrated before our eyes on this matter.

Also, remember that "The heart is deceitful above all things, and desperately wicked" (Jer. 17:9; NKJV). There is "none who understands; none who seeks after God" (Rom. 3:11; NKJV). Proverbs 1:29 reminds us that these people "hated knowledge."

And don't be surprised when certain religious leaders oppose those who stand for the truth of God's Word. The prophets of old spoke about this — when Jesus walked on earth as the "God-man," He had to deal with the religious leaders of the day.

> Beware of the false prophets, who come to you in sheep's clothing, but inwardly are ravenous wolves (Matt. 7:15).

> Their shepherds have led them astray (Jer. 50:6).

So be advised that listening to lectures, reading text books, writing papers, exploring research, completing assignments, attending class, and all the things that are virtues of the collegiate academic experience are no guarantee that you will become smarter. The increase in knowledge must go hand in hand with the pursuit of wisdom — placing God's Word first! Wisdom is knowledge being applied. It is seeing life through God's eyes, through God's perspective. Wisdom means thinking God's thoughts after Him. It is the ability to have insight and discretion. It is having a discerning spirit.

Wisdom leads us to do what is right, being righteous, which is simply that — doing right in the eyes of God. It is being just and fair. Wisdom means we value the life God has given us and value the lives of others. Wisdom guides us in our plans for the future and places confidence in our hearts that everything is in control of the One who is greater than ourselves and that He wants the absolute best for us in every way. It is wisdom that teaches us to "fear" the Lord in the sense, not that we are afraid of Him, but that we revere Him and honor Him and live *Coram Deo* — which means before the face of God and under His authority. Instructing students in the pursuit of wisdom is in fact the moral imperative of a Christian college. It is the moral imperative for this institution.

We tell you on the basis of the truth of the Word of God that seeking after wisdom, putting God and His Word first, is the greatest blessing known to man, and ignoring it will lead to your ultimate destruction. But you must first know that your Father in heaven wishes to bless you today and give victory in the face of any issue of life. Listen to these words from Proverbs 2:1–11:

> My son, if you accept my words and store up my commands within you, turning your ear to wisdom and applying your heart to understanding — indeed, if you call out for insight and cry aloud for understanding, and if you look for it as for silver and search for it as for hidden treasure, then you will understand the fear of the LORD and find the knowledge of God. For the LORD gives wisdom; from his mouth come knowledge and understanding. He holds success in store for the upright, he is a shield to those whose walk is blameless, for he guards the course of the just and protects the way of his faithful ones. Then you will understand what is right and just and fair — every good path. For wisdom will enter your heart, and knowledge will be pleasant to your soul. Discretion will protect you, and understanding will guard you (NIV).

Proverbs 3:1–8 reads:

> My son, do not forget my teaching, but keep my commands in your heart, for they will prolong your life many years and bring you prosperity. Let love and faithfulness never leave you; bind them around your neck, write them on the tablet of your heart. Then you will win favor and a good name in the sight of God and man. Trust in the LORD with all your heart and lean not on your own understanding; in all your ways acknowledge him, and he will make your paths straight. Do not be wise in your own eyes; fear the LORD and shun evil. This will bring health to your body and nourishment to your bones (NIV).

Think of it: You are promised victory when you honor God's Word. You will be protected, for God Himself will become a shield for you. He guards you and guides you and protects you. You will find a long, productive, and prosperous life. You will be full of love and faithfulness. You will find favor and have a good name and reputation with both God and men and you will enjoy good health, being nourished by the very hand of God. Who could possibly promise so much and make good on all that is promised besides God? No one! What a blessing these words are. They are life and light, they are sustenance and prosperity. They are promised by God the Father, delivered in Jesus Christ His Son, and reserved for all who believe in the Holy Spirit.

Will you, to your own peril, reject the promises of God? Consider these words from Proverbs 1:20–33:

Wisdom calls aloud in the street, she raises her voice in the public squares; at the head of the noisy streets she cries out, in the gateways of the city she makes her speech: "How long will you simple ones love your simple ways? How long will mockers delight in mockery and fools hate knowledge? If you had responded to my rebuke, I would have poured out my heart to you and made my thoughts known to you. But since you rejected me when I called and no one gave heed when I stretched out my hand, since you ignored all my advice and would not accept my rebuke, I in turn will laugh at your disaster; I will mock when calamity overtakes you — when calamity overtakes you like a storm, when disaster sweeps over you like a whirlwind, when distress and trouble overwhelm you. Then they will call to me but I will not answer; they will look for me but will not find me. Since they hated knowledge and did not choose to fear the LORD, since they would not accept my advice and spurned my rebuke, they will eat the fruit of their ways and be filled with the fruits of their schemes. For the waywardness of the simple will kill them, and the complacency of fools will destroy them; but whoever listens to me will live in safety and be at ease, without fear of harm" (NIV).

If you are in Christ, God is for you today and willing and more than able to bless you beyond your wildest imagination. He alone is able to heal all your hurts, to forgive all your sin. He alone has written a personal plan for your life. He knows you and calls you by name. You can belong to Him. You can seek Him and find Him, for He is as near as your very breath. One of the greatest blessings of wisdom is that it alone will open the door for you to a life of significance — something that God puts in the hearts of the creatures He loves. We are destined for a life of purpose — a life that will glorify our Creator. It is a life of joy and enthusiasm.

But it is a life different from what many typically expect. It is not necessarily a life full of the trappings of our culture. It may or may not include vast resources of financial or physical assets; it is rather a life of significance available to those who through wisdom seek what only God can give.

But it all starts when you jump in and pursue the living Word of God on your own. Again, this is something that no one else can do for you. You may or may not sit under gifted spiritual teachers during college, but nothing, *nothing*, can be a substitute for the time that you will spend in the Word of God yourself, experiencing its wisdom and power as the truth sets you free to be all that God created you to be.

3. Church and para-church involvement

The Christian life was not designed to be lived alone. Repeatedly, God describes us as a body that works together and encourages each other for His purposes. No matter where you go, we feel that it is imperative to surviving and thriving in the college years to find committed fellowship under the guidance of spiritual leaders who both know and apply the authority of God.

Many students will find this in a local church where the Body of Christ is alive and well, and where the truth of the Word is lived out naturally. It is vital that you find a local church where the Word of God is preached and the members live in light of that teaching as the body of Christ. You may also find support on campus in a para-church ministry (but beware — many of them compromise in the same way we have seen from the research we have detailed in this book). On both Christian and secular campuses, these para-church organizations can be spiritual lifesavers, and often times they are the training and equipping stations that can ignite you for a lifelong strategic mission. Sadly, there are those that do more harm than good because they do not stand on God's Word as they should — you will need to be discerning and judge what they believe and teach against the authority of God's Word. No matter where you go to school, supplement your academic education with dynamic fellowship, teaching, and worship experiences. We all need that. That's how God created us! It is simply an essential.

4. Prepare for battle

The surveys that were conducted by America's Research Group for this book clearly showed that the biblical worldview is under attack by secular influences within the Christian colleges. These enemies of faith have, to a certain degree, succeeded in infiltrating and influencing Christian institutions. We are in a battle with the world's system. You must prepare yourself, no matter where you go. Listen again to what's at stake. These kinds of quotes should awaken us and call us to action:

> Dr. Richard Dawkins: "Faith is one of the world's great evils . . . it is capable of driving people to such dangerous folly . . . it seems to me to qualify as a kind of mental illness."[2]

> Dr. Steven Weinberg: "If scientists can destroy the influence of religion on young people, then I think it may be the most important contribution we can make."[3]

Richard Rorty: Secular professors should "arrange things so that students who enter as bigoted, homophobic religious fundamentalists will leave college with views more like our own."[4]

5. Keep your guard up wherever you go

Students, even if you think you're going into a conservative Christian educational institution, our research has proven that you need to be wary and enter with a healthy skepticism of what will be taught. Your commitment to the Bible as your authority means that you must check *everything* that you are taught by *anyone* by comparing it to the truth of Scripture.

Don't let your guard down by letting anything except the Bible become your final authority. Hopefully you'll meet many committed and caring professors along the way, but they are not your source of truth. Just because your parents endorsed you going to this school does not mean that your teachers know best. In many situations liberal professors are more personable than staunch conservatives who come across as closed-minded and impersonal. (That's not always the case, just a generalization here.) If you allow their position and personality to justify their theology (which may be seriously compromised), you're setting yourself up for problems. Truth is determined by the Word, not by someone's social skills. Keep your guard up, and protect your soul by the truth of Scripture.

6. Have a mission

The last message that we have from the Apostle Paul is 2 Timothy, written as final advice to his close friend and young disciple. Consider this challenge from 2 Timothy 2:22:

> Now flee from youthful lusts and pursue righteousness, faith, love and peace, with those who call on the Lord from a pure heart.

If you want to survive and thrive, having a clear mission is not an option. It's imperative. The account of David and Bathsheba in 2 Samuel is a clear warning: Anyone who is not engaging in the battle as they should becomes an easy target for sin and compromise. God has designed you to go for it! During college you have an unprecedented opportunity to allow the Lord to work through you to minister somewhere in some specific way. Pursue this with brothers and sisters in the Lord who share your passion. It's the best way to flee from the lusts and the lies of the world that seek to bring you down.

7. Plan on victory

A few years ago, Warner University experienced the fury and devastation of four killer hurricanes. The school had damages of $3 million. In Florida, losses totaled $42 billion. But what was experienced in Florida in the summer of 2004 is overshadowed by overwhelming power and destruction of the events of December 26, 2004, when a 9.0 magnitude earthquake struck 100 miles from the western coast of Sumatra Island. It was the strongest quake in the world since 1964. It was the fourth-strongest quake since recording began in 1899. This slippage of the tectonic plates caused a tsunami that traveled 500 miles an hour and made landfall in several locations with catastrophic devastation. The earthquake that caused the tsunami was calculated as having the power of 23 atomic bombs, the like of which destroyed Hiroshima and Nagasaki. It was a power so great that seismologists detected the earth literally shaking on its axis. These natural disasters revealed just how fragile the world really is, and is an illustration of how the kingdom of this world is shaking at its very foundations. This earthly kingdom will pass away and it will be far more dramatic than the most recent earthquake and tsunami. According to 2 Peter 3:10:

> The heavens will pass away with a roar and the elements will be destroyed with intense heat, and the earth and its works will be burned up.

We understand why Jesus said we should not love the kingdom of this world. It is passing away in the physical sense and in the spiritual sense too. If we are feeling any consolation or any confidence in being part of this world we are missing the point of the message of the gospel.

Jesus explained to us that the kingdom of this world promotes and encourages everything that God is against. The earthly kingdom is full of pride, jealousy, hatred, malice, murder, and deceit. It promotes everything that is unwholesome and ungodly. Those who oppose God and everything He stands for lead it. And so as it says in 1 John 2:15–17:

> Do not love the world or anything in the world. If anyone loves the world, the love of the Father is not in him. For everything in the world — the cravings of sinful man, the lust of his eyes and the boasting of what he has and does — comes not from the Father but from the world. The world and its desires pass away, but the man who does the will of God lives forever (NIV).

God will eventually judge the kingdom of this world and expose its darkness by turning on His light. And this light is Jesus. And He is shining on the world to expose our evil deeds. Everything about the ways of the earthly kingdom God will destroy. And not just the earth, but all the spiritual wickedness and unrighteousness that goes with it. It is one thing to honestly struggle with our persistent sin . . . God is *for* that person, not against him or her . . . but He is dead set against us when we sin, acting like we do so with impunity and never understanding the need we have for the Savior.

God plays no games on this account. He has offered full forgiveness and mercy by the sacrifice for sin, taking the responsibility for our salvation on Himself alone. He requires us only to repent of our sin and believe in His name to enter the eternal kingdom. He is justified in destroying those who sin against Him and reject this offer of salvation. We must realize God is under no obligation to save anyone. He does so only as He exhibits His own nature and character. Consider the sobering words of Hebrews 2:1–3:

> We must pay more careful attention, therefore, to what we have heard, so that we do not drift away. For if the message spoken by angels was binding, and every violation and disobedience received its just punishment, how shall we escape if we ignore such great salvation? (NIV).

The signs are all around us that the shaking of the kingdom of this world is imminent. As college students, you must choose for yourselves whether you will become a servant to this worldly kingdom or choose the Kingdom of God. Staying connected to this world means living in fear instead of knowing peace. It is remaining as a slave to sin instead of being set free. It is being lost instead of rescued.

To refuse Him is to wallow in that tormenting guilt instead of knowing forgiveness and grace. Instead, God is offering you right now the choice to be part of a Kingdom that cannot be shaken. It is the eternal Kingdom of God and Jesus said it is with you and shall be in you. It is the kingdom of peace and righteousness and holiness. It is the kingdom of victory and power. It is the kingdom of deliverance. It is the kingdom of life and light. And it cannot be shaken. And of His Kingdom there shall be no end. Hebrews 12:25–29 reads:

> See that you do not refuse Him who speaks. For if they did not escape who refused Him who spoke on earth, much more shall we not escape if we turn away from Him who speaks from heaven, whose voice then shook the earth; but now He has promised, saying, "Yet once more I shake not only the earth, but also heaven." Now this, "Yet once more," indicates the removal of those things that are being shaken, as of things that are made, that the things which

cannot be shaken may remain. Therefore, since we are receiving a kingdom which cannot be shaken, let us have grace, by which we may serve God acceptably with reverence and godly fear. For our God is a consuming fire (NKJV).

Consider this quote from Malcolm Muggeridge.

We look back upon history and what do we see, empires rising and falling, revolutions and counter-revolutions, wealth accumulated and wealth disbursed. Shakespeare has spoken of the rise and fall of the great ones. I look back upon my own fellow countrymen, once upon a time dominating a quarter of the world, most of them convinced of the words of what is still a popular song, that the God who made the mighty shall make them mightier yet. I heard a crazed Austrian announce to the world the establishment of a Reich that would last a thousand years. I've seen an Italian clown saying he was going to stop and restart the calendar with his own ascension to power. I met a murderous Georgian Brigand in the Kremlin acclaimed by the intellectual elite of the world as wiser than Solomon, more humane than Marcus Aralias, more enlightened than Ashoka, all in one lifetime, all gone. Gone with the wind. England, part of a tiny island off the coast of Europe, threatened with dismemberment and even bankruptcy, Hitler and Mussolini dead, remembered only in infamy. Stalin a forbidden name in the regime he helped found and dominate for some three decades, all in one lifetime, all in one lifetime, gone. Still behind the debris of these self-styled Solomon supermen and imperial diplomatist, stands the gigantic figure of one person because of whom, by whom, in whom, and through whom mankind might still have hope, the person of Jesus Christ. And He has given a kingdom that cannot be shaken, and of this kingdom there shall be no end.[5]

Our charge to you as students, therefore, is to not be afraid. Be strong and courageous for the Lord your God is with you wherever you go. Consider these words from Haggai 2:6–7:

For thus says the LORD of hosts, "Once more (it is a little while) I will shake heaven and earth, the sea and dry land; and I will shake all nations, and they shall come to the Desire of All Nations, and I will fill this temple with glory" (NKJV).

There is no way we will lose the war. The heavens and earth shake, but we are receiving a kingdom that will not be shaken. We are the ultimate survivors and victors. We need not be discouraged or be in despair. We may falter and exhibit our frailties, but Jesus said, "I will build My church, and the gates of Hades will not overpower it" (Matt. 16:18).

And so, with all that has been said and done in this book, we have little left to say, and nothing left to do but to release you, as students and future leaders and servants of the Church, into the hands of God. You're entering institutions of higher learning that to one degree or another are already compromised. You're stepping across the threshold into a fallen world, and this is where God calls you to be — to be in this world, yet not of it. The battles will be many, but we believe that you can do more than just survive; we believe that you can thrive as you grow in intimacy with God in Christ like you have never, never experienced before. And we firmly believe that you are part of the Kingdom that cannot be shaken, even as the fallen world around you proceeds from bad to worse.

Would you allow us to leave you with this one final blessing?

May the Lord bless you, and keep you and cause his face to shine upon you. May his peace, which surpasses all comprehension, guard your hearts and your minds in the knowledge of Christ Jesus, always. In any and every circumstance may you know the secret of contentment: You can do all things through Christ who strengthens you, yet apart from Him, you can do nothing. May the truth of His living Word, and the reality of His Spirit within you, be your ultimate authority in all things. As you learn and grow in knowledge, may your hearts and minds be receptive to the life-giving truths of Scripture, which is living and active and sharper than any two-edged sword. By God's grace and mercy, may you know the truth. And may the truth set you free.
Amen.

Endnotes

1. Brother Yun with Paul Hattaway, *The Heavenly Man: The Remarkable True Story of Chinese Christian Brother Yun* (Peabody, MA: Hendrickson Publishers, 2009).
2. Richard Dawkins, *The selfish Gene* (New York: Oxford University Press, 1989), p. 330–31; Richard Dawkins, "Is Science a Religion?" *The Humanist* (January–February 1997); Richard Dawkins, "The Improbability of God," *Free Inquiry*, vol. 18, no. 3.
3. Remarks by Steven Weinberg at the Freedom from Religion Foundation, San Antonio, November 1999.
4. Cited by Jason Boffetti, "How Richard Rorty Found Religion," *First Things* (May 2004).
5. Quoted by Ravi Zacharias in a sermon, "Jesus Christ Among Other Gods," 1993; www.urbana.org/articles/jesus-christ-among-other-gods-1993.

Chapter 11

Final Thoughts: A Plea for Unity

Ken Ham and Greg Hall

My prayer is not for them alone. I pray also for those who will believe in me through their message, that all of them may be one, Father, just as you are in me and I am in you. May they also be in us so that the world may believe that you have sent me (Jesus, in John 17:20–22; NIV).

We have taken a look at the state of Christian higher education in this book. The survey gave us dependable statistics to form logical conclusions. As a result, we have dared to question the very core and foundation of colleges functioning in the name of Christ. Reputation and pride is at stake. As often is the case, the first responses are accusations that we are being divisive, causing unnecessary conflict, and stirring waters that should be left alone. We are often told we should be concentrating on our unity in Christ alone. The accusations usually sound like this: "Only Christ should matter and those elements of the gospel message essential for salvation — and differing interpretations in Genesis should be acceptable and tolerated."

But this view ignores a larger question — can we separate the centrality of Christ from the authority of His Word? Surely we would all agree that our unity should be centered in Christ. After all, it is only through faith in

Jesus Christ that one can be saved. The question, however, is not whether we are saved, but what Christians should hold as being essential for Christian unity. The Christian Church can only know about Jesus Christ through His Word. If the Word of God is not an authoritative document, then how can we know that the message of Jesus and the gospel is reliable? It's easy to say wonderful statements about how Jesus is all we need for unity and quickly forget that Christ is not only the Christ of the Cross but also the giver of His Word. Shouldn't this then mean that we need to be united in the authority of the document He has given as His message?

What about the history that provides the foundational understanding for His gospel? Is it possible to de-unify the God of creation from the God of redemption by being willing to accept only one truth in the gospel while accepting the world's views in origins? The Bible tells us that the God of creation IS the God of redemption, so surely this means that unity in Jesus has much wider ramifications than many are realizing. Sadly, the modern Church has been very selective about what aspects of Jesus we are willing to be unified in. If the Church continues to go down a path that restricts Jesus simply to what we are willing to be unified in, we will end up with an undefined Christ.

Since the Apostles, the Church has increased in number and divided in doctrines and established denominational boundaries. America has over 20 Baptist denominations alone; each one is distinctive in its own emphases. Even within each of the evangelical denominations, we have numerous factions according to the persuasions of pastors, pew sitters, denominational leaders, and college faculties. Before any finger is pointed in the area of division, perhaps we should first admit to the distinctive characteristics we allow to divide us every day.

Many of those denominational differences disappear at Answers in Genesis (AiG) conferences. AiG staff routinely sees great cross-denominational unity as people are taught to defend their faith. People become excited when they can have increased confidence in His revealed Word, and greater understanding for His redemptive history recorded in His Word from the very first verse.

Answers in Genesis is a para-church ministry that has a specific calling to support the local church in defending the authority of the Word of God from the very first verse against the attacks of the world. Even when teaching people apologetics, AiG does so with the ultimate view of pointing to the person and work of Jesus Christ, and He can never be disjoined from the authority of His Word. Why teach people to defend the Bible simply for defense sake?

After all, our only assurance and hope of salvation is in Jesus Christ. AiG's ultimate purpose and unifying factor is always Jesus, and He can never be disjoined from the authority of His Word.[1]

It is Christ and His Word that uncovers the ugliness and consequences of our sin. Nobody likes to be exposed — because of the sinful nature within us. We desire to cling to our own foolishness rather than accept the truth that Christ has revealed to us in His Word. Every human struggles in this area and it really does expose the war we have with sin. It is this sin that we should struggle against as Paul does in Romans 7 and that we should be dead to as explained in Romans 6. Human pride often causes us to be greatly offended in the light of God's truth. This is why Christ Himself divided one against another (Luke 12:51). Nobody likes to be exposed.

One major and foundational area where God's Word is exposing the compromising positions of many Christian leaders today is in the area of biblical history in Genesis that relates to geology, astronomy, anthropology, biology, etc. This is also the area where the world's attack against the gospel of Jesus Christ is most heavily pointed.

A proper biblical defense of this attack will support and strengthen the Church to preach Christ and Him crucified. Our hearts should desire that the Church would preach the centrality of Christ with the strongest possible foundations, and not with a history that contradicts or causes someone to question the validity of the gospel message:

> How do we know man is a sinner?
> How do we know we are all sinners?
> How do we know that death is the penalty for sin?
> How do we know that God's Son became a man — the God/man, Jesus Christ?
> How do we know Jesus died and rose again physically?
> How do we know Jesus paid the penalty for sin on the Cross?

We know because the Bible tells us so. Scripture is an accurate account of the redemptive history between God and His people. We know because we believe the *authority* in which this is revealed — the Bible. Biblical authority is therefore essential for Christian unity and foundational faith.

Jesus Himself teaches that He is the way, the truth, and the life (John 14:6). Evangelical Christians should know this and rejoice in it. It wouldn't be difficult to get a room full of evangelical Christian leaders agreeing to and preaching the centrality of Jesus Christ in the message of Scripture. When it comes to accepting and preaching Jesus as the revealer and Creator, and everything that it means, unity starts to fray. Certainly the Bible testifies to Jesus being the revealer of truth. In John 1 we read that Jesus is the Word, is God, is light and life who created all things and became flesh. John 1 teaches us that Jesus is the revealer, the Creator, and the central point of redemption.

If Jesus is the pre-eminent, supreme revealer of truth, then the search for truth must start with His pre-eminence over man's philosophies. Our unity must come through Scriptures given to us by Jesus shedding light on this world, and not on man's interpretations of this world supposedly telling us what Jesus is saying. To do otherwise is essentially shifting the power of supremacy from Jesus to man. And this is something those committed to the centrality of Jesus cannot tolerate.

This begs a very important question: Is the Church today trying to find unity in Christ as the center of truth, without recognizing Him as the revealer of truth in the entirety of the biblical account — from Genesis 1:1 to Revelation 22:21?

Christ taught that truth is important. Today, however, one of the most common definitions of "Christian unity" revolves around a consensus of fallible man's opinion rather than the truth of God's infallible Word. Depending on which circles you are in, you will find varying levels of pressure to accept the consensus of opinion as truth. Particularly in today's academic circles, immense pressure is placed upon students to accept this consensus-centered view.

Every word of man must be viewed and scrutinized in the light of the revealed Word of God. While great respect should be given to our teachers, we must be careful that we are not placed in a situation similar to the time before the Reformation where it was proposed only "clergy" could understand the Bible. We must not allow the ideas of professors to become the final word. Nowhere in Scripture are we taught that unity comes through consensus of opinion. The truth of God trumps consensus every time.

It is in the biblical Book of John that we get the first key points of insight in answering these crucial issues. In John 17 Christ prays for the unity of the Church:

> I will remain in the world no longer, but they are still in the world, and I am coming to you. Holy Father, protect them by the power of your name, the name you gave me, so that they may be one as we are one. While I was with them, I protected them and kept them safe by that name you gave me. None has been lost except the one doomed to destruction so that Scripture would be fulfilled.

I am coming to you now, but I say these things while I am still in the world, so that they may have the full measure of my joy within them. I have given them your word and the world has hated them, for they are not of the world any more than I am of the world. My prayer is not that you take them out of the world but that you protect them from the evil one. They are not of the world, even as I am not of it. Sanctify them by the truth; your word is truth. As you sent me into the world, I have sent them into the world. For them I sanctify myself, that they too may be truly sanctified (John 17:11–19; NIV).

In verse 11, Jesus prays unity may be kept with the Apostles, as it is in the Trinity. The unity Jesus was looking for did not come from consensus. Jesus is talking about a unity that is already perfectly present in Christ; it is the *supremacy* of Christ.

In verses 17–19, He prays that we may be kept in the *truth* — *His* truth. Unity for the believer is full in Christ rather than something to be obtained by consensus of opinion. This unity is to be kept, not established. It is unity that is separate from this world, and maintained in the truth of Christ and His Word.

Is the division over the interpretation of Genesis a result of an earnest desire to be unified around the Word of God, or a desire to be unified around the words of sinful fallible human beings (regardless of whether they are highly qualified scientists or theologians)? Richard Baxter said:

Indeed, no truth is inconsistent with any other truth: but yet when two dark or doubtful points are compared together, it is hard to know which of them to reject. But here it is easy; nothing that contra-dicteth the true nature of God or man or any principle, must be held.[2]

Logic tells us that something cannot be both true and false at the same time, and truth is always consistent with itself. For the sake of unity, this logic particularly applies to the nature of God and man. God is holy, pure, and perfect. Man however has a heart that is "deceitful above all things, and des-perately wicked" (Jer. 17:9; NKJV).

The only truth consistent with the nature of both God and man is the literal interpretation of the historical narrative in Genesis. Genesis tells us of a perfect and unblemished creation free of death, disease, or suffering. Scripture tells us that man is a creation of God. It tells us God's creations were good. Therefore, evil and death cannot be a part of man's beginning (or of any part of the creation for that matter), as it would contradict the truth of who God is.

Death, thorns, carnivorous diet, a cursed ground, groaning physical creation, and eternal judgment are the consequences of sin. Such things were
not in existence before the Fall. It is only this understanding that is consistent
with the truth that Jesus came to physically die and then rise again to conquer the consequences of man's sin. Later Scripture also tells us that man is
essentially evil, destined to die, and then face judgment for sin.

Back in chapter 1 we mentioned the theodicy of Dr. William Dembski
(which is further elaborated on in the appendix). He comes up with what we
consider to be a bizarre scenario to try to maintain "unity" on what God's Word
teaches and "unity" on what fallible man teaches. In doing so, he creates division and undermines biblical authority. The question that must be answered is:
Can that which contradicts God's Word really be considered truth?

Truth is important in unity; this is echoed and emphasized throughout
Scripture. Consider Ephesians 4:11–13:

> And He Himself gave some to be apostles, some prophets, some
> evangelists, and some pastors and teachers, for the equipping of the
> saints for the work of ministry, for the edifying of the body of Christ,
> till we all come to the unity of the faith and of the knowledge of the
> Son of God, to a perfect man, to the measure of the stature of the
> fullness of Christ (NKJV).

It is the job of the officers in the Church to utilize the unity we have in
the foundation of truth and lead us toward the fullness of Christ. This foundation is essential for Christian growth and Church leadership. We don't see
that kind of unity today. Our survey certainly illustrates there is division, and
sometimes division is actually necessary. But is it the right sort of division? Is
it division for the sake of unity on God's Word? Or is it division for the sake
of unity on man's word? Therein lies the issue. Sadly, the division we see in
regard to Genesis really comes down to a unity many Christian academics
want to have in regard to fallible man's word. This is the problem with the
Church — and really has been the problem with man since Genesis 3 when
the temptation was one of getting man to question God's Word, but decide
truth for one's self (trusting man's word).

It is in Ephesians 4:14 that we find a very strong warning. We are to grow
in the knowledge of Christ and His fullness "that we should no longer be
children, tossed to and fro and carried about with every wind of doctrine, by
the trickery of men, in the cunning craftiness of deceitful plotting" (NKJV).

Unity is not only in Christ and His truth, but is maintained by commit-
ting to *that* truth and not being persuaded otherwise by men. In Colossians,

a similar warning is given by Paul to a newly established church as he desires to keep a strong unity within:

> Beware lest anyone cheat you through philosophy and empty deceit, according to the tradition of men, according to the basic principles of the world, and not according to Christ (Col. 2:8; NKJV).

You will not find millions of years or evolution anywhere in the text of Scripture. Nor can such teachings fit consistently into the text of Scripture. Yet those who have not allowed the intrusion of man's ideas of millions of years into the first chapter of Genesis are often accused of causing division. These beliefs are philosophies and "empty deceit" according to the "traditions of men." The Church is warned to be on the lookout for this and to shut the door to the compromise of human philosophies. Paul wrote to encourage them to keep the truth and maintain the unity.

To others, Paul wrote to rebuke them for divisions that were already among them. In 1 Corinthians we find a church that was full of contentions. Some were following Paul, others Apollos or Peter. There was in-fighting and factions and a general rebellion against God's truth. Paul spends considerable time discussing the difference between men and God when it comes to wisdom:

> Where is the wise? Where is the scribe? Where is the disputer of this age? Has not God made foolish the wisdom of this world? For since, in the wisdom of God, the world through wisdom did not know God, it pleased God through the foolishness of the message preached to save those who believe. For Jews request a sign, and Greeks seek after wisdom; but we preach Christ crucified, to the Jews a stumbling block and to the Greeks foolishness, but to those who are called, both Jews and Greeks, Christ the power of God and the wisdom of God. Because the foolishness of God is wiser than men, and the weakness of God is stronger than men (1 Cor. 1:20–25; NKJV).

Paul exhorts the Corinthians to come back to the essential truth of Christ and to unity within *that* truth, emphasizing that the true teaching of Christ was not compatible with the signs required by the Jews, or the man-centered philosophies of the Greeks.

To bring the unity of Christ to the Jews, Peter preached to them the gospel of Christ. We see a great example of this in the account of Pentecost in Acts 2. They already believed in one God and the history concerning Adam and Eve, the entrance of sin, and thus the need for a Savior and Messiah. The

Jews, however, did not believe that Jesus was the Messiah (there was division over this), but they had unity on all of the history that lead up to Jesus from creation (sin, the law, and the prophets foretelling the coming Messiah). The history was understood and the message of Jesus was consistent with the history. As a result of Peter's preaching, many were saved.

In Acts 17, Paul had a much more difficult challenge. Paul was preaching to the Greeks, with particular mention given to his encounter with the Epicureans and the Stoics. Neither group had any real understanding of the history as understood by the Jews. To offer unity in Christ, Paul first had to ground them in a new history (the same history the Jews understood). This was a new foundation of truth to enable them to understand who Jesus was and what He had done for them on the Cross.

The Epicureans must have found this to be a new revelation since they held to atheistic evolutionary philosophies. The Epicureans believed that all life came from the basic component of all matter and formed over long ages of time. Without a rewrite of their history, the Epicureans were lost to understand the truth of Christ. The message of Jesus made no sense to them without an understanding of what sin is and what it did to God's perfect creation — and thus their standing before a Holy Creator God as judge. As a result of Paul's foundational teaching on the true God and the true history of humanity as a lead up to the message of the Cross, some were saved.

How would Paul feel to see many in the Church today embracing a new version of Epicurean (Greek) philosophy and rewriting a history that undermines and contradicts the biblical truth of history within Genesis that points to Christ? Many Christian leaders and scholars are leading people in the Church back to the type of evolutionary philosophies of the Epicureans and compromising this with God's Word — a compromise with the very philosophies that were causing these Greeks to see the message of the Cross as mere foolishness.

In today's Church, the compromise with millions of years and evolution has undeniably increased the problem of division within the Church. It is time for the Church to again review the prayer of Christ in John 17 and commit to return to the keeping of the unity that is only in Christ. It is time to take heed of the warning in Colossians 2:8 and beware of the philosophies of men that keep us from the truth *that is in Christ.*

People have been persuaded into thinking that if they don't adhere to the consensus of the scientific and or theological establishment, they have checked their brains at the door. The many PhD scientists who do start with the truth of Scripture and use all of the principles of logic in operational science to confirm biblical history might have something to say about that.

In Christian academic settings today, there is a great appeal to experts as the authority. They say we need to follow Professor X, or Dr. Y on this point or that, seeking a unity around the words of an academic, instead of one based on the clear teaching of the Word of God. No matter the stature of a leader, the number of the consensus, or the multitude of letters in a title, our unity is not in man or his philosophies but in Christ and His truth. This is why Paul warned the Corinthians not to follow men even though he was one of them being mentioned with Cephas and Apollos.

This phenomenon of people following the teachings of so-called great men rather than Christ is not new. In studying the Puritan pastors of the 1600s, Dr. Martyn Lloyd-Jones commented on the voluminous writings on Christian unity by John Owen. In relation to schisms in the Church, Dr. Lloyd-Jones offers the following in reference to Owen:

> The trouble, as he points out repeatedly, over the whole question of schism is that people will defend the position that they are in. They shut their minds; they are not ready to listen, to be instructed, and to change.[3]

What Dr. Lloyd-Jones understood was that Owen in his day found that rather than being conformed to the truth that is in Christ and His Word, men were more likely to hold strong to their own belief. This is called pride.

The great divide in the Church today has its roots in this pride. Few people are able to admit error, even when it comes to biblical truth. Yet all want to rejoice and find unity in Christ. The Church is in need of those who will unite uncompromisingly on God's Word, because of the division caused by those who use man's fallible word to reinterpret Scripture. In doing such, we are really calling for a new reformation as it happened in the 16th century. Yes, we call for a new reformation in our churches and Christian academic institutions!

Our closing prayer echoes that of Christ. Throughout this book we have shown the division within the Body of Christ caused by the compromise of scriptural authority starting with the first verse. We see the division between the leadership of Christian colleges. We see it between the departments of respected Christian universities. And we see this division causing the same compromise that brought down once-strong institutions like Dartmouth and Princeton. Yes, we pray and strive not for division, but for unity, that we might all be one, in truth, as Jesus prayed we would be.

God's grace to you all,

Ken Ham (with thanks to Steve Ham for his assistance in putting this chapter together)

Greg Hall

> I have given them the glory that you gave me, that they may be one as we are one — I in them and you in me — so that they may be brought to complete unity. Then the world will know that you sent me and have loved them even as you have loved me (Jesus, in John 17:22–23; NIV).

Endnotes

1. It should be noted that Scripture, such as Romans 10:9, makes it clear that salvation is conditioned upon faith in Christ, not what a person believes about the age of the earth or evolution. Many born-again Christians do believe in millions of years and many also believe in evolution. AiG would not question their salvation when they testify to being born again as the Scripture defines, but challenge these people to understand that such acceptance of fallible man's ideas and reinterpreting parts of Scripture is an undermining of the authority of the Word of God. The consequences of this particularly show up in the next generation, who tend to open the door of undermining God's Word even further — until eventually generations arise who, by and large, reject biblical authority. This is what we observe across our Western world today.
2. Richard Baxter (1615–1691) *Christian Directory* (Morgan, PA: Soli Deo Gloria Publications, 2008).
3. Martyn Lloyd-Jones discussing John Owen and his teaching on schisms, *Diversity in Unity* (London: A.G. Hasler and Co.), The Puritan and Reformed Studies Conference December 1963, p. 63.

Want to know which colleges were contacted as part of the ARG study? Visit www.creationcolleges.org and also find a growing list of Christian colleges we recommend you search out.

Appendix A

Speaking of Newspeak

Ken Ham

n the late 1700s and early 1800s, the idea of a long age (millions of years) for the earth was being popularized by deists, atheists, and other non-Christians.[1] They were attempting to use a so-called "scientific investigation of the world" to justify their rejection of God and His Word. At the time, their primary target was to undermine the plain reading of the Bible concerning the Flood of Noah (and its consequence of rock layers and worldwide fossil deposits) and a young age for the earth. It was really their attempt to undermine the authority of the entire Bible.

At that time, there were church leaders who adopted these ideas (millions of years) into Scripture (e.g., Thomas Chalmers with gap theory, Hugh Miller with day-age ideas, etc.). This was no different than today, and really no different than what happened with the religious leaders in the Apostle Paul's day, and also no different to what was happening with the priests and false prophets in ancient Israel.

Fallible, sinful man, ever since Genesis 3, has had the propensity to believe the fallible words of humans rather than the infallible Word of God. That is really our nature. At heart, because of sin, we are against God and what He teaches. People will go out of their way to trust in man rather than trust what God has clearly revealed.

In the early 1800s, there were church leaders in England who began to reinterpret the days of creation and the Flood account in Genesis to fit in the millions of years. Some advocated the idea of a gap between Genesis 1:1 and 1:2, like Chalmers. Others said that Christians could interpret the creation days as long ages, like Hugh Miller. Others realized that if one interpreted the fossil layers as representing millions of years, then how could one believe in the global Flood of Noah's day? Such a flood would destroy those layers and deposit more layers with fossils. Thus, it was postulated that Noah's Flood was only a local (regional) flood in the Mesopotamian Valley (modern-day Iraq).

As the 19th century progressed, Darwin popularized his ideas of biological evolution, which built on the ideas of geological evolution. There were church leaders who then reinterpreted Genesis to fit into evolution, even human evolution. When the idea of the big bang (astronomical evolution) was popularized in the early 20th century, in the same manner many church leaders then adopted this into God's Word.

Over the past two hundred years, many different positions regarding the creation account of Genesis have arisen in the Church, such as the following:

- Day-age idea
- Gap theory
- Local flood
- Theistic evolution
- Progressive creation
- Framework hypothesis

There are other positions or variations on those listed above, but they all have one thing in common: trying to fit man's ideas of millions of years into the Bible.

A number of Christian scientists actually opposed these compromise positions. Various books and articles were written to challenge the Church to stand on God's Word and not compromise with the fallible ideas of man that, intentionally or unintentionally, seriously undermined the authority of the Bible.

Biblical-creation scientists and theologians have been able to conduct tremendous research and have provided many answers in geology, biology, astronomy, anthropology, archaeology, and theology, which have equipped Christians to stand uncompromisingly on Genesis. The several thousand articles on the Answers in Genesis website[2] are a good example of providing such answers, as well as the hundreds of books, DVDs, and other resources now available there.

The modern biblical-creation movement has been highly successful at informing Christians of the numerous inconsistencies that try to add millions of years and evolution into the Bible. Many articles on the AiG website (or in the *Answers* magazine) deal with this issue.

Even with this wonderful research and its dissemination, the spiritual battle is intensifying. We don't fight against flesh and blood but "principalities and powers" (Eph. 6:12). As more and more answers have been given and inconsistencies pointed out, the arguments against God's Word in Genesis move on to different topics. This is why we continually need to be on our guard as we "contend for the faith" (Jude 3).

Word-twisting, truth-skewing newspeak is happening in the debate over the creation account in Genesis. Dr. William Dembski *says* that he believes in the inspired inerrant Word of God and in a literal Adam and Eve. But what does he *really* mean by this?

Dr. William Dembski (Southern Baptist)

Because he believes in billions of years and evolution (which means death, disease, and suffering before sin), consider what he does in an attempt to convince people he believes in a literal Adam and Eve, with death, disease, and suffering coming after sin. Here are some quotes from one of his latest books:

> For the theodicy I am proposing to be compatible with evolution, God must not merely introduce existing human-like beings from outside the Garden. In addition, when they enter the Garden, God must transform their consciousness so that they become rational moral agents made in God's image.[3]
>
> Any evils humans experience outside the Garden before God breathes into them the breath of life would be experienced as natural evils in the same way that other animals experience them. The pain would be real, but it would not be experienced as divine justice in response to willful rebellion. Moreover, once God breathes the breath of life into them, we may assume that the first humans experienced an amnesia of their former animal life: Operating on a higher plane of consciousness once infused with the breath of life, they would transcend the lower plane of animal consciousness on which they had previously operated — though,

after the Fall, they might be tempted to resort to that lower consciousness.[4]

Now when a Christian reads the above quotes, the average believer responds with, "What? This is bizarre!" But it is more than bizarre — it undermines the authority of the Word of God. But please keep in mind as I make these statements that I am not questioning anyone's Christian faith. We are encouraged to know that many Southern Baptist leaders (e.g., the late Dr. Adrian Rogers, Dr. Paige Patterson, and others) have been standing up for biblical inerrancy, but we are greatly concerned that there are some professors in Southern Baptist schools (as well as many other schools) who are actually undermining biblical authority — contrary to what they claim.

So why does Dr. Dembski propose ideas such as those above? Let's hear from his own words:

> The young-earth solution to reconciling the order of creation with natural history makes good exegetical and theological sense. Indeed, the overwhelming consensus of theologians up through the Reformation held to this view. I myself would adopt it in a heartbeat except that nature seems to present such a strong evidence against it. I'm hardly alone in my reluctance to accept young-earth.[5]

Notice his admission that if one takes God's Word as authoritative ("makes good exegetical and theological sense"), then it is obvious the earth is young. However, note the "except" word when he states that "*except* that nature seems to present such a strong evidence against it" (emphasis added).

So what does Dr. Dembski mean by stating that "nature seems to present such a strong evidence against it"?

He further states:

> A young earth seems to be required to maintain a traditional understanding of the Fall. And yet a young earth clashes sharply with mainstream science.[6]

In an article, he wrote:

> Dating methods, in my view, provide strong evidence for rejecting this face-value chronological reading of Genesis 4–11.[7]

It really comes down to the fact that Dr. Dembski accepts the fallible secular dating methods (based on numerous fallible assumptions[8]) and uses their results to trump the Word of God! That is the problem with many in the

Church — accepting man's words over God's Word. And yet, he claims to believe in inerrancy.

But without even dealing with the age of the earth issue (there are numerous articles on the www.answersingenesis.org website dealing with this topic), let us compare parts of his "theodicy" with Scripture — and you can be the judge.

Consider these statements concerning his above quotes:

> God must not merely introduce existing human-like beings from outside the Garden. In addition, when they enter the Garden, God must transform their consciousness so that they become rational moral agents made in God's image. . . . We may assume that the first humans experienced an amnesia of their former animal life: Operating on a higher plane of consciousness once infused with the breath of life, they would transcend the lower plane of animal consciousness on which they had previously operated.

Could God have introduced "human-like beings" into the Garden? Dr. Dembski is saying the Garden was perfect, but because of his belief in billions of years, death and suffering existed in the world with animals eating each other, etc. What I understand him to be saying is that because God is infinite and knew man would fall, He created a world in which there would be billions of years of death and suffering — so that when God gave Adam and Eve souls and they were then made in the image of God, they would fall (sin) in a perfect Garden and then see the effects of their sin in the death and suffering outside the Garden (which chronologically existed before sin but is actually a result of their sin, as God knew they would fall)!

Let's consider this passage of Scripture:

> Then the LORD God formed man of dust from the ground, and breathed into his nostrils the breath of life; and man became a living being (Gen. 2:7).

Note the order here: God made man from dust, added the divine breath, and this caused Adam to become a living being. The Hebrew words translated "living being" are the same Hebrew words used to describe sea creatures, birds, and land animals in Genesis 1:21, 24, 30, and 9:10. So the Bible is absolutely clear: God did *not* make some human-like living being and then add the divine breath that became man. The Scriptures teach man plus divine breath equals living being, *not* living being plus divine breath equals man. Paul affirms the literal truth of Genesis 2:7 when he says (in 1 Cor. 15:45) that "the first man Adam was made a living soul" (KJV). This is further confirmed by the judgment of God in Genesis 3:19. Adam was made from dust, and when he died, he returned to dust — he did not return to a human-like or ape-like being! Also, consider these passages of Scripture:

> Then the LORD God took the man and put him into the garden of Eden to cultivate it and keep it (Gen. 2:15).

> Then the LORD God said, "It is not good for the man to be alone; I will make him a helper suitable for him" (Gen. 2:18).

> The man said, "This is now bone of my bones, and flesh of my flesh; she shall be called Woman, because she was taken out of Man" (Gen. 2:23).

Note that Eve was made *from* Adam (by supernatural surgery, not by any natural process) after Adam was *in* the Garden. Eve did not come into the Garden as some "human-like" being and then get transformed by God into a full human being.

Note also what the Apostle Paul wrote as part of the infallible Scriptures:

> For as woman came from man . . . (1 Cor. 11:12; NIV).

> For man did not come from woman, but woman from man (1 Cor. 11:8; NIV).

> For Adam was formed first, then Eve (1 Tim. 2:13; NIV).

These passages all quote from Genesis 2:23 and Genesis 2:24 as literal history — so the literal history from Genesis is that the woman was made *from* Adam after he was already *in* the Garden.

Also, while in the Garden, God had made the animals and brought certain land animals to Adam for him to name and to show that he was alone. Obviously these animals weren't aggressive, so God had to have non-aggressive animals in the Garden, but outside the Garden, according to Dr. Dembski, there was a world that was "red in tooth and claw," as the poet Tennyson stated. (Actually, Gen. 1:30 states that all the animals were plant eaters originally — not sure how Dr. Dembski handles this, but maybe he would suggest this was just for the animals in the Garden.)

Another fatal flaw in Dr. Dembski's theodicy (i.e., the question of evil) is that he proposes that God judged the world with millions of years of animal death, disease, and extinction and other natural evil — and this judgment was because of man's sin, which occurred *after* all this natural evil had been occurring for billions of years. What kind of judge would punish a man with prison resulting in great suffering for his family *before* he committed a crime? Dr. Dembski's theodicy turns God into a grossly unjust Judge. But as Genesis 18:25 says, "Shall not the Judge of all the earth deal justly?"

There are many other inconsistencies in Dr. Dembski's beliefs. But what they show are the outrageous lengths some Christian academics will go in order to blend billions of years with the Scriptures. Yet they try to keep their belief in a literal Adam and Eve and the original sin, telling unsuspecting parents and prospective students that they believe in inerrancy.

Now many might believe we are just being divisive, or splitting hairs. Why does it really matter anyway? Let me explain by once again considering the writings of Dr. William Dembski quoted earlier. I have had interaction with a Christian leader concerning why we see the writings of Dr. Dembski as a major problem for the Church. This leader said that the world is the enemy and we shouldn't critique someone who believes in the inerrancy of Scripture. In my response I stated:

> I believe there is a misunderstanding in regard to the emphasis of our Answers in Genesis ministry and why our presenters (including myself), at appropriate times, quote scholars like Dembski, Sailhamer, Grudem, Waltke, Kline, Archer, Young, Falk, Giberson, Bohlin, Harlow, Craig, Hodge, Warfield, and others. We have never called into question these men's salvation. And we are not attacking them personally. But we are convinced that they are making a serious and significant mistake regarding the age of the earth (and in some cases evolution, too), and thereby (no doubt unintentionally) undermining the gospel and the authority of Scripture, which seriously hurts the church and her witness.

I went on to state:

> Over the years, we have written many articles (most are available on our website) to help people understand that we are first and foremost a ministry standing on the authority of the Word of God and proclaiming the saving gospel of Jesus Christ. We do not just want to see people converted to believe in creation, or an intelligent designer, but to believe in and trust the Creator, the Lord Jesus Christ, for salvation. Many people have the erroneous idea that our main emphasis is that of arguing against evolution and teaching a young earth. However, like you I am sure, the reason we believe in a young earth/

universe and reject evolution is because of our stand on the authority of God's Word. In other words, our belief in a young earth/ universe is part of the greater belief that the Bible is true and should be taken as written (e.g., 2 Cor. 4:2; Prov. 8:8–9). An abundance of biblical evidence in the Old and New Testament shows that Genesis is written as literal history and therefore our stand is that it should be interpreted as such. I believe you wholeheartedly agree.

I have included with this letter one of our latest publications (*Already Gone*) in which we detail the results of research conducted by renowned researcher Britt Beemer from America's Research Group. This research deals with why the majority of our young people are leaving their theologically conservative churches after they graduate from high school. Actually, this research also showed that the belief in millions of years was a significant contributing factor to creating doubt in these young people about the Bible's accuracy. We all know that churches have problems with the younger generation and their commitment to church and the Christian faith. We also observe the massive decline of Christianity throughout Europe and the United Kingdom — and we know that the USA is also moving rapidly down the same path.

This research and other studies (and our own experiences) have convinced us that a major contributing factor in the youth exodus has been the undermining of biblical authority. Of course, we all know that God's Word has come under attack since Genesis 3, and the Apostle Paul warns us in 2 Corinthians 11:3 that Satan is going to use the same method on us as he did on Eve. That method has been used to lead people to doubt God's Word and put them on a slippery slide of unbelief. In this era of history (beginning in the late 18th and early 19th centuries), there has been a very specific attack on the history of the first eleven chapters of the Bible.

We insist that what Dr. Dembski proposes in his book *The End of Christianity* is undermining the clear teaching of Scripture and thereby also undercutting biblical authority. God's people need to be warned concerning this serious slide.

And I further stated:

If there is truly an undermining of the authority of God's Word in a publication that is now very public, then I believe we should firmly and graciously confront this issue. Did not Paul set an example for us in Galatians 2:11–14, when he "withstood him [Peter] to the face" for compromising the gospel by his eating habits, which on the surface seemed so insignificant?

Dr. Karl Giberson and Dr. Darrel Falk (Nazarene)

We could obtain examples of "newspeak" and compromise from a variety of denominations. Here is an example from the Nazarene denomination. As you read below, keep in mind this quote about one of the founders and the first president (Phineas Bresee) of Point Loma Nazarene University in San Diego:

> There is a Bible on campus, encased in protective glass. This Bible belonged to Phineas Bresee. It's opened to Isaiah 62, the chapter Bresee claimed for the school. Permanently marked with his fingerprints, it displays a double message: God's words in Isaiah 62 and Bresee's love for those words. It's a message of being grounded in Scripture, of pursuing a well-rounded education and serving the poor out of a first and intense love for God and His Word. Bresee died in 1915, but his message still resonates. In fact, it defines Point Loma Nazarene University.[9]

Now consider the following in regard to that college and another Nazarene college. Students at Eastern Nazarene College (Boston), and Point Loma Nazarene University (San Diego) who came under the teaching of ardent evolutionists Dr. Karl Giberson and Dr. Darrel Falk respectively, would not only have been taught evolution as fact, but sadly, probably came under such teaching described below and endorsed by these same professors in the roles of vice-president and president of the BioLogos Foundation:

> Belief in a supernatural creator always leaves open the possibility that human beings are a fully-intended part of creation. If the Creator chooses to interact with creation, he could very well influence the evolutionary process to ensure the arrival of his intended result.... Furthermore, an omniscient creator could easily create the universe in such a way that physical and natural laws would result in human evolution....
> God planned for humans to evolve to the point of attaining these characteristics.... For example, in order to reflect God's Image by engaging in meaningful relationships, the human brain had to

evolve to the point where an understanding of love and relationship could be grasped and lived out. God's intention for humans to have relationships is illustrated in the opening chapters of Genesis, where many fundamental truths about God and humankind are communicated through the imagery of a creation story. After placing Adam in the Garden of Eden, Genesis 2 describes God's decision to provide Adam with a partner. . . . The Image of God also includes moral consciousness and responsibility. Humans did not have a fully formed moral consciousness prior to the time of Adam and Eve. . . . However, general consciousness must have already evolved so that a moral consciousness and the associated responsibility were possible. . . . When Adam and Eve received God's image, they had evolved to where they could understand the difference between right and wrong. It seems that Adam and Eve first demonstrated their new moral prowess when, using their free will, they chose wrong by eating from the forbidden tree of knowledge of good and evil. Adam and Eve then knew the difference between right and wrong in a more personal way than before, having experienced the guilt and shame that accompanied their decision (see Genesis 3:1–13). . . . When Did Humans Receive the Image of God?

We cannot know the exact time that humans attained God's image. In fact, it may be that the image of God emerged gradually over a period of time. Estimates of the historical time of Adam and Eve are varied. . . . While some literalist interpreters of Genesis argue that God created Adam and Eve in their present form, the evidence of DNA and the fossil record establishes that humans were also participants in the long evolutionary continuum, and God used this process as his means of creation. . . .

We also do not know if humanity received the image of God by the immediate onset of a relationship with God or by a slower evolutionary process. In either case, this development occurred before the fall of Adam and Eve, since moral responsibility and a broken relationship with God are both involved in the story of the fall. Perhaps God used the evolutionary process to equip humankind with language, free will and culture, and then revealed God's will to individuals or a community so that they might then enter into meaningful relationship with God through obedience, prayer, and worship. In this scenario, the evolutionary process is necessary but not sufficient to encompass the biblical teaching on the image of God.[10]

This is just a small amount of the teaching these Nazarene professors endorse — certainly not consistent with orthodox Christianity.

Dr. Giberson was also the co-author of an opinion column that appeared on the *USA Today* website and in the print edition.[11] The piece began:

> We believe in evolution — and God. Nearly half of Americans still dispute the indisputable: that humans evolved to our current form over millions of years. We're scientists and Christians. Our message to the faithful: Fear not. . . . The "science" undergirding this "young earth creationism" comes from a narrow, literalistic and relatively recent interpretation of Genesis, the first book in the Bible.[12]

What many parents don't realize is these two Nazarene professors (like certain other Christian college professors) don't just teach students evolution — it is much worse than that. The section above from the BioLogos website is just a tiny sample of the incredible attack on the authority of Scripture such teachers are imparting to students while the unsuspecting parents think they are doing a great thing in paying thousands of dollars for the children to be educated in a Christian school — but educated against the Bible!

In the *USA Today* article,[13] Dr. Giberson (and Dr. Falk) state: "We have launched a website to spread this good news (www.biologos.org) and — we hope — to answer the many questions those of faith might have. . . . The project aims to counter the voices coming from places such as the website Answers in Genesis. . . ."

By the way, the "good news" includes the statements above from the BioLogos website,[14] as well as such things as:

> The Everyman Reading of the creation story provides a very different metaphorical take on the text. This view understands the Fall as an allegorical story representing every human's individual rejection of God. In this light, the Fall was not a historical event but an illustration of the common human condition that virtually everyone agrees is deeply flawed and sinful. In this view, it does not matter if Adam and Eve were historical figures. Their deeds simply represent the actions of all humans and remind us of this troubling part of our natures.
>
> . . . where did the wife of Cain, Adam's son, come from? The only possibility is that she was Cain's sister, but this conflicts with later Biblical commands against incest. Even more problematic are

the people whom Cain fears when he is banished from his homeland for killing his brother Abel. It is highly implausible that the people Cain fears are also offspring of Adam and Eve; the text certainly does not suggest this. The people trying to kill Cain would have to be his extended family — siblings, nieces, nephews and so on — all united in trying to kill him. Along the same lines, Genesis mentions the city that Cain built and named after his son (Genesis 4:17). Who would populate this city or help to build it? The scientific evidence suggests a dramatically larger population at this point in history. Recently acquired genetic evidence also points to a population of several thousand people from whom all humans have descended, not just two.

So, no literal Fall, no literal Adam and Eve — so much for Christianity! And all people have descended from several thousand people, not just two — which means the Apostle Paul in Romans 5 and 1 Corinthians 15 is wrong concerning the gospel! And if that's the case, then Jesus didn't even tell the truth in Matthew 19 when he quoted Genesis and built the doctrine of marriage on the literal history in this account.

It seems the atheists understand theology better than these compromised Christians. They realize that if a literal Fall and a literal Adam and Eve are indeed false, then there is no use being a Christian because it undermines the very basis for the Gospel. One leading atheist claims:

> Christianity has fought, still fights, and will fight science to the desperate end over evolution, because evolution destroys utterly and finally the very reason Jesus' earthly life was supposedly made necessary. Destroy Adam and Eve and the original sin, and in the rubble you will find the sorry remains of the son of god. Take away the meaning of his death. If Jesus was not the redeemer that died for our sins, and this is what evolution means, then Christianity is nothing.[15]

For Christmas 2010, the American Atheists sponsored a billboard for people to see as they exited the Lincoln Tunnel. The billboard read: "You KNOW it's a Myth — This Season, Celebrate REASON!" It then directed people to their website. A statement on this website illustrates clearly that atheists do understand the importance of a literal Adam and Eve and a literal Fall to Christianity. They stated:

> Chances are, if you're reading this, you don't believe in the fable of Adam and Eve and the talking snake. You probably think it's a

story, created out of ignorance, to explain the origin of life. You probably don't believe that Adam literally ate a fruit, resulting in God expelling him and Eve out of the idyllic Garden of Eden.

In other words, you know that's a myth.

Right so far? So if Adam and Eve and the Talking Snake are myths, then Original Sin is also a myth, right? Well, think about it. . . .

Jesus' major purpose was to save mankind from Original Sin.

Original Sin makes believers unworthy of salvation, but you get it anyway, so you should be *grateful* for being saved (from that which does not exist).

Without Original Sin, the marketing that all people are sinners and therefore need to accept Jesus falls moot.

All we are asking is that you take what **you know** into serious consideration, even if it means taking a hard look at all you've been taught for your whole life. No Adam and Eve means no need for a savior. It also means that the Bible cannot be trusted as a source of unambiguous, literal truth. It is completely unreliable, because it all begins with a myth, and builds on that as a basis. No Fall of Man means no need for atonement and no need for a redeemer. You know it.[16]

But atheists aside, there is so much more on the BioLogos website — I actually encourage you to read all their questions and answers. If you stand on God's infallible Word, you will be shocked at some of the things you read. The trouble is most people in our churches do not know the reality of what is being taught at these colleges and through the books and websites! "Giberson has been on the faculty at Eastern Nazarene College in Quincy, Massachusetts, since 1984, where he teaches interdisciplinary honors seminars and the history of science. He is also the director of the Forum on Faith and Science at Gordon College in Wenham, Massachusetts, codirector of the Venice Summer School on Science & Religion and a fellow of the American Scientific Affiliation."[17]

May God have mercy on us when one considers this is the shocking state of a growing number of seminaries and Christian colleges in this nation.

Dr. William Lane Craig (Talbot School of Theology)

Some of you may have heard of Dr. William Lane Craig, research professor of philosophy at Talbot School of Theology in La Mirada, California. He says he believes in biblical inerrancy.[18] However, listen to the podcast referenced to understand what he means by inerrancy. And then of course it is not surprising to hear him in this television interview as he discusses the question of the age of the earth and Genesis:[19]

> Coren: How old is the world?
>
> Dr. Craig: The best estimates today are around 13.7 billion years.
>
> Coren: Now this is good, you see. This is a position I can embrace. Because there are people who will sit here and say, "No, it's six and a half thousand years old." That is not a tenable position?
>
> Dr. Craig: I don't think it's plausible. The arguments that I give are right in line with mainstream science. I'm not bucking up against mainstream science in presenting these arguments. Rather I'm going with the flow of what contemporary cosmology and astrophysics supports.
>
> Coren: Is there a contradiction or an inconsistency between the biblical account of the age of the earth and your statement?
>
> Dr. Craig: That's interesting because there isn't any biblical account of the age of the earth. There's nothing in Genesis or elsewhere in the Bible that says how old the universe is, so no, I don't think it is incompatible.
>
> Coren: We often hear the rather caricatured argument that Christians believe that man and dinosaur coexisted.
>
> Dr. Craig: There are some creationists — they typically style themselves "young earth creationists" — who believe that. I've even seen children's books where Noah takes dinosaur eggs on the ark with him. Well, all of this is reading between the lines. There's nothing like that in the book of Genesis.

What does inerrancy really mean? This is a major problem within Christianity. The point we make over and over again is that when we teach the next generation to reinterpret God's Word this way (i.e., by using the majority view in secular science), it unlocks a door that undermines all of biblical authority. Subsequent generations will continue to push that door open wider, which has already happened all across our Western world. After all, the majority of secular scientists also insist that virgins don't have babies and dead men don't rise from the dead. So should we also reinterpret Matthew 1 and Matthew 28 accordingly and just go with the flow of mainstream science?

Now I have observed an interesting phenomenon that is permeating Christian colleges and seminaries, which influences future church leaders and what they take to the pulpit, mission field, etc.

I believe many Christian academics recognize the inconsistency in trying to add millions of years and evolution to Genesis. The compromise is obvious. Many of them recognize that one has to totally change the meaning of the words in Genesis to allow such compromise. For example, creating Adam out of dust and Eve from a rib have to be changed to mean that ape-men and ape-women changed into Adam and Eve. But this ignores many details in the biblical text and ends up playing language games. Various articles on the Answers in Genesis website point out the numerous problems with such compromise.

Ultimately, of course, the result of this compromise undermines the authority of God's Word. And in the Church today, we see two-thirds of young people leaving the Church by the time they reach college age, and it's largely because the reliability and authority of God's Word has been undermined (as our research for the book *Already Gone* has shown).

Today, the same battle rages, but we see a change in what is being foisted on the Church as the enemy continues to attack God's Word. Remember, the attack has always been on God's Word, as it started with the questioning of what God said to Adam and Eve in Genesis 3 and has never let up.

That attack just manifests itself in different ways in different eras. I have observed that more and more Christian academics, in their attempt to adopt man's ideas of evolution and millions of years, are continuing this attack in a different sort of way. The following is a specific example from a professor at Wheaton College, Illinois.

Dr. John Walton (Wheaton College, Illinois)

Dr. John Walton is professor of Old Testament at Wheaton College in Illinois and is author of *The Lost World of Genesis One*.[20]

A summary of what Dr. Walton teaches is that Genesis 1 is not history in regard to the material world; it has to do with what he calls God's "Cosmic Temple." He basically insists that one can only understand Genesis if one has an understanding of ancient Near Eastern thinking — and surprise, surprise — this has been lost for thousands of years. Now a few academics like Dr. Walton have unearthed this thinking so now they can tell us what the writer of Genesis 1 really meant! It is an academic elitism.

Dr. Walton tries (unsuccessfully) to insist that he is not coming up with this new idea of his because of the influence of evolution/millions of years — but the clear fact is that he is doing just that! He knows that young people today have a conflict between the secular view of origins and the Bible — so his solution is to relegate Genesis 1 as having nothing to do with material origins and thus people are free to believe whatever they want — though he is obviously convinced that evolution and millions of years should be believed.

The bottom line is, it is just another way of trying to come up with a "solution" to fitting millions of years and evolution into the Bible. Because Dr. Walton knows (and admits) that the days of creation are ordinary days in Genesis 1, according to the Hebrew language, he had to come up with a way to allow for millions of years and evolution and yet agree that the days of creation are ordinary days. So his solution? Relegate Genesis 1 to mean it is the creation of God's Cosmic Temple, and not allow it to have anything to do with material origins. Then he can say that students will have no conflict — they can believe in millions of years/evolution/or whatever — and it doesn't matter!

And of course, the reason the Church greats of the past (whether Luther, Calvin, Gill, or whomever) never thought of this is because they did not discover how ancient Near Eastern cultures were thinking! This has now been discovered by an elite few who can now tell us for the first time in thousands of years what Genesis 1 really means. Sound bizarre? I encourage you to read the book for yourself! Following are just a few quotes from the book.

Were Adam and Eve two real people? Dr. Walton states:

> This archetypal understanding applies also to Genesis 2. An individual named Adam is not the only human being made of the dust of the earth, for as Genesis 3:19 indicates, "Dust you are and to dust you will return." This is true of all humans, men and women. It is an archetypal feature that describes us all. It is not a statement of chemical composition nor is it describing a material process by which each and every human being is made. The dust is an archetypal feature and therefore cannot be viewed as a material ingredient. It is indicative of human destiny and mortality, and therefore is a functional comment, not a material one.[21]

Is Genesis 1 an account of material origins? Dr. Walton states:

> When we thought of Genesis 1 as an account of material origins, creation became an action in the past that is over and done with. God made objects and now the cosmos exists (materially). Viewing Genesis 1 as an account of functional origins offers more opportunity for understanding that God's creative work continues.[22]

> Genesis 1 would be viewed as a temple text — we gain a different perspective on the nature of the Genesis creation account. Genesis 1

can now be seen as a creation account focusing on the cosmos as a temple. It is describing the creation of the cosmic temple with all of its functions and with God dwelling in its midst.[23]

Was the Garden of Eden a real garden? Dr. Walton states:

The garden of Eden is not viewed by the author of Genesis simply as a piece of Mesopotamian farmland, but as an archetypal sanctuary, that is a place where God dwells and where man should worship him. Many of the features of the garden may also be found in later sanctuaries particularly the tabernacle or Jerusalem temple. These parallels suggest that the garden itself is understood as a sort of sanctuary.[24]

Does Dr. John Walton believe in millions of years?

The day-age theory and others that attempt to mitigate the force of the seven days do so because they see no way to reconcile seven twenty-four-hour days of material creation with the evidence from science that the earth and the universe are very old. They seek a solution in trying to stretch the meaning of yôm, whereas we propose that once we understand the nature of the creation account, there is no longer any need to stretch yôm.[25]

Some variation exists as to whether the cosmic origins go back 10,000–20,000 years as some would allow, or only go back about 6,000 years from the present (as promoted at the Creation Museum in Petersburg, Kentucky). The challenge they face is to account for all of the evidences of great age of the earth and of the universe.[26]

Of course he believes in millions of years, and despite his insistence to the contrary, this is part of his ultimate motivation to relegate Genesis 1 to something other than material history.

So what does Dr. Walton say Genesis 1 means?

In summary, we have suggested that the seven days are not given as the period of time over which the material cosmos came into existence, but the period of time devoted to the inauguration of the functions of the cosmic temple, and perhaps also its annual reenactment. It is not the material phase of temple construction that represents the creation of the temple; it is the inauguration of the functions and the entrance of the presence of God to take up his rest that creates the temple. Genesis 1 focuses on the creation of the (cosmic) temple, not the material phase of preparation. In the next chapter we will track the implications of the idea that the seven days are not related to the material phase of creation.[27]

There is so much more. He does not believe in a global Flood and believes there was death of animals (and disease and thorns because he allows for millions of years) millions of years before man (however man came into existence.)

There is a very telling statement from his book:

> This is not a conclusion designed to accommodate science — it was drawn from an analysis and interpretation of the biblical text of Genesis in its ancient environment. The point is *not* that the biblical text therefore supports an old earth, but simply that there is not biblical position on the age of the earth. If it were to turn out that the earth is young, so be it. But most people who seek to defend a young-earth view do so because they believe that the Bible obligates them to such a defense. I admire the fact that believers are willing to take unpopular positions and investigate all sorts of alternatives in an attempt to defend the reputation of the biblical text. But if the biblical text does not demand a young earth there would be little impetus or evidence to offer such a suggestion.[28]

Well he is correct here in one sentence — biblical creationists do insist on a young earth because we "believe the Bible obligates" us "to such a defense." Of course! But notice he is trying to see his conclusion is not "designed to accommodate science" — yet as one reads the book, one finds that is *exactly* what it is all about.

What does Dr. John Walton teach in regard to the Flood of Noah's day?

I will use the almost one-thousand-page *Dictionary of the Old Testament Pentateuch* edited by T. Desmond Alexander and David W. Baker[29] to document Dr. Walton's teaching on the Genesis Flood. Starting on page 315, there is 12-page section on the Genesis Flood account written by Dr. John Walton, professor of Old Testament at Wheaton College in Illinois.

In the section above, I outlined Dr. Walton's approach to Genesis, pointing out that he believes Genesis 1 is not an account of material origins, but an account of God's "Cosmic Temple." Dr. Walton believes that a person needs to understand ancient Near Eastern thinking and culture in order to understand Scripture. He argues that such an understanding has been lost for ages, but that academics, like himself, have been able to regain an understanding of this ancient Near Eastern thinking so the rest of us in the Church can finally (after thousands of years) understand what Genesis 1 means.

Dr. Walton certainly has a different view of inspiration to that of Drs. Whitcomb and Morris who authored the famous *The Genesis Flood* publication, our AiG staff, and millions of other Christians around the world. Dr. Walton, though, looks at the person(s) who wrote Genesis and the pagan cultures of the day as authoritative. Drs. Morris and Whitcomb (and Answers in Genesis and the Institute for Creation Research — two of the leading creation apologetics organizations), however, understand that it is the *words* of Scripture that are inspired.

I think of this passage of Scripture: "All Scripture is inspired by God, and profitable for teaching, for reproof, for correction, for training in righteousness" (2 Tim. 3:16).

In the original Greek language, "inspiration of God" is one word and it means literally "God-breathed." This verse clearly states that the words of Scripture are God-breathed! Every one of them came from Him as the Spirit of God worked through the prophets and Apostles. We are also told that God's Word will stand forever. If the infinite God, who created language, cannot move people to write His "God-breathed" words so all people (regardless of culture) can understand them, then there is something dreadfully wrong. If it is only now, after thousands of years, that we can finally understand what Genesis means because of what a few academics claim about ancient Near Eastern thinking, how can we be sure we know anything? How do we know those academics like Dr. Walton have it right? No wonder Scripture cautions us that "knowledge puffs up" (1 Cor. 8:1; NIV). We are seeing academia in the Christian world going mad as "Protestant popes" are popping up all over the Christian world.

Regarding the Flood, Dr. Walton applies the same misguided approach as he does in Genesis 1. He states the following:

> The theological message of the Bible was communicated to people who lived in the ancient Near Eastern world. If we desire to understand the theological message of the text, we will benefit by positioning it within the worldview of the ancient cultures rather than simply applying our own cultural perspectives.[30]

Dr. Walton then discusses ancient Near Eastern mythology and relates it to Scripture and its Book of Genesis. In essence, he is using pagan, idolatrous mythology to supposedly help enable us to understand what God and Moses really meant!

But really, the whole underlying reason for what he is doing (as I noted previously) relates to the ideas of millions of years and evolution. Dr. Walton recognizes that you can't fit millions of years and evolution into Genesis, so he is hoping to popularize an idea that Genesis is not revealing an account of material origins. Genesis chapter 1, for instance, is supposed to be about God's Cosmic Temple and the function of the different creatures in that temple (which came into existence who knows when)!

So what does the Flood account mean then? Dr. Walton declares the following:

> It has already been suggested that the boat in Mesopotamian accounts may have served as a floating shrine. In its dimensions, the Genesis ark is much more realistic for a boat, though conceptually it may also represent a sanctuary where order is maintained floating on a sea of resurgent chaos. In this sense the Mesopotamian ark appears as a physical representation of a sanctuary, while the Genesis ark appears as a functional representation of a sanctuary. Creation both in the Bible and in the ancient Near East entailed deity bringing order while pushing back chaos. . . . The forces of chaos were most consistently represented in the cosmic waters. In this sense, the flood represents a reversal of creation. This is more the case in the biblical account than in the ancient Near Eastern accounts, for in the latter there is no textual representation of re-creation.[31]

Now that makes sense to the average person, doesn't it? Why didn't any Jews or Christians before the 20th century ever think of this? Obviously, the answer to this is that they trusted the Bible as the authority, whereas today many trust man's ideas as being *greater* than God's and therefore demote God's Word to be lesser than their own ideas (Ps. 118:8).

While Dr. Walton insists that he does not propose his views as a response to millions of years and evolution, that is exactly what his underlying motive is. It is obvious when you read his writings carefully. For instance, Dr. Walton objects to a global Flood by bringing up the same old arguments that Drs. Morris and Whitcomb were confronted with and answered in their book!

For instance, Dr. Walton makes the following claims:

1. It would be impossible to cover Mt. Ararat with the waters of the Flood. Answer: this assumes Mt. Ararat existed before the Flood! This mountain is one that has undergone massive volcanism and uplift. If you were to smooth out the earth's surface and oceans basins, there is enough water on the earth's surface right now to cover the earth to a

depth of about two miles. The oceans were not as deep and the mountains not as high before the Flood. There has been a lot of uplift — particularly associated with the ending of the Flood (as Ps. 104:6–9 tells us — and the promise in verse 9, which reflects God's rainbow promise in Genesis 9, shows that this passage is not referring to day 3 of Genesis 1). That is why marine fossils are found near the top of Mt. Everest (and other high mountains); the mountains were not covered by the Flood but the once-horizontal sediments were tilted and raised up at the end of the Flood. One also can see evidence of this uplift at the Grand Canyon, where layers supposedly millions of years old were uplifted while they were still soft.

2. Dr. Walton brings up the old accusation that there are too many species of animals to fit on the ark. Answer: First of all, God brought the animals to Noah; Noah didn't have to locate them. Second, God sent two (seven of some) of every *kind*, not species. There are good biblical and scientific reasons to conclude that many species or even genera are descended genetically from each original created kind. For example, only one male and one female of the dog kind (not two wolves, two jackals, two dingoes, two poodles, two Great Danes, etc.) were needed. Far fewer animals were required than what Dr. Walton is imagining and claiming.

3. Dr. Walton states, "one must also explain how the animals today found only in Australia could have gotten to that continent."[32] He needs only to purchase our *New Answers Book 1* — or just go to the Answers in Genesis website — for a very plausible answer of land bridges during the Ice Age that followed the Genesis Flood. Frankly, this academic has not done his homework.

4. Dr. Walton states, "How could Noah and his family and animals such as elephants and hippopotami make the trek down the mountain (Mt. Ararat)."[33] First, the Bible does not say the ark landed on Mt. Ararat; it landed on the "mountains of Ararat," which this Hebrew expert should have known. So the Bible doesn't tell us what particular mountain it was. The Mt. Ararat Dr. Walton refers to has undergone massive changes since the Flood: volcanism, earthquakes, and uplift. Answers in Genesis's geologist, Andrew Snelling, Ph.D., has stated that based on technical data that has been publicly available in maps and scientific papers for more than a decade, he is convinced that modern Mt. Ararat is almost certainly a post-Flood volcano, with most of its lavas having erupted during the post-Flood Ice Age. Therefore, the ark most

likely landed on some other mountain in that range. And unless Dr. Walton is going to say the Flood account is a myth, then it is obvious that Noah's family and all the animals could safely descend the mountain they landed on so that they could repopulate the earth.

There are many more problems with what Dr. Walton states. But the bottom line is that he does not believe in a global Flood, and he does believe in an earth that is millions of years old. In this section of the book, he certainly speaks positively about a possible regional event millions of years ago. He states, "If the reader finds it difficult to put the flood 5.5million years ago, the Black Sea theory may be more palatable."[34] He really sums it up when he states, "There is presently no convincing archaeological evidence of the biblical flood." So does he believe it was a myth? That belief would be contrary to the teaching of Jesus (Matt. 24:37–39) and the Apostle Peter (2 Pet. 2:4–6 and 3:3–7).

So the battle rages. It is the same battle Drs. Morris and Whitcomb were dealing with in their classic *The Genesis Flood*. These great scholars were passionate for the Word of God. In the 50 years since their book's publication, the biblical creation movement is more passionate than ever for the Word of God. At the same time, we now see Christian academics like Dr. Walton using the argument that Genesis is not an account of material origins and that a Christian has to understand ancient Near Eastern thinking to know what Genesis really means.

Dr. Walton's own arguments can be summed up this way; he states the following:

> Some feel they are protecting theories that account of the details of the traditional interpretation of the text. Too often, however, these theories prove to be implausible and are easily discredited by the scientific thinkers whom they intend to win over.[35]

Let me reword this for you (my words are interspersed in Dr. Waltons' and are in brackets to help explain what I believe Dr. Walton is saying):

> Some [those like Drs. Whitcomb and Morris] feel they are protecting theories [protecting the clear teaching of the text] that account for details of the traditional interpretation of the text [the interpretation that greats like Luther, Calvin, Wesley, Gill, and others held because of what the text clearly states]. Too often, however, these theories [their views based clearly on the text — Scripture alone] prove to be implausible [to unbelievers, but not

to Bible-believers] and are easily discredited by scientific thinkers [fallible, sinful humans whose hearts are "deceitful above all things and desperately wicked," and who arrogantly claim that "science" has disproved the Bible's account because they insist millions of years are a fact] whom they intend to win over [who need to listen to God's Word, but instead "suppress the truth in unrighteousness" (Rom. 1:18)].

Today, let's praise God for the faithfulness of scholars like Drs. Whitcomb and Morris and for the publication of their book *The Genesis Flood*. In some ways, this was the beginning of a new "reformation" in the modern church, which continues to this day as organizations like Answers in Genesis, Institute for Creation Research, Creation Research Society, etc., continue to challenge the Church and culture to return to the authority of the Word of God.

Why are we seeing more and more bizarre and elitist ideas (like those of Dr. Dembski and Dr. Walton) coming out of Christian academia? I believe it is an academic pride, from academic peer pressure, because ultimately some of these people love "human praise more than praise from God" (John 12:43; NIV).

Why should we bother bringing such matters to the attention of the Church? I believe we need to be watchmen as described in Ezekiel, warning people about the teaching that is in the public arena that attacks biblical authority. We must be willing to defend God's Word and warn God's people of the damage some of these teachers are doing. Also, some of them must be called to return to God's sovereign authority, and we invite any and all educators to privately dialogue with us on these fundamentally important and essential matters.

> Son of man, speak to the children of your people, and say to them: "When I bring the sword upon a land, and the people of the land take a man from their territory and make him their watchman, when he sees the sword coming upon the land, if he blows the trumpet and warns the people, then whoever hears the sound of the trumpet and does not take warning, if the sword comes and takes him away, his blood shall be on his own head. He heard the sound of the trumpet, but did not take warning; his blood shall be upon himself. But he who takes warning will save his life. But if the watchman sees the sword coming and does not blow the trumpet, and the people are not warned, and the sword comes and takes any person from among them, he is taken away in his iniquity; but his blood I will

require at the watchman's hand."

So you, son of man: I have made you a watchman for the house of Israel; therefore you shall hear a word from My mouth and warn them for Me (Ezek. 33:2–7; NKJV).

I have included more quotes below from professors associated with well-known Christian colleges to help people understand the extent of such compromise in these institutions. (Of course, this is just scratching the surface of this problem ingrained in most such academic institutions across the nation.)

Calvin College, Michigan

1. Dr. Davis A. Young, emeritus professor of geology, Calvin College

The Bible has traditionally been read to imply that the universe is young; astronomy concludes that the universe is billions of years old. The Bible has been widely interpreted as saying that the Earth was created in six days; geology concludes that the Earth has undergone a long and complex history spanning 4.5 billion years. The Bible has been interpreted as implying fixity of animal and plant species; paleontology and biology conclude that organisms have developed from one another through time, that they have evolved. Some believe that the Bible teaches that all death entered the world only after human beings appeared and fell into sin; paleontology concludes that animals and plants died, and in some cases died violently by being devoured by other animals, before human beings were even on the Earth. Many Christians have a very difficult time accepting such conclusions since they cannot see how the Bible can possibly be in accord with them.[36]

Contrary to the view held by many Christians, we believe that historical reconstructions by modern astronomy and geology are neither uncontrolled speculations nor founded upon unbiblical presuppositions. We hold that these reconstructions are firmly grounded in a wealth of carefully gathered data and have been repeatedly tested by the respected canons of science.[37]

If rocks are historical documents, we are driven to the related conclusion that the available evidence is overwhelmingly opposed to the notion that the Noahic flood deposited rocks of the Colorado Plateau only a few thousand years ago or that the rocks were formed from a diminishing ocean.[38]

2. Dr. Howard J. Van Till, emeritus professor of physics, Calvin College

According to contemporary cosmological models, which incorporate evidence drawn from a variety of phenomena, the beginning of the universe took place about fifteen billion years ago, the exact figure depending on the evaluation of certain model parameters. We call this fifteen billion years the "age" of the universe, and we call the first episode of cosmic history the "big bang."[39]

I have often suggested that the historic Judeo-Christian doctrine of creation is better summarized by saying that *the universe is God's creation* than by saying *that the universe was created by God.*[40]

3. Dr. Deborah B. Haarsma, chair, Department of Physics and Astronomy, Calvin College

Because of this kind of evidence, by about 1840 virtually all practicing geologists, including Christian geologists, believed that the earth must be at least millions of years old. Moreover, if a flood had occurred, it must have been local, not global. The data from many locations indicated that the world's stratified rocks and fossils could not have been deposited in a single global flood. While local floods certainly did take place here and there, a longer time period and more gradual processes are required to explain the entire picture. Scientific study indicated that the earth had long geological history *before* humans arrived on the scene.[41]

The careful structure of this passage [Genesis 1] shows that the author selected the sequence of events and number of days with symbolism and thematic order in mind rather than our modern scientific concept of historical sequence. The organization and structure of the text support non-concordist interpretations of Genesis 1, since it appears that historical sequence was not the top priority for the original author.[42]

Thus, if Christians today wish to interpret Genesis 1 completely literally, they must believe that:

- The earth is flat rather than spherical.
- The earth rests on pillars rather than orbiting the sun.
- The sky is a solid dome rather than a transparent atmosphere.
- An ocean of water is above the sky.

Any other so-called *literal* interpretation of Genesis 1 is, at best, a semi-literal interpretation in which the reader picks and chooses some pieces to view literally and others to view figuratively.[43]

4. Dr. Loren Haarsma, associate professor of physics, Calvin College

The Bible teaches that God can precisely select the outcome of events that appear random to us. It is also possible that God gives his creation some freedom, through random processes, to explore the wide range of potentials he has given it. Either way, randomness within natural processes is not the absence of God. Rather, it is another vehicle for God's creativity and governance.[44]

5. Dr. Daniel C. Harlow, associate professor of religion, Calvin College

Roberts accuses Calvin of propounding "dangerous beliefs" that foster "misguided views" among our students on such topics as homosexuality. He then charges the Religion faculty with feeding a generation of Calvin students "the lie that what they are learning is Christian orthodoxy rather than 20th century modernism." Our "lie" is that we deny that the Bible is inerrant. In defending my department, I am speaking only for myself and not for the rest of my colleagues, who would doubtless want to word things differently.

To begin with, the Bible itself nowhere claims that it is inerrant (free of factual errors of any sort). . . .

Mr. Roberts is also mistaken when he asserts that the doctrine of inerrancy represents "the historic position of the Church on Scripture." The fact of the matter is that no ancient Church council ever debated the issue of inerrancy, let alone pronounced favor of it. No ecumenical creed even addresses the issue — not the Apostle's Creed, not the Nicene Creed, not the Athanasian Creed. None of the Reformed confessions that Calvin College adheres to asserts Scripture's inerrancy, but rather its "sufficiency." As the Belgic Confession states, "We believe that this Holy Scripture contains the will of God completely and that everything one must believe to be saved is sufficiently taught in it" (Article 7). The great theologians of the Church, including Protestant Reformers like Luther and Calvin, had the highest regard for Scripture's inspiration, authority and truthfulness, and at times they used words like "infallible" and even "unerring" when affirming its truth claims. But they also acknowledged factual discrepancies and other problems in the Bible and recognized the cultural limitations of its human authors. So if inerrancy is supposedly the "historic position of the Church," as Roberts asserts, how is it that the Church's great councils, creeds, confessions and theologians missed the boat? . . .

When thoughtful Christians turn to the historical narratives in the Bible, they see ancient authors who wrote according to the methods and standards of their own day. By those ancient standards, which involved the use of a variety of sometimes conflicting oral and written traditions, they were very good historians. But they made occasional errors of fact in areas like geography, chronology and political history. To acknowledge this is not to demean Scripture but to accept it as it is. It's rather like noticing one day that your beloved has a small mole or other blemish; instead of considering the feature a defect, you come to regard it as an endearment.[45]

Dr. Dan Harlow as professor of biblical and early Jewish studies in the Department of Religion at *Calvin College* stated the following in a recent paper:

Recent research in molecular biology, primatology, sociobiology, and phylogenetics indicates that the species *Homo sapiens* cannot be traced back to a single pair of individuals, and that the earliest human beings did not come on the scene in anything like paradisal physical or moral conditions. It is therefore difficult to read Genesis 1–3 as a factual account of human origins. In current Christian thinking about Adam and Eve, several scenarios are on offer. The most compelling one regards Adam and Eve as strictly literary figures — characters in a divinely inspired story about the imagined past that intends to teach theological, not historical, truths about God, creation, and humanity.

Taking a nonconcordist approach, this article examines Adam and Eve as symbolic-literary figures from the perspective of mainstream biblical scholarship, with attention both to the text of Genesis and ancient Near Eastern parallels. Along the way, it explains why most interpreters do not find the doctrines of the Fall and original sin in the text of Genesis 2–3, but only in later Christian readings of it. This article also examines briefly Paul's appeal to Adam as a type of Christ. Although a historical Adam and Eve have been very important in the Christian tradition, they are not central to biblical theology as such. The doctrines of the Fall and original sin may be reaffirmed without a historical Adam and Eve, but invite reformulation given the overwhelming evidence for an evolving creation.[46]

In response to feedback the college has received about what this professor believes and teaches (and he is just one of many with compromising beliefs at this Christian college), the office of the president of Calvin College stated the following:

What does Calvin College teach about evolutionary biology? Calvin affirms that the one true God is the creator and designer of the universe. The Calvin College Biology Department also clearly maintains that God, as the creator and designer of the universe, brought the world into being. With this as a firm foundation, the department also accepts the biological theory of evolution (descent with modification over time) to be the best explanation for understanding the commonality and diversity seen among all living creatures on earth.[47]

Dr. John Collins, Covenant Theological Seminary, St. Louis, Missouri

Basically, as long as you believe the human race started with Adam and Eve (whatever that means) and you believe there was a Fall (whatever that means) and believe sin entered the human race (whatever that means) and you believe God created (whatever that means) then you are being academic in the Christian world!

What you will find is what he means by "historical" is certainly not what many Christians mean by "historical" in regard to Adam and Eve. This is the typical "newspeak" discussed throughout this book as a result of the research results from the Christian institutions.

This, sadly, is an example of the typical type of "academia" being taught in most Christian colleges/seminaries across the nation.

Following are excerpts from a paper entitled "Adam and Eve as Historical People, and Why It Matters," by Dr. Jack Collins, professor of Old Testament at Covenant Theological Seminary in St. Louis, Missouri:

Quite briefly, I take the biblical storyline to imply that Adam and Eve are historical persons at the headwaters of the distinctly human kind. To say that they are "historical," of course, lays on us no requirement of "literalism" for reading Genesis, if the material itself does not invite it. I think, for example, that the account of Cain and Abel uses "anachronism," describing aspects of older times in terms of what the writer and his audience were familiar with. Therefore those who find that the farming and the crafts of Genesis 4 imply a Neolithic setting, are being unduly literalistic. Further, it is well established that the genealogies of Genesis 5 do not intend to list every generation; gaps are to be expected. There is no way to know what size gaps the literary conventions allow, or even if there are any limits at all; this is not the kind of information these genealogies aim to convey. Nothing in Genesis 2–4 tells us how long these events are supposed to have taken, which means the other people Cain fears could be his siblings, or their descendants. Of those who think of contemporary humans, collateral with Adam and Eve, the best are careful about what Genesis 4 does and does not imply.

From the paleontologists, we learn that Adam and Eve, if they are indeed at the headwaters of the human race, must come before such events as the arrival of modern humans in Australia, which means before about 40,000 BC. According to John Bloom's survey, there are two important gaps in the available record of human development. The first occurs with the appearance of anatomically modern humans around 130,000 BC. The second gap occurs when culture appears, around 40,000 BC. At this point, we find that art and "the complexity and variety of artifacts greatly increases." As Bloom observes, "At present either of these transitions seems sharp enough that we can propose that the special creation of man occurred in one of these gaps and that it was not bridged by purely natural means."

The geneticists give us two matters to account for. First, they conclude from the genetic similarities between humans and chimpanzees that humans and chimpanzees have some kind of "common ancestor." Second, some infer from features of the human genome that the human population needs to have been a thousand or more individuals, even at its beginning. I will not assess this DNA evidence; I do not know whether the evidence is only compatible with these conclusions, or strongly favors them. I cannot predict whether future geneticists will still think the same way about DNA as contemporary ones do. I do know that biologists' understanding of DNA (e.g., so-called "junk DNA" now appears to have a function) has changed over the years, but I cannot say what biologists might think in the future. Hence, rather than try to say whether these inferences are good or bad, I have sought ways to allow advocates of these conclusions to stay within the bounds of sound thinking. In other words, even if someone is persuaded that humans had "ancestors," and that the human population has always been more than two, he or she does not necessarily have to ditch all traditional views of Adam and Eve; I have tried to provide for these possibilities more than to contend for my particular preferences on these matters.

Young-earth creationists, and many old-earth creationists, commonly think of Adam and Eve as fresh creations, with no animal forebears. Others allow for God to have refurbished a preexisting hominid into Adam. While I am not making an issue of this, my first criterion (p. 159) shows why I think it is nevertheless crucial to affirm that, whatever the process, it was not a purely natural one. Regardless of where God got the raw material, we can say that humans are the result of "special creation."[48]

In his book *Science and Faith* Dr. Collins makes this statement:

Since I am not a cosmologist, I have no way of knowing whether the technical details of the Big Bang theory are sound or not. My own reading of Genesis means that I have no problem with the amount of time the theory calls for. The conclusion from these three lines of evidence seems to be fair, so far as I can tell. As long as we recognize that it's a theory in physics. I see no reason to reject it, I say this because this kind of theory can't tell us *why* we're here, only *how* we came to be here.[49]

It is interesting that he states he has "no way of knowing," but then goes on to basically accept it!

Further on, he states:

I conclude, then, that I have no reason to disbelieve the standard theories of the geologists, including their estimate for the age of the earth. They may be wrong, for all I know; but if they are wrong, it's not because they have improperly smuggled philosophical assumptions into their work.[50]

That's a sad statement illustrating he accepts man is neutral — instead of the biblical understanding that fallible man suppresses the truth in unrighteousness (Rom. 1).

Dr. Bruce Waltke, Knox Theological Seminary, Florida

Dr. Bruce Waltke, formerly a professor at Reformed Theological Seminary in Orlando, Florida, is now listed as distinguished professor of Old Testament for Knox Theological Seminary. The seminary website describes Dr. Waltke as one of the preeminent Old Testament scholars.

On the Biologos website, Dr. Waltke stated:

> I think that if the data is overwhelming in favor of evolution, [then] to deny that reality will make us a cult, some odd group that's not really interacting with the real world, and rightly so. We're not using our gifts nor trusting God's providence that brought us to this point of our awareness. Because I see all of history is in God's providence, and I think we're at a unique moment in history. So many strands are coming together. We're at almost, to my mind, the pinnacle of history. We're aware of these things, and to deny the reality would be to deny the truth of God in the world, and would be to deny truth. So I think it would be our spiritual death if we stopped loving God with all of our minds and thinking about it. I think it's our spiritual death.
>
> It's also our spiritual death in our witness to the world — that we're not credible, that we are bigoted, we have a blind faith, and this is what we are accused of. So I see this all as part of the growth of the church. We are much more mature by this dialogue that we're having, and I think this is how we come to the unity of the faith is that we wrestle with these issues.
>
> We're all in the body of Christ — one Lord, one faith, one baptism — and we may disagree with one other but we are really interacting in a very serious way, trusting God as truth and that we are testing what is true and holding fast to that which is good and we are the richer for it and if we don't do that we are going to die. And I think it's essential to us, or we'll end up like some small sect somewhere that retains a certain dress or certain language and then end up marginalized, totally marginalized, and I think that would be a great tragedy for the church, for us to become marginalized in that way.[51]

In his treatise on Old Testament theology Dr. Waltke also states:

> The best harmonious synthesis of the special revelation of the Bible, of the general revelation of human nature that distinguishes

between right and wrong and consciously or unconsciously craves God, and of science is the theory of theistic evolution.[52]

Of course, many more examples could be offered. The above I consider to be representative of where the majority of Christian academics at Christian institutions across the United States (and in fact, around the world) stand in regard to what they teach and write on the Book of Genesis and their approach to Scripture. This is generally the sad state of Christendom in the academic world. It is time for Christians to take a stand for biblical authority and go forth and demolish false unbiblical views.

Endnotes

1. Some of these were Comte de Buffon, James Hutton, Abraham Werner, and others, but it culminated with Charles Lyell in the 1830s. For more, see Ken Ham, editor, *The New Answers Book 2*, "How Old Is the Earth?" by Bodie Hodge (Green Forest, AR: Master Books, 2008).
2. www.answersingenesis.org.
3. William Dembski, *The End of Christianity: Finding a Good God in an Evil World* (Nashville, TN: Broadman & Holman Academic, 2009), p. 159.
4. Ibid., p. 154–155.
5. Ibid., p. 55.
6. Ibid., p. 77.
7. William A. Dembski, paper, "Christian Theodicy in Light of Genesis and Modern Science," p. 49.
8. The assumptions can be revealed in these questions: Initial amounts? Was any parent amount added? Was any daughter amount added? Was any parent amount removed? Was any daughter amount removed? How has the rate changed due to the environmental effects?
9. http://www.pointloma.edu/discover/about-plnu/history
10. http://biologos.org.
12. For a refutation of this, see Ken Ham, editor, *The New Answers Book 2*, "How Old Is the Earth?" by Bodie Hodge (Green Forest, AR: Master Books, 2008).
13. http://blogs.usatoday.com/oped/2009/08/we-believe-in-evolution-and-god-.html.
14. http://biologos.org.
15. G. Richard Bozarth, "The Meaning of Evolution," *American Atheist*, 20 Sept. 1979, p. 30.
16. http://atheists.org/atheism/Christmas.
17. www.nes.edu/NewsEvents/?NewsID=1610.
18. http://www.rfmedia.org/RF_audio_video/RF_podcast/What_is_Inerrancy_.mp3.
19. Transcription of William Lane Craig and Michael Coren on the Michael Coren Show. http://www.youtube.com/watch?v=_IQoLg7w-_4, accessed 4 Mar 2010 and again on 9 Aug 2010. The interview was on 6 Feb 2009 with Canadian TV host, Michael Coren (http://www.michaelcoren.com/bio.html).
20. John Walton, *The Lost World of Genesis One* (Downers Grove, IL: IVP Academic, 2009).
21. Ibid., proposition 6, p. 70.
22. Ibid., proposition 7, p. 77.
23. Ibid., proposition 8, p. 84.
24. Ibid., proposition 8, p. 82–83.

25. Ibid., proposition 9, p. 92.
26. Ibid., proposition 12, p. 108–109.
27. Ibid., proposition 9, p. 92.
28. Ibid., proposition 10, p. 95.
29. T. Desmond Alexander and David W. Baker, editors, *Dictionary of the Old Testament Pentateuch* (Downers Grove, IL: InterVarsity Press, 2003).
30. Ibid., p. 315.
31. Ibid., p. 322.
32. Ibid., p. 321.
33. Ibid., p. 321.
34. Ibid., p. 325.
35. Ibid., p. 320.
36. Howard J. Van Till, Robert E. Snow, John H. Stek, and Davis A. Young, *Portraits of Creation: Biblical and Scientific Perspectives on the World's Formation* (Grand Rapids, MI: W.B. Eerdmans Pub. Co., 1990), p. 6.
37. Ibid., p. 11.
38. Ibid., p. 80.
39. Ibid., p. 105–106.
40. Keith B. Miller, editor, *Perspectives on an Evolving Creation,* "Is the Universe Capable of Evolving?" by Howard J. Van Till (Grand Rapids, MI: Wm. B. Eerdmans Publ., 2003), p. 313–314.
41. Deborah B. Haarsma and Loren D. Haarsma, *Origins: A Reformed Look at Creation, Design, and Evolution* (Grand Rapids, MI: Faith Alive Christian Resources, 2007), p. 89.
42. Ibid., p. 111.
43. Ibid., p. 115.
44. Miller, *Perspectives on an Evolving Creation,* "Does Science Exclude God? Natural Law, Chance, Miracles, and Scientific Practice," by Loren Haarsma, p. 77.
45. Daniel C. Harlow, "Consensus in CRC: Bible Is Not Inerrant," *Chimes* (April 20, 2007): p. 17.
46. Daniel C. Harlow, "After Adam: Reading Genesis in an Age of Evolutionary Science," *Perspectives on Science and Christian Faith,* volume 62, number 3 (September 2010), p. 179.
47. http://www.calvin.edu/admin/provost/origins-discussion. The department's Statement on Evolution can be found at http://www.calvin.edu/academic/biology/why/evolution-statement10May2010.pdf.
48. Jack Collins, "Adam and Eve as Historical People, and Why It Matters," *Perspectives on Science and Christian Faith,* volume 62, number 3 (September 2010): p. 147–165.
49. C. John Collins, *Science and Faith: Friends or Foes?* (Wheaton, IL: Crossway Books, 2003), p. 233.
50. Ibid., p. 250.
51. Bruce Waltke, "Why Must the Church Come to Accept Evolution?" http://biologos.org/blog/why-must-the-church-come-to-accept-evolution/, posted March 24, 2010, and accessed and downloaded March 29, 2010. This was pulled from the website on about April 2, 2010.
52. Bruce K. Waltke, *An Old Testament Theology* (Grand Rapids, MI: Zondervan, 2007), p. 202–203.

Appendix B

Do You Really Understand "Worldview"?

Greg Hall

"Worldview" is not a uniquely Christian term. It is more of a philosophical term and was first used by German philosophers. In German, the word is *weltanshung*. Generally, it refers to how we view reality and life. In order for the concept of worldview to have significance for us, it pays to see what scholars have said about it, and how they define it. Dr. James W. Sire, in *The Universe Next Door* gives this definition:

> A worldview is a commitment, a fundamental orientation of the heart, that can be expressed as a story or in a set of presuppositions (assumptions which may be true, partially true or entirely false) which we hold (consciously or subconsciously, consistently or inconsistently) about the basic constitution of reality, and that provides the foundation on which we live and move and have our being.[1]

Though not originally a "Christian" word, Christian philosophers and theologians have used the word to help Christians understand that Christian faith is intended to be a framework (built upon the authority of the Word of God), by which we build the correct way of thinking about the reality and core view of life intended by our Creator. Being a Christian is not a matter of having a compartment of life that is religious and others that are secular — with the false idea that such a position is non-religious. In fact, there are ultimately only two religions in the world — you either start with God's Word or man's word.

The Scripture teaches us there is a God who expects us to live the whole of our lives, not part, in correspondence to His truth and purpose for all of life, based on the foundational propositional truths of God's Word.

For those interested in a very scholarly overview of the worldview discussion, you should have as a resource, *Worldview, the History of a Concept,* by Dr. David K. Naugle.[2] This book gives us a historical perspective on the various definitions offered by scholars including:

> "Worldview" in a Christian perspective implies the objective existence of the trinitarian God whose essential character establishes the moral order of the universe and whose word, wisdom, and law define and govern all aspects of created existence.[3]

I have had the fortune of being part of the Centurions Program, a ministry of *Prison Fellowship* devoted to helping believers understand the significance of worldview thinking. Even though there are some areas of concern regarding Genesis, nonetheless, I agree with Chuck Colson when he defines worldview like this:

> It is the sum total of our beliefs about the world, the "big picture" that directs our daily decisions and actions."[4]

The definition of "worldview" is the first step in understanding this important topic, but there is more to it than definition. It is important to understand the "content" of what goes into making a worldview.

In *The Universe Next Door*, Dr. Sire lists seven basic worldview questions. "If a worldview can be expressed in propositions, what might they be? Essentially, they are our essential, rock-bottom answers to the following seven questions:

1. *What is prime reality — the really real?* To this we might answer God, or the gods, or the material cosmos. Our answer here is the most fundamental. It sets the boundaries for the answers that can consistently be given to the other six questions.
2. *What is the nature of external reality, that is, the world around us?* Here our answers point to whether we see the world as created or autonomous, as chaotic or orderly, as matter or spirit; or whether we emphasize

our subjective, personal relationship to the world or its objectivity apart from us.

3. *What is a human being?* To this we might answer: a highly complex machine, a sleeping god, a person made in the image of God, a naked ape.

4. *What happens to a person at death?* Here we might reply: personal extinction, or transformation to a higher state, or reincarnation, or departure to a shadowy existence on "the other side."

5. *Why is it possible to know anything at all?* Sample answers include the idea that we are made in the image of an all-knowing God or that consciousness and rationality developed under the contingencies of survival in a long process of evolution.

6. *How do we know what is right and wrong?* Again, perhaps we are made in the image of a God whose character is good, or right and wrong are determined by human choice alone or what feels good, or the notions simply developed under an impetus toward cultural or physical survival.

7. *What is the meaning of human history?* To this we might answer: to realize the purposes of God or the gods, to make a paradise on earth, to prepare a people for a life in community with a loving and holy God, and so forth."[5]

So how does a worldview get developed? Where does it come from? As I stated earlier, in an ultimate sense (as exhibited in Genesis 3 concerning the temptation), there are only two worldviews. Either one bases one's thinking on the word of one who knows everything, who has always been there, who doesn't tell any lies, and has revealed to us what we need to know, or one has to build one's thinking on the fallible word of fallible man.

Now, we need to understand that there are many versions of these two ultimate worldviews. There are many that will compete for your attention. On what basis is one right? Aren't they all simply a matter of choosing (this would default to the religion of humanism, as humans would be the ultimate authority on the subject)? And further to this, who is to say one has merit, and others do not? Aren't they all equally valid (again, this would be more humanism)? But even so, these are questions with which we must contend. How will you answer?

According to Dr. Ronald Nash, three major tests should be applied when evaluating worldviews. They are: the test of reason, the test of experience, and the test of practice.[6]

The test of reason has to do with logic — and ultimately the only logical starting point is the infinite God of the Bible (who is the basis for the logic and its existence). In other words, if there is no God of the Bible, there is no basis for logic in the first place. Logic is predicated on the existence of the God of the Bible.

Regarding logic, students should know about the law of non-contradiction as fundamental to our ability to reason. It states: A cannot be B and non-B at the same time and in the same relationship. This is an important philosophic notion in the study of logic. Simply put, it means: two contradictory ideas cannot both be true. Where there is contradiction, one side or the other is in error. Not all ideas are equally valid. To employ the test of reason in worldview development is to determine, among competing ideas, which are reasonable and which might we believe to be true. Ultimately only one passes the test — the rest will exhibit logical fallacies. The only true worldview is that which begins with the infinite Creator God and His written revelation to man.

The test of reason alone is not enough upon which to build the content of a worldview. Dr. Nash says, "Worldviews must pass not only the test of reason; they must also satisfy the test of experience. Worldviews should be relevant to what we know about the world and ourselves."[7]

Here is a truth that many students need to connect with: *Your experience counts.* Sure it is considered subjective, but your experiences in life matter because the knowledge it represents is valuable and pertinent to your life. I am not suggesting that your personal observations are in any sense the exclusive test for developing worldview, but rather is *coherence* as a whole, where all aspects of reality work together. If your personal experience is your *only* criteria for developing worldview you are greatly mistaken. I am simply saying that your experience does matter.

The test of practice is how we evaluate our worldview in the circumstances of daily life (i.e., consistency). It is about how we actually live in a practical, down-to-earth way, with the ideas we profess to be true. For example, in an evolutionary worldview, people are merely animals that have no basis in wearing clothes. Yet inconsistently, these evolutionists betray their worldview by wearing clothes that come from a literal Genesis 3. The question is this: can the ideas and concepts stand up as a real explanation for the way you experience your life, and do they have application beyond your own life?

The content of a biblical Christian worldview must also be well developed and be solidly built on the authority of Scripture. You need to know the basic time-honored truths of the scriptural history and doctrine that serve as a basis for Christian theism — a biblical understanding of the nature and character of God and the true history of the universe as revealed by Him in His Word. Here is a short list of the many aspects of Scripture that provide a foundation for our worldview:

- He (through His Son, Jesus) created the universe *ex nihilo* (out of nothing) because He is the sovereign God.
- Though He is transcendent and other worldly, He is personal and immanent and longing to be involved in the lives of His creation.
- He has accomplished this through His Son Jesus who is God incarnate, Immanuel, God "with us."
- Jesus is the exact representation of God the Father.
- The Father has redeemed those who will believe in His Son as the atoning sacrifice for sin.
- God makes it possible to be connected with Him through His Holy Spirit who is God, "in us."
- His Spirit is our comforter and teacher and guide. He leads us into truth and is God's guarantee of His presence with us until the end of our lives.
- The Garden of Eden was real and our fore bearers made a decision of disobedience recorded in Genesis that affected the human family. Original sin is a reality.
- God gave the plan of redemption, the sacrifice of His Son, as the payment for the debt owed a Holy God for such an offense.

Beyond this, you need to have a command on why Christians believe the Bible to be God's Word to us. And you also need to know the evidence that confirms the fact His Word is trustworthy and true. You need to know how to answer the basic secular attacks of our day that cause people to doubt that God's Word is the true starting point for our worldview.

This is just an example to show you how your Christian worldview must start with the content we gain from the truths revealed in Scripture about God, His Son, Jesus, and the Holy Spirit. They are the building blocks upon which your worldview is built. To not understand them or to understand them wrongly is to build a faulty foundation. Christians must think clearly and scripturally about the basic tenets of theism if their worldview is to be biblical.

The Worldview of Naturalism

Contrary to the Christian worldview is the worldview of naturalism (which is an essential tenant in similar worldviews like humanism, materialism, and atheism). Keep in mind that when a person mixes naturalistic thinking with God's Word, their starting point really is man's word. Once fallibility is introduced to one's starting point — then that starting point is man's word, even if it is mixed with God's revelation. As was said earlier, there are ultimately only two worldviews.

The thinking behind naturalism goes something like this: the world and universe as you see it is all there is. There is no God, no Creator, no one to whom humans give an account of their lives. The naturalist believes death marks the end of life in this world with no prospect of life beyond in any form. For the naturalist, the universe is a closed system and therefore there is no need for humans to seek the involvement of a transcendent being.

Naturalism is a worldview that assumes it has succeeded at getting God out of the picture in every area of life. It is also intent in getting the biblical God and His written revelation out of our educational process. In large measure, it has been successful due to an often subtle influence as well as an overt and militant influence. The naturalistic worldview is the basis for the development of the public education curriculum of our schools. As Ben Stein so aptly put it in a movie,[8] God has been "expelled."

I think for the most part that this is a subtle fact among educators today. I don't think that most of them are even aware that they are part of the naturalist indoctrination. Try asking this question of your public school leadership: "What is the worldview or educational philosophy behind the curriculum of your school?" They will probably find it hard if not impossible to answer. If probed, they may think that Judeo-Christian principles are at the core of our public education system curriculum. Many are committed to the "Character Counts" movement, which borrows certain Christian values, but is completely mute on the source of those values.

I honestly think that many educators would be greatly concerned if they were aware of the naturalistic presuppositions beneath their work. One of the problems is they have been convinced that including God and His Word (the Bible) is religion, but eliminating them results in a neutral position. They don't understand there is no neutral position. One is either "for Christ or against." What they perceive wrongly as a neutral position is in reality an anti-God position — it is a religious position — the religion of naturalism/ atheism. We have much work to be done in pointing this out to the Church, let alone the secular world.

The naturalistic worldview holds steadfastly to the idea of evolution and millions of years, as "the" explanation of the origin of life. The two are virtually inseparable in the Western mind. If there is no God, and if the physical reality is all there is, then life must have come into being by itself . . . somehow. That's where evolution (which needs millions of years to even be postulated) comes in. What is "evolution"? Dr. Michael Behe, who is basically a theistic evolutionist but is against pure naturalism, in *Darwin's Black Box*, defines it this way:

> Evolution is a flexible word. It can be used by one person to mean something as simple as change over time, or by another person to mean the descent of all life forms from a common ancestor, leaving the mechanism of change unspecified. In its full-throated, biological sense, however, evolution means a process whereby life arose from non-living matter and subsequently developed entirely by natural means. That is the sense that Darwin gave the word, and the meaning that it holds in the scientific community.[9]

Why Naturalism Survives

Despite massive amounts of scientific and philosophical arguments against it, the worldview of naturalism and the idea of evolution persist. Today there is a huge cloud of doubt hanging over the science of evolution. As Christians, we must pursue this information and honestly explore and openly criticize it when we see it for what it is.

It is all part of defending what we believe and know to be true. Disclosing such faulty ideas helps us make the case for the authenticity of the biblical account of the origin of life (2 Cor. 10:4–5). Evolution and naturalism as a belief about the origin and development of life is being shown by scientists to be no explanation for the origin of life at all. How then do we account for its persistence as the *only* explanation for the origin and diversification of life in the textbooks our students must read in our public schools?

The first reason is that those promoting evolution and naturalism are in control. They currently control the debate on the issues and they control what goes into textbooks. They do not include any other explanations for life because they don't want to. This intellectual dishonesty has been enabled by those of us who believe in God and creation, as we have abdicated our responsibility long ago for intellectual rigor on the major issues of our times. Basically, we walked away; they took over, and now we find it a stronghold in the educational process that is very hard to deal with. Also, many of us have succumbed to the false idea of neutrality, and thus backed off on defending the Christian position — only to allow these secularists to now be able to impose their religion on the education system and thus generations of our kids.

The second reason evolution persists is because it is absolutely necessary for the philosophical worldview of naturalism. The real battle about evolution is not one of operational science, but of philosophy. The belief in evolution as an explanation for the origin of all life on earth is religious — it is man's attempt to explain life without God. The religion of naturalism (or atheism) that is being taught to generations of students is the philosophy that attempts to totally remove God from the picture. For the naturalist, there is no God, no supernatural, and no life beyond death. That is their philosophical starting point — one, they are not prepared to question, regardless of the evidence that conflicts with it.

As Dr. Carl Sagan said, "The Cosmos is all there ever was or ever will be."[10] This is the naturalistic mantra. And it becomes very circular in its reasoning. People believe in evolution because of the naturalist worldview (naturalism is the focal point for their starting point but in reality, man being the ultimate authority is the underlying starting point). But the same people who believe in the naturalist worldview say they do so because of evolution. In reality, because they won't question their naturalistic starting point, they won't question evolution. See the problem? Why is this important? Why should anyone care?

1. The growing issues of concern in our culture have as their foundational cause the transition from a Christian worldview to principles now based on naturalism. The question about life's origin is used to justify this wrong foundation. Lose the battle here and you lost that battle in its entirety.
2. The philosophical assumptions of those who teach your children have the power, if left unchecked, to determine their destiny. This might scare you. It should. Those who control the textbooks and curriculum of our public education system have capitulated to naturalistic thinking and God has been removed, and we are paying the price.

Currently, we are losing the battle. By and large, we send our children away each morning to public schools, or have sent them to secular colleges or universities, to be inculcated with the subtle but pervasive ideas about naturalism and any other number of godless philosophies.

Lately, however, the subtlety of those who promote naturalism as the philosophy behind public education has been replaced by militancy — and our students and parents are increasingly feeling it. The goal of the current educational philosophy is certainly not neutral as is claimed (Matt. 12:30).

We can see that more clearly as this militancy emerges. The new goal is to convince students there is no such thing as transcendent or supernatural truths. The *only* source of truth is man, and God doesn't exist.

Of course, students are told that "science" confirms this naturalistic position. However, students are not being taught the distinction between historical science (beliefs about the past) and operational science (knowledge based on observation/repeatability/experimentation that builds technology). Students have been led to believe that if they don't believe in naturalism, they are giving up the science that built our technology. Sadly, this brainwashing in false ideas has had a devastating effect on these students. They, in essence, have been thoroughly indoctrinated in a secular worldview and convinced that this is a neutral position that is supported by unbiased scientists who are merely seeking the truth.

By systematically training our children from a biblical starting point, we can instill in them the necessary components of a biblical worldview. We must also consider that none of these arguments matter if our children are not followers of Christ. Preaching the gospel to them and helping them understand the true nature of repentance and faith in Christ is a crucial starting point. As we teach them apologetics and help them learn how to study the Bible to feed their own souls, we will be fostering a faith that will withstand the attacks from the world. We can help them understand the philosophies that have set themselves up against Christ and that through the empowering of the Holy Spirit they can fight these battles. Firmly grounding their worldview in Scripture offers them great hope and assurance that they can conquer the challenges from the world.

Endnotes

1. James W. Sire, *The Universe Next Door* (Downers Grove, IL: InterVarsity Press, 4th Edition, 2004), p. 17.
2. David K. Naugle, *Worldview* (Grand Rapids, MI: Wm. B. Eerdmans Publishing Co., 2002).
3. Ibid., p. 260.
4. Charles Colson, *How Now Shall We Live?* (Wheaton, IL: Tyndale House Publishers, Inc., 1999), p. 14.
5. Sire, *The Universe Next Door,* p. 20.
6. Ronald H. Nash, *Worldviews in Conflict* (Grand Rapids, MI: Zondervan Publishing House, 1992), p. 55.
7. Ibid., p. 57.
8. *Expelled: No Intelligence Allowed* is a 2008 documentary film, directed by Nathan Frankowski and hosted by Ben Stein.
9. Michael J. Behe, *Darwin's Black Box* (New York, NY: Free Press, 2006).
10. Carl Sagan, *Cosmos* (New York: Random House, 1980), p. 4.

Appendix C

The Documentary Hypothesis:
Moses, Genesis, and the JEDP?

Terry Mortenson and Bodie Hodge

In the past few hundred years, the Bible has been under severe attack by scientific and philosophical skeptics of all sorts. In this scientific age the most-attacked book of the Bible has arguably been Genesis, particularly the first 11 chapters. Long-age geology, big-bang cosmology, secular archaeology, liberal theology, and philosophical attacks on miracles in the Bible have deceived many people to believe that the Bible is not true and therefore cannot be trusted.

One of the major attacks on the Bible in the past three hundred years has been directed against Moses and his authorship of the Pentateuch, the first five books of the Old Testament (Genesis–Deuteronomy). Such attacks on these foundational books of the Bible come both from non-Christians as well as professing Christians.

Seminary courses, theology books, introductions to the Pentateuch in Bibles, and the secular media have promoted the man-made idea that Moses did not write the Pentateuch (also known as the Law or Torah). Instead, it is claimed that at least four different authors (or groups of authors) wrote various portions of these books over many centuries and then one or more redactors (editors) over many years combined and inter-wove everything together into its present form. For example, one translation of the Bible we surveyed said this in its introduction to the Pentateuch:

Despite its unity of plan and purpose, the book is a complex work, not to be attributed to a single original author. Several sources, or literary traditions, that the final redactor used in his composition are discernable. These are the Yahwist (J), Elohist (E), and Priestly (P) sources which in turn reflect older oral traditions.[1]

The introduction to the Old Testament in another Bible translation says that the J document was written by someone much later than Moses in the southern kingdom of Judah and the E document was written by someone in the northern kingdom of Israel.[2] Let's evaluate the arguments put forth in defense of this hypothesis.

The Documentary (or JEDP) Hypothesis

Various sections of the Pentateuch are assigned to various authors who are identified by the letters J, E, D, and P. Hence, it is called the *documentary hypothesis* (or the *JEDP model*[3]). As this hypothesis was developed by a number of Jewish and theologically liberal Christian scholars in the late 17th to the late 19th centuries, there were a number of different proposals of who wrote what and when. But by the end of the 19th century, liberal scholars had reached general agreement. The letters stand for:

J documents are the sections, verses, or in some cases parts of verses that were written by one or more authors who preferred to use the Hebrew name *Jahweh* (Jehovah) to refer to God. It is proposed that this author wrote about 900–850 B.C.

E documents are the texts that use the name *Elohim* for God and were supposedly written around 750–700 B.C.

D stands for Deuteronomy, most of which was written by a different author or group of authors, perhaps around the time of King Josiah's reforms in 621 B.C.

P stands for Priest and identifies the texts in Leviticus and elsewhere in the Pentateuch that were written by a priest or priests during the exile in Babylon after 586 B.C.

Then around 400 B.C. some redactors (i.e., editors) supposedly combined these four independently written texts to form the Pentateuch as it was known in the time of Jesus and modern times.

Development of the Documentary Hypothesis

Ibn Ezra was a very influential Jewish rabbi in the 12th century. While he believed in the Mosaic authorship of the Pentateuch, he noticed that a few verses (e.g., Genesis 12:6, Genesis 22:14) had some phrases that seemed mysteriously out of place.[4] But he never pursued these mysteries to resolve them.[5]

About five hundred years later, the famous Jewish philosopher Baruch (Benedict) Spinoza (1632–1677) picked up on what Ibn Ezra had stated and asserted that Ibn Ezra did not believe Moses wrote the Pentateuch. Others disagreed, pointing to other statements by Ibn Ezra that contradicted Spinoza's conclusion. In his book *Tractatus Theologico-Politicus* (1670), Spinoza, who was a pantheist and was subsequently excommunicated from the Jewish community and denounced by Christians, argued that Moses did not write the Pentateuch. Besides using the verses noted by Ibn Ezra, Spinoza offered a few other brief arguments against Mosaic authorship, which were easily answered by Christian writers in the following few decades.[6]

Nevertheless, further attacks on the Mosaic authorship of the Pentateuch began taking hold in France through Jean Astruc, whose book *Conjectures About the Original Memoirs Which It Appeared That Moses Used in Composing the Book of Genesis with Certain Remarks Which Help Clarify These Conjectures* was published in 1753. He believed Moses was the author of the Pentateuch, but he unlocked the door for the skepticism of later scholars.

Astruc basically questioned, as others had before him, how Moses knew what happened prior to his own life, (i.e., the history recorded in Genesis). In other words, where did Moses get information on the patriarchs? Of course, there are several ways Moses could have obtained this information: divine revelation, previously written texts passed down through the generations, and/or oral tradition from his ancestors.[7] Regardless, under the guidance of the Holy Spirit (2 Pet. 1:20–21), the books of Moses would be completely true and without error.

Astruc also noticed that *Elohim* (the Hebrew name for God in Genesis 1:1–2:3) was used in Genesis 1, but then the text switches to *Yahweh* (Jehovah) in chapter 2. Astruc claimed that these name changes indicated different sources that Moses used. Specifically, he thought that Genesis 1:1–2:3 was one creation account and Genesis 2:4–24 was a different creation account. Hence, we have the *Elohim* and *Jehovah* sections (or E and J documents).[8] Thus, the first assumption of the documentary hypothesis became established: The use of different divine names means different authors of the text.

The German scholar Johann Eichhorn took the next step by applying Astruc's idea to the whole of Genesis. Initially, in his 1780 *Introduction to the Old Testament*, Eichhorn said that Moses copied previous texts. But in later editions he apparently conceded the view of others that the J–E division could be applied to the whole of the Pentateuch, which was written after Moses.[9]

Following Eichhorn, other ideas were advanced in denial of the Mosaic authorship of the first five books of the Old Testament. In 1802, Johann Vater insisted that Genesis was made from at least 39 fragments. In 1805, Wilhelm De Wette contended that none of the Pentateuch was written before King David and that Deuteronomy was written at the time of King Josiah.

From here, the door flew open to profess that other portions of the Law were not written by Moses. Not only was there a J-document, E-document, and D-document, but then it was argued that Leviticus and some other portions of the Pentateuch were the work of Jewish priests, hence the P-documents.

And today, several variant views of documentary hypothesis exist, but perhaps the most popular is that of Dr. Julius Wellhausen proposed in 1895. Dr. Wellhausen put dates to the alleged four sources and none were earlier than around 900 B.C.[10] As noted Old Testament scholar Gleason Archer remarks, "Although Dr. Wellhausen contributed no innovations to speak of, he restated the documentary theory with great skill and persuasiveness, supporting the JEDP sequence upon an evolutionary basis."[11]

Even though a great many scholars and much of the public have accepted this view, is it really true? Did Moses have little or nothing to do with the writing of the Book of Genesis or the rest of the Pentateuch? Several lines of evidence should lead us to reject the documentary hypothesis as a fabrication of unbelievers.

Reasons to Reject the Documentary Hypothesis

There are many reasons to reject this skeptical attack on the Bible. First, consider what the Bible itself says about the authorship of the Pentateuch.

Biblical Witness to Mosaic Authorship

1. The chart below shows that the Pentateuch states that Moses wrote these books: Exod. 17:14; 24:4; 34:27; Num. 33:1–2; and Deut. 31:9–11. In his rejection of Mosaic authorship, Dr. Wellhausen nowhere discussed this biblical evidence. It is easy to deny Mosaic authorship if one ignores the evidence for it. But that is not honest scholarship.

2. We also have the witness of the rest of the Old Testament: Josh.1:8; 8:31–32; 1 Kings 2:3; 2 Kings 14:6; 21:8; Ezra 6:18; Neh. 13:1; Dan. 9:11–13; and Mal. 4:4.

3. The New Testament is also clear in its testimony: Matt. 19:8; John 5:45–47; 7:19; Acts 3:22; Rom. 10:5; and Mark 12:26. The divisions of the Old Testament were clearly in place in the Jewish mind long before

the time of Christ, namely, the Law of Moses (first five books of the Old Testament), the Prophets (the historical and prophetic books) and the Writings (the poetic books of Job, Psalms, Proverbs, etc.). So when Jesus referred to the Law of Moses, His Jewish listeners knew exactly to what He was referring.

Table 1: Selected Passages Confirming Mosaic Authorship

Old Testament		
1	Exodus 17:14	Then the Lᴏʀᴅ said to Moses, "Write this for a memorial in the book and recount it in the hearing of Joshua, that I will utterly blot out the remembrance of Amalek from under heaven" (NKJV).
2	Number 33:2	Now Moses wrote down the starting points of their journeys at the command of the Lᴏʀᴅ. And these are their journeys according to their starting points. . . .
3	Joshua 1:7–8	Only be strong and very courageous, that you may observe to do according to all the law which Moses My servant commanded you; do not turn from it to the right hand or to the left, that you may prosper wherever you go. This Book of the Law shall not depart from your mouth, but you shall meditate in it day and night, that you may observe to do according to all that is written in it. For then you will make your way prosperous, and then you will have good success.
4	Joshua 8:31	As Moses the servant of the Lᴏʀᴅ had commanded the children of Israel, as it is written in the Book of the Law of Moses: "an altar of whole stones over which no man has wielded an iron tool." And they offered on it burnt offerings to the Lᴏʀᴅ, and sacrificed peace offerings. (See Exodus 20:24–25.)
5	Joshua 23:6	Therefore be very courageous to keep and to do all that is written in the Book of the Law of Moses, lest you turn aside from it to the right hand or to the left.
6	1 Kings 2:3	And keep the charge of the Lᴏʀᴅ your God: to walk in His ways, to keep His statutes, His commandments, His judgments, and His testimonies, as it is written in the Law of Moses, that you may prosper in all that you do and wherever you turn.
7	2 Kings 14:6	But the children of the murderers he did not execute, according to what is written in the Book of the Law of Moses, in which the Lᴏʀᴅ commanded, saying, "Fathers shall not be put to death for their children, nor shall children be put to death for their fathers; but a person shall be put to death for his own sin." (See Deuteronomy 24:16.)

8	1 Chronicles 22:13	Then you will prosper, if you take care to fulfill the statutes and judgments with which the LORD charged Moses concerning Israel. Be strong and of good courage; do not fear nor be dismayed.
9	Ezra 6:18	They assigned the priests to their divisions and the Levites to their divisions, over the service of God in Jerusalem, as it is written in the Book of Moses. (This is taught in the Books of Exodus and Leviticus.)
10	Nehemiah 13:1	On that day they read from the Book of Moses in the hearing of the people, and in it was found written that no Ammonite or Moabite should ever come into the assembly of God. (See Deuteronomy 23:3-5.)
11	Daniel 9:11	Yes, all Israel has transgressed Your law, and has departed so as not to obey Your voice; therefore the curse and the oath written in the Law of Moses the servant of God have been poured out on us, because we have sinned against Him.
12	Malachi 4:4	Remember the Law of Moses, My servant, which I commanded him in Horeb for all Israel, with the statutes and judgments.
New Testament		
13	Matthew 8:4	And Jesus said to him, "See that you tell no one; but go your way, show yourself to the priest, and offer the gift that Moses commanded, as a testimony to them." (See Leviticus 14:1–32.)
14	Mark 12:26	But concerning the dead, that they rise, have you not read in the Book of Moses, in the burning bush passage, how God spoke to him, saying, "I am the God of Abraham, the God of Isaac, and the God of Jacob"? (See Exodus 3:6.)
15	Luke 16:29	Abraham said to him, "They have Moses and the prophets; let them hear them."
16	Luke 24:27	And beginning at Moses and all the Prophets, He expounded to them in all the Scriptures the things concerning Himself.
17	Luke 24:44	Then He said to them, "These are the words which I spoke to you while I was still with you, that all things must be fulfilled which were written in the Law of Moses and the Prophets and the Psalms concerning Me."
18	John 5:46	For if you believed Moses, you would believe Me; for he wrote about Me.
19	John 7:22	Moses therefore gave you circumcision (not that it is from Moses, but from the fathers), and you circumcise a man on the Sabbath.
20	Acts 3:22	For Moses truly said to the fathers, "The LORD your God will raise up for you a Prophet like me from your brethren. Him you shall hear in all things, whatever He says to you." (See Deuteronomy 18:15.)

21	Acts 15:1	And certain men came down from Judea and taught the brethren, "Unless you are circumcised according to the custom of Moses, you cannot be saved."
22	Acts 28:23	So when they had appointed him a day, many came to him at his lodging, to whom he explained and solemnly testified of the kingdom of God, persuading them concerning Jesus from both the Law of Moses and the Prophets, from morning till evening.
23	Romans 10:5	For Moses writes about the righteousness which is of the law, "The man who does those things shall live by them." (See Leviticus 18:1–5.)
24	Romans 10:19	But I say, did Israel not know? First Moses says: "I will provoke you to jealousy by those who are not a nation, I will move you to anger by a foolish nation." (See Deuteronomy 32:21.)
25	1 Corinthians 9:9	For it is written in the law of Moses, "You shall not muzzle an ox while it treads out the grain." Is it oxen God is concerned about? (See Deuteronomy 25:4.)
26	2 Corinthians 3:15	But even to this day, when Moses is read, a veil lies on their heart.

Take note of some the references back to Moses' work. For example, John 7:22 and Acts 15:1 refer to Moses giving the doctrine of circumcision. Yet John also reveals that this came earlier — in Genesis, with Abraham. Nevertheless, it is credited to Moses because it was recorded in his writings. The New Testament attributes all the books from Genesis through Deuteronomy as being the writings of Moses. So to attack the Mosaic authorship of the first five books of the Old Testament then is to attack the truthfulness of the rest of the biblical writers and Jesus Himself.

Moses' Qualifications to Write

Not only is there abundant biblical witness that Moses wrote the Pentateuch, Moses was fully qualified to write the Pentateuch. He received an Egyptian royal education (Acts 7:22) and was an eyewitness to the events recorded in Exodus to Deuteronomy, which contain many references or allusions to Egyptian names of places, people, and gods, as well as Egyptian words, idioms, and cultural factors. He also consistently demonstrated an outsider's view of Canaan (from the perspective of Egypt or Sinai).[12] And as a prophet of God he was the appropriate recipient of the written records or oral traditions of the patriarchs from Adam to his own day, which the Holy Spirit could use to guide Moses to write the inerrant text of Genesis. There is no other ancient Hebrew who was more qualified than Moses to write the Pentateuch.

Fallacious Reasoning of the Skeptics

A final reason for rejecting the documentary hypothesis and accepting the biblical testimony to the Mosaic authorship of the Pentateuch is the erroneous assumptions and reasoning of the liberal scholars and other skeptics.

1. They assumed their conclusion. They assumed that the Bible is not a supernatural revelation from God and then manipulated the biblical text to arrive at that conclusion. They were implicitly deistic or atheistic in their thinking.

2. They assumed that Israel's religion was simply the invention of man, a product of evolution, as all other religions are.

3. Based on evolutionary ideas, they assumed that "the art of writing was virtually unknown in Israel prior to the establishment of the Davidic monarchy; therefore there could have been no written records going back to the time of Moses."[13] This claim not only attacks the intelligence of the ancient Israelites, but also the Egyptians who trained Moses. Were the Egyptians incapable of teaching Moses how to read and write? Since the time the documentary hypothesis was first proposed, archaeologists have discovered scores of written records pre-dating the time of Moses. It is hard to believe that Israel's ancient neighbors knew how to write, but the Jews could not.

4. Liberal Bible scholars allegedly based their theories on evidence from the biblical text and yet they evaded the biblical evidence that refutes their theories. Theirs was a "pick and choose" approach to studying the Bible, which is hardly honest scholarship in pursuit of truth.

5. They arbitrarily assumed that the Hebrew authors were different from all other writers in history — that the Hebrews were incapable of using more than one name for God, or more than one writing style regardless of the subject matter, or more than one of several possible synonyms for a single idea.

6. Their subjective bias led them to illegitimately assume that any biblical statement was unreliable until proven reliable (though they would not do this with any other ancient or modern text) and when they found any disagreement between the Bible and ancient pagan literature, the latter was automatically given preference and trusted as a historical witness. The former violates the well-accepted concept known as Aristotle's dictum, which advises that the benefit of the doubt should be given to the document itself, rather than the critic. In other words, the Bible (or any other book) should be considered

innocent until proven guilty or considered reliable until its unreliability is compellingly demonstrated.

7. Although many examples have been found of an ancient Semitic author using repetition and duplication in his narrative technique, skeptical scholars assume that when Hebrew authors did this, it is compelling evidence of multiple authorship of the biblical text.

8. The skeptics erroneously assumed, without any other ancient Hebrew literature to compare with the biblical text, that they could, with scientific reliability, establish the date of the composition of each book of the Bible.[14]

9. To date, no manuscript evidence of the J-document, E-document, P-document, D-document, or any of the other supposed fragments have ever been discovered. And there are no ancient Jewish commentaries that mention any of these imaginary documents or their alleged unnamed authors. All the manuscript evidence we have is for the first five books of the Bible just as we have them today. This is confirmed by the singular Jewish testimony (until the last few centuries) that these books are the writings of Moses.

Is JEDP/Documentary Hypothesis the Same Thing as the Tablet Model of Genesis?

These two ways of dividing Genesis are not the same at all. The tablet model is based on the Hebrew word *toledoth*, which appears 11 times in Genesis (2:4; 5:1; 6:9; 10:1; 11:10; 11:27; 25:12; 25:19; 36:1; 36:9; 37:2) and helps to tie the whole book together as a single history. Our English Bibles translate *toledoth* variously as "this is the account" or "these are the generations" of Adam, Noah, Shem, etc. Scholars disagree about whether each *toledoth* follows or precedes the text with which it is associated, though we are inclined to agree with those scholars who conclude the former. In this case, the name associated with the *toledoth* is either the author or custodian of that section (see, for example, table 2 below). Regardless, the 11 uses of *toledoth* unite the book as a history of the key events and people from creation to the time of Moses.

Unlike the JEDP model, the tablet model shows a reverence for the text of Genesis and attention to these explicit divisions provided by the book itself. These divisions represent either oral tradition or written texts passed down by the Genesis patriarchs to their descendants,[15] which Moses then used to put Genesis into its final form under the inspiration of the Holy Spirit.

We think it very likely that Moses was working with written documents because the second *toledoth* (Gen. 5:1) reads "this is the book of the generations of Adam" where "book" is a translation of the normal Hebrew word meaning a written document. Also, the account of the Flood after the third *toledoth* (Gen. 6:9) reads like a ship's log. Only evolutionary thinking would lead us to conclude that Adam and his descendants could not write. Early man was very intelligent: Cain built a city (Gen. 4:17), six generations later people were making musical instruments and had figured out how to mine ores and make metals (Gen. 4:21–22), Noah built a huge boat for his family and thousands of animals to survive a year-long flood, etc.[16]

Table 2: Breakdown of the *Toledoth* Sections from Genesis 1–11

Beginning	End	Probable author of original work from which Moses drew
Genesis 1:1	Genesis 2:4a	Adam by direct divine revelation, so not connected with Adam's name
Genesis 2:4b	Genesis 5:1a	Adam
Genesis 5:1b	Genesis 6:9a	Noah
Genesis 6:9b	Genesis 10:1	Shem, Ham, and Japheth
Genesis 10:2	Genesis 11:10a	Shem
Genesis 11:10b	Genesis 11:27a	Terah
Genesis 11:27b	Genesis 25:12a	Abraham
Genesis 25:12b	Genesis 25:19a	Ishmael
Genesis 25:19b	Genesis 36:1a	Esau
Genesis 36:1b	Genesis 36:9a	Jacob?[17]
Genesis 36:9b	Genesis 37:2	Jacob
Genesis 37:2b	Genesis 50:26	Joseph

The biblical doctrine of the inspiration of Scripture does not require us to conclude that all the books of the Bible were written by God dictating to the human authors. Dictation was one means employed, very often in the prophetic books (e.g., the prophet says, "The Word of the Lord came to me saying …"). But much of the Bible was written from the eyewitness experience of the authors (e.g., 2 Pet. 1:16) or as a result of research by the author (e.g., Luke 1:1–4). And just as Christian authors today can quote truthful statements from non-Christian sources without thereby endorsing their wrong ideas, so the biblical authors could quote non-believers or non-biblical sources without introducing false statements into their divine writings (e.g., Josh. 10:13; 2 Sam. 1:18; Acts 17:28; Titus 1:12; Jude 14–15). So it is perfectly reasonable to think that Moses wrote Genesis from pre-existing, well-preserved oral tradition and/or written documents from the patriarchs.

Unlike those who affirm Mosaic authorship of Genesis and divide the text by the *toledoths*, JEDP adherents divide the text on the basis of the names of God that were used and say that, at best, Moses simply wove these texts together, often in contradictory ways. However, most JEDP advocates would say that Moses had nothing to do with writing Genesis or the rest of the Pentateuch, which were written much later by many authors and editors.

Answering a Few Objections

A number of objections have been raised by the proponents of the documentary hypothesis. Space allows us to respond to only a few of the most common ones, but the other objections are just as flawed in terms of logic and a failure to pay careful attention to the biblical text.

1. Moses couldn't have written about his own death, which shows that he didn't write Deuteronomy.

The death of Moses is recorded in Deuteronomy 34:5–12. These are the last few verses of the book. Like other literature, past and present, it is not uncommon for an obituary to be added at the end of someone's work after he dies, especially if he died very soon after writing the book. The obituary in no way nullifies the claim that the author wrote the book.

In the case of Deuteronomy, the author of the obituary of Moses was probably Joshua, a close associate of Moses who was chosen by God to lead the people of Israel into the Promised Land (for Moses was not allowed to because of his disobedience), and who was inspired by God to write the next book in the Old Testament. A similar obituary of Joshua was added by an inspired editor to the end of Joshua's book (Josh. 24:29–33).

2. The author of Genesis 12:6 seems to imply that the Canaanites were removed from the land, which took place well after Moses died.

> Abram passed through the land to the place of Shechem, as far as the terebinth tree of Moreh. And the Canaanites were then in the land (Gen. 12:6; NKJV).

So another argument against Mosaic authorship of the Pentateuch is that an author, *after* Moses, had to have written this verse (Gen. 12:6). The very reason they argue this is due to the fact that Moses died prior to the Canaanites being removed, which occurred in the days of Joshua who began judging the Canaanites for their sin.

Two things can be said in response. First, Moses could have easily written this without knowing that the Canaanites would be removed after his death because, due to warring kingdoms or other factors, people groups did get removed from territories. So it was just a statement of fact about who was living in the land at the time of Abraham. But second, it could also be a comment added by a later editor working under divine inspiration. The editorial comment would in no way deny the Mosaic authorship of the Book of Genesis. Editors sometimes add to books by deceased authors and no one then denies that the deceased wrote the book.[18]

3. Genesis 14:14 mentions the Israelite region of Dan, which was assigned to that tribe during the conquest led by Joshua after Moses died. So Moses could not have written this verse.

> Now when Abram heard that his brother[19] was taken captive, he armed his three hundred and eighteen trained servants who were born in his own house, and went in pursuit as far as Dan. He divided his forces against them by night, and he and his servants attacked them and pursued them as far as Hobah, which is north of Damascus (Gen. 14:14–15; NKJV).

Genesis 14:14 mentions Dan. However, Dan in this context is not the region of Dan, that Israelite tribe's inheritance given when the Jews took the Promised Land, but a specific ancient town of Dan, north of the Sea of Galilee. It was in existence long before the Israelites entered the land. Jewish historian Josephus, just after the time of Christ, said:

> When Abram heard of their calamity, he was at once afraid for Lot his kinsman, and pitied the Sodomites, his friends and neighbours; and thinking it proper to afford them assistance, he did not delay it, but marched hastily, and the fifth night attacked the Assyrians, near Dan, for that is the name of the other spring of Jordan; and before they could arm themselves, he slew some as they were in their beds, before they could suspect any harm; and others, who were not yet gone to sleep, but were so drunk they could not fight, ran away.[20]

This specific place was known to Abraham as one of the springs of Jordan. It is possible that Rachel was already aware of that name, as it meant "judge," and used it for the son of her handmaiden (Gen. 30:6). It seems Rachel viewed this as the Lord finally turning the tide in judgment and permitting her a son. In the same way, this was where the Lord judged his enemies through Abraham.

But again, even if "near Dan" was added by a later inspired editor, this would not mean that it was inaccurate to say that Moses wrote Genesis.[21]

4. The author of Genesis 36:31 obviously knew about kingdoms in Israel which were only present well after Moses, so Moses could not have written this.

Such a claim is without warrant. Moses was clearly aware that this had been prophesied about the nation of Israel when the Lord told Abraham (Gen. 17:6) and Jacob (Gen. 35:11) that Israel would have kings. Also, Moses, himself, prophesied in Deuteronomy 17:14–20 that Israel would have kings. So knowing that kings were coming was already common knowledge to Moses.

Conclusion

There is abundant biblical and extra-biblical evidence that Moses wrote the Pentateuch during the wilderness wanderings after the Jews left their slavery in Egypt and before they entered the Promised Land (about 1445–1405 B.C). Contrary to the liberal theologians and other skeptics, it was not written after the Jews returned from exile in Babylon (c. 500 B.C.). Christians who believe Moses wrote the Pentateuch do not need to feel intellectually intimidated. It is the enemies of the truth of God that are failing to think carefully and face the facts honestly.

As a prophet of God, Moses wrote under divine inspiration, guaranteeing the complete accuracy and absolute authority of his writings. Those writings were endorsed by Jesus and the New Testament Apostles, who based their teaching and the truth of the gospel on the truths revealed in the books of Moses, including the truths about a literal six-day creation about 6,000 years ago, the Curse on the whole creation when Adam sinned, and the judgment of the global, catastrophic Flood at the time of Noah.

The attack on the Mosaic authorship of the Pentateuch is nothing less than an attack on the veracity, reliability, and authority of the Word of Almighty God. Christians should believe God, rather than the fallible, sinful skeptics inside and outside the Church who, in their intellectual arrogance, are consciously or unconsciously trying to undermine the Word so that they can justify in their own minds (but not before God) their rebellion against God. As Paul says in Romans 3:4, "Let God be true but every man a liar" (NKJV).

Endnotes

1. *The New American Bible* (Nashville, TN: Memorial Bible Publishers, 1976), p. 1.
2. *The Dartmouth Bible* (Boston, MA: Houghton Mifflin, 1961), p. 8–9.
3. Some scholars rearrange these letters as JEPD, based on the order they believe the sections were written.
4. "Now the Canaanite was then in the land" (Gen. 12:6) and "as it is said to this day" (Gen. 22:14) might suggest that those phrases were written later than the rest of the verses they are in. In other words, they look like editorial comments.
5. Allan MacRae, *JEDP: Lectures on the Higher Criticism of the Pentateuch* (Hatfield, PA: Interdisciplinary Biblical Research Institute, 1994), p. 63.
6. Ibid., p. 63-64. Spinoza's arguments included these: 1) Numbers 12:3 says that Moses was the most humble man of his day, but a humble man would not write that about himself; 2) Moses is spoken of in the third person in the Pentateuch, which he would not do if he was the author; and 3) Moses could not have written his own obituary (Deuteronomy 34:5–6). In reply, even if the few verses (Genesis 12:6; 22:14, Numbers 12:3; Deuteronomy 34:5–6) are comments added by an inspired editor many years after Moses, that does not undermine the accuracy of the biblical testimony that Moses is the author of the Pentateuch. Second, modern authors often write about themselves in the third person, so this is nothing unusual.
7. On this point, see Bodie Hodge, "How Was Moses Able to Read Pre-Tower of Babel Texts?" http://www.answersingenesis.org/home/area/feedback/2006/1027.asp, October 23, 2006.
8. MacRae, *JEDP,* p. 70–72.
9. MacRae, *JEDP,* p. 72–84.
10. Josh McDowell, *A Ready Defense* (Nashville, TN: Thomas Nelson, 1993), p. 137–139.
11. Gleason Archer, *A Survey of Old Testament Introduction* (Chicago, IL: Moody Press, 1985), p. 89 (p. 95 in the 1994 edition).
12. Archer, *A Survey of Old Testament Introduction,* p. 114–123.
13. Ibid., p. 175.
14. The points are explained in Archer, *A Survey of Old Testament Introduction,* p. 109–113.
15. All people need to know where they came from, where their place in history is, or they will be very confused people. Every culture, no matter how "primitive" (by our arrogant Western standards), teaches history to their children (how accurate that history may be is a separate question). It is therefore most unreasonable to think that the Genesis patriarchs would not record and pass on the history they had to the next generation. And studies of non-literate people groups have shown that they have much better memories for maintaining the accuracy of their oral traditions than people groups that rely primarily on written communication to learn and pass on information. See Kenneth E. Bailey, "Informal Controlled Oral Tradition and the Synoptic Gospels," Themelios 20.2 (January 1995): 4–11 (http://www.biblicalstudies.org.uk/article_tradition_bailey.html, accessed January 21, 2011), and "Oral Traditions — Oral Traditions as a Source and as a Method of Historical Construction," http://science.jrank.org/pages/10523/Oral-Traditions-Oral-Traditions-Source-Method-Historical-Construction.html, accessed January 21, 2011.
16. For more on this topic, see Henry Morris, *The Genesis Record* (Grand Rapids, MI: Baker Book House, 1976), p. 22–30; and Curt Sewell, "The Tablet Theory of Genesis Authorship," *Bible and Spade,* vol. 7:1 (Winter 1994), http://www.trueorigin.org/tablet.asp.
17. The record of Esau's descendants contains a toledoth before and after it, which is problematic for either view of the connection of the toledoth to the text. Perhaps it signifies

that the account of Esau (Gen. 36:1–9) was inserted into the account written by Jacob (Gen. 25:19–37:2), since Jacob (not Esau) was the son of promise in the Messianic line from Adam.

18. Though modern editors do this usually in a footnote, we cannot demand the same literary convention be applied to the ancient editors.

19. Just as "son of" in Hebrew doesn't always mean a literal father-son relationship, so the Hebrew word translated here as "brother" doesn't always mean a literal brother, but can refer more generally to a familial or tribal relative. In this case, Lot was Abraham's brother's son, i.e., Abraham's nephew.

20. "Revised Works of Josephus," Chapter 10: The Assyrian army pursued and defeated by Abram — Birth of Ishmael — Circumcision instituted, 1912–1910 B.C., taken from: The Online Bible, by Larry Pierce.

21. But let's assume for a moment that it was referring to the region Dan, where Israelites, who were from the tribe of Dan settled. Would this be a problem for Moses? No. It was Moses who wrote where the allotments would be! In Numbers 34:1–15, Moses described the general vicinity of the borders of the various tribes. So this would actually be further confirmation of Mosaic authorship, had this been referring to descendants of Israelite Dan's territory.

Appendix D

Institution Questionnaire

Bodie Hodge

In today's culture, where evolution and millions of years has infiltrated many schools (and churches), it is difficult to even begin looking for a college or university that stands on the authority of the Bible from the very first verse.

In an effort to help parents and students find a college or university (or even a Bible-believing church), *Answers in Genesis* put together a short "Institution Questionnaire."

This quick 15-question survey can be used to present to a pastor at a church or a Christian college to see if the institution really believes what the Scriptures say, whether they admit they adhere to biblical authority or not.

This questionnaire is written to carefully see what the institution believes. This should help you discern if the institution is truly biblical or not. Keep in mind none are perfect, but some are usually much better than others. What follows are merely 15 questions that could be helpful. Following that we have short answers, a couple of references, and brief explanations of what you can learn.

Name: _____

Name of Institution: _____

Date: _____

1. Is God triune (Father, Son, and Holy Spirit) or not?
2. When did death and suffering enter into the world (for man and for animals)?
3. Do you believe Jesus Christ is the Creator?
4. Do you believe the days in Genesis are literal approximate 24-hour days or not?
5. Is it proper to interpret Genesis to conform to what one already believes about the past, or should one change one's belief to conform to what Genesis says? In other words, should Genesis be interpreted in the style it is written (literal history) or should it be interpreted in some other fashion (i.e., in light of millions of years and evolution)?
6. Have human male and female been around since the beginning of creation, did they evolve from a lower life form, or did God create them millions of years after creation?
7. Do you believe there are intelligent alien life forms?
8. Did God use a big bang?
9. Was the Flood of Noah's day global or local (regional)?
10. Do you believe Satan/Lucifer rebelled before or after the end of day 6 of the creation week discussed in Genesis 1–Genesis 2:3?
11. Why don't people today believe the Gospel when we boldly preach it?
12. How many races of people did God create?
13. Was the fossil record primarily laid down by Noah's Flood and how does this relate to the age of the earth?
14. Is Genesis important when preaching the gospel in today's culture?
15. Are there any legitimate contradictions in the Bible?

College Questionnaire Answers with References
(similar to these are acceptable)

1. They better say yes!

Question 1 helps you realize if a school is mainstream or if it has been influenced by a cult that may deny the deity of Jesus Christ (John 1, Col. 1, and Heb. 1). Also, this should be an easy question to answer for most Christian institutions.

> References: "God Is Triune," by Bodie Hodge, *Answers in Genesis* website, AiG–U.S., February 20, 2008, http://www.answersingenesis. org/articles/2008/02/20/god-is-triune, and "The Trinity," by Dr. Mark Bird, Answers in Genesis website, God's Bible School and College, July 30, 2008, http://www.answersingenesis.org/articles/aid/ v3/n1/the-trinity.

2. When Adam and Eve rebelled, resulting in the Curse and the sentence to die from Genesis 2:17, Genesis 3:17, and Romans 5:12. If they believe death (of either mankind or animals) has been around prior to this, then they have a major problem. Also, animals were vegetarian in the beginning as was man (Gen. 1:29–30), so this points to no animal death prior to sin either.

Question 2 allows you to find out if the institution really believes in a literal curse in Genesis 3 and provides an answer for the common question "Why did God make the world like this?" Biblically, God made the world perfect (Gen. 1:31; Deut. 32:4) and due to man's sin, death and suffering came into the world. This is why we need a Savior to save us from sin and death and provide a new heaven and a new earth. Adam and Eve rebelled, resulting in the Curse and the sentence to die (Gen. 2:17; Gen. 3:17; Rom. 5:12). After sin, we find the first recorded death of an animal (Gen. 3:21) and from here, we find a relationship between human sin and animal death.

> References: Ken Ham, editor, *New Answers Book 1*, "How Did Defense/ Attack Structures Come About?" by Andy McIntosh and Bodie Hodge (Green Forest, AR: Master Books, 2006), http://www.answersingenesis. org/articles/nab/origin-of-attack-defense-structures, and "Biblically, Could Death Have Existed before Sin?" by Bodie Hodge, Answers in Genesis website, March 2, 2010, http://www.answersingenesis.org/arti-cles/2010/03/02/satan-the-fall-good-evil-could-death-exist-before-sin.

3. Yes!

Question 3 reiterates question one, but more directly. With these questions up front, the institution should feel comfortable answering the survey questions. So at this point we can start getting into the meat of the subject.

> References: John 1; Col. 1; and Heb. 1. (See also the references from Question 1.)

4. Yes! This is confirmed by Exodus 20:11 and Exodus 31:17, also, Mark 10:6 (marriage came at the beginning of creation, thus only five days before, not millions of years, otherwise it would be the "end" of creation.

Question 4 allows you to really start testing to see if the institution believes the Bible as the authority, or if man's ideas about millions of years has begun to creep in. The Bible is clear that it was six days, not millions of years (Exod. 20:11 and 31:17). Otherwise, our basis for a "week" makes no sense.

> References: Ham, *The New Answers Book 1*, "Could God Really Have Created Everything in Six Days?" *http://www.answersingenesis. org/Home/Area/answersbook/sixdays2.asp*, and the technical article, "The Days of Creation: A Semantic Approach," by James Stambaugh, first published in the *TJ* 5(1):70–78, April 1991, later revision published at the *Evangelical Theological Society*, *http://www. answersingenesis.org/docs/4204tj_v5n1.asp*.

5. No. Second Corinthians 4:2 and Proverbs 8:8–9 make it clear the Scriptures should be interpreted plainly/straightforwardly. This means metaphors are metaphors, literal history is literal history, poetry is poetry, parables are parables, etc. Thus, we should learn about history from a perfect, all-knowing God who has always been there, instead of trying to reinterpret what God says to conform to current imperfect and fallible beliefs about the past by those who weren't there.

Question 5 is important because you can determine how the institution thinks — whether biblically or "humanistically." Humanism is a religion that has humans as the ultimate authority. If the Bible is the authority, then we as fallible sinful human beings should change our views to conform to what God says in the Bible. But if one can simply reinterpret the Bible because of one's own thinking (e.g., the days in Genesis can't be ordinary because other humans say it was millions of years), then what is the real authority? It would be that person or humans in general. So humans would be sitting in authority over God and His Word in this case. This is one way to see if humanism, even if subtly, has crept into their thinking.

> References: Ham, *The New Answers Book 1*, "Don't Creationists Believe Some 'Wacky' Things?" by Bodie Hodge, http://www.answersingenesis.org/articles/nab/creationists-believe-wacky-things.

6. Human male and female (Adam and Eve) have been around since the beginning of creation on day 6 specifically. This is confirmed by Mark 10:6 and Mathew 19:4. This means it cannot be billions of years after creation.

Question 6 reveals if the institution believes in long ages of some sort. If one answers that humans evolved, then they obviously don't believe the Bible in Genesis. But many say they believe Genesis literally but are really tacking on man's ideas about millions of years by reinterpreting Genesis. However, Jesus reveals the glitch from His own words in Mark 10:6. The context of Jesus' response is about divorce, which concerns marriage. Jesus referred back to Genesis 1 and 2 and even quoted them in the parallel passage in Matthew 19 and stated that at the *beginning* of creation God made them male and female. If Jesus was speaking about four thousand years [according to genealogies] after the creation week of six approximately 24-hour days, then day 6 and even soon after, would be the "beginning of creation." If one has long ages, then human male and female came about 13 to 15 billion years after the creation, which is the *end* of creation, thereby making Jesus out to be speaking a falsehood. So with this verse, Jesus is affirming a relatively young age of the earth.

> References: "But from the Beginning of . . . the Institution of Marriage? by Dr. Terry Mortenson, Answers in Genesis website, November 1, 2004, http://www.answersingenesis.org/docs2004/1101ankerberg_response. asp, and "Feedback: Are the Bible and Evolution Compatible?" by Bodie Hodge, Answers in Genesis website, AiG–U.S., June 13, 2008, http://www. answersingenesis.org/articles/2008/06/13/feedback-bible-evolution-incompatible.

7. No.

Question 7 reveals how much evolutionary thinking may have infiltrated.

> Reference: Ham, *The New Answers Book 1*, "Are ETs & UFOs Real?" by Dr. Jason Lisle, http://www.answersingenesis.org/articles/ nab/are-ets-and-ufos-real.

8. No.

Question 8 exposes progressive creation, theistic evolution, and other compromised views. If an institution believes in the big bang, then they are holding to the atheistic view over God's view given in Scripture (astronomical evolution). In the big bang, it simply doesn't mesh with Scripture (i.e., see a few below in the chart). The big bang starts itself, it does not need God, so when Christians try to add the idea that God started the big bang, they basically say God didn't really do anything.

	Big Bang/Millions of Years	Genesis
1.	Sun before earth	Earth before sun
2.	Dry land before sea	Sea before dry land
3.	Atmosphere before sea	Sea before atmosphere
4.	Sun before light on earth	Light on earth before sun
5.	Stars before earth	Earth before stars
6.	Earth at same time as planets	Earth before all planets
7.	Death before man	Death after man
8.	Sun before plants	Plants before the sun

Reference: Ken Ham, editor, *The New Answers Book 2*, "Does the Big Bang Fit with the Bible?" by Dr. Jason Lisle (Green Forest, AR: Master Books, 2008), http://www.answersingenesis.org/articles/nab2/does-big-bang-fit-with-bible.

9. Global — it is clearly stating that it was a worldwide event in Genesis 6–8 (specifically Gen. 7:19–20).

Question 9 also reveals if one believes in long ages but from a different perspective. If the bulk of the fossil layers represent long ages, then a global Flood is impossible because it would have ripped up the layers and redeposited them. A local Flood also makes a mockery of the promise God made after the Flood to not send another Flood like this. It was clearly a global Flood as Genesis 6–8 teaches, because we have numerous local floods all the time.

Reference: Ham, *The New Answers Book 1*, "Was There Really a Noah's Ark & Flood?" http://www.answersingenesis.org/articles/nab/really-a-flood-and-ark, and Ken Ham, editor, *The New Answers Book 3*, "Was the Flood of Noah Global or Local?" by Ken Ham and Dr. Andrew Snelling (Green Forest, AR: Master Books, 2010).

10. Satan had to rebel after day 6 (probably not day 7 because God sanctified that day and made it holy). Otherwise, rebellion from God (sin) would have been declared "very good" in Genesis 1:31.

Question 10 reveals if the compromised view of gap theory is being held at the institution. Gap theorists have millions of years thrown in between Genesis 1:1 and 1:2. As the gap theory goes, the fossils layers are primarily from an alleged Luciferian Flood when Satan fell. This is strange since the bulk of the fossil layers would no longer be representative of atheism's long ages, which was what this alleged gap was trying to mix with Scripture in the first place! Also, if this were the case, then Lucifer's actions of rebellion would be very good because God declared all things very good at the end of day 6 (Gen. 1:31). So Satan had to have fallen after day 6, and likely not on day 7 which was holy, but soon after.

References: Ham, *The New Answers Book 1*, "What About the Gap and Ruin-Reconstruction Theories?" http://www.answersingenesis. org/articles/nab/gap-ruin-reconstruction-theories, and "When Did Adam and Eve Rebel?" By Bodie Hodge, Answers in Genesis website, AiG–U.S., April 20, 2010, http://www.answersingenesis.org/articles/2010/04/20/satan-the-fall-good-evil-adam-eve-rebel.

11. People today have the wrong foundational beliefs (an "evolutionary/millions of years" foundation) that teaches the Bible is wrong. We need to teach them the true history in the Bible so they will have a foundation for understanding why they need Jesus Christ as their Savior.

Question 11 reveals if the institution really understands *why* people are walking away from the Church at an alarming rate, or if they even realize the gravity of the problem. If people don't believe Genesis is true, then why would they believe the gospels (John 3:12)? Having generations of people brought up with teaching of long ages and evolution has seen nations like England have hardly any semblance of Christianity left. The same is now happening to the United States. Yet people toss out many ideas about why the Church is dying, but they rarely get to the root of the problem. Basically, the Church as a whole let the world train its children to believe humanism (evolution and millions of years are subsets of the religion of humanism). Thus, the next generation has been taught the Bible is not true and is walking away. See Proverbs 22:6.

Reference: Ham, *The New Answers Book 1*, "How Can I Use This Information to Witness?" http://www.answersingenesis.org/articles/ nab/how-use-information-to-witness.

12. There is one race, the human race, where each person is a descendant of Noah and ultimately Adam and Eve.

Question 12 allows you to see if the institution really believes that all people came from Adam and Eve or if they have worldly racist ideas that have crept in. Evolutionary thinking has infiltrated the Church in many areas and on the issue of racism it has contributed significantly over the years. Christians should be leading the fight against racism.

> Reference: Ham, *The New Answers Book 1*, "Are There Really Different Races?" http://www.answersingenesis.org/Home/Area/AnswersBook/races18.asp.

13. The global Flood of Noah would have laid down billions of dead things buried in sedimentary rock layers. Of course, there have been some changes since then that will add and remove some sediment (places affected by the post-Flood Ice Age, volcanoes, earthquakes, etc.)

Question 13 is a reiteration of Question 9 but focuses on the age of the earth, to see if they are consistent with a global Flood or not, so be sure to compare their answers to Question 9 with this answer.

According to the genealogies, from Adam to Christ is about four thousand years by most chronologists. This would give an age of the earth at about six thousand years. Any long age view, however, adopts man's ideas *over* God's Word in Genesis.

> Reference: Ham, *The New Answers Book 2*, "How Old Is the Earth?" by Bodie Hodge, http://www.answersingenesis.org/articles/nab2/how-old-is-the-earth.

14. Yes. How can people fully understand the good news of being saved, if they don't understand the bad news in Genesis of why we are lost in the first place?

Question 14: Not everyone will get this correct, but if they do, then they've been listening to creation ministries — which is a good sign! In today's culture where basic Bible knowledge has severely suffered, how can people fully understand the good news of being saved, if they don't understand the bad news in Genesis of why we are lost in the first place? Don't be hard on a church or institution if they get this wrong. This is like a "bonus question" to see if they really get the message. But also note that this is not saying if one does not see the importance of Genesis, it does not mean they are not saved. It simply means they fail to realize the importance of the foundation of the gospel. One can believe in an old earth, for example, and be saved, but they are inconsistent in their treatment of the Word of God.

Reference: "What Does It Mean to Be 'Saved'?" by Bodie Hodge, Answers in Genesis website, April 21, 2009, http://www.answersingenesis.org/articles/2009/04/21/what-does-it-mean-to-be-saved.

15. No.

Question 15 gives you an understanding of how they view the Bible. Hopefully, they answer that the Bible is inerrant in the original autographs and that no legitimate contradictions exist, since God cannot contradict Himself (2 Tim. 2:13). But some Christians have a very low view of Scripture due to evolutionary influence, whether they realize it or not.

References: "Contradictions: Introduction," by Dr. Jason Lisle, Answers in Genesis website, September 29, 2008, http://www.answersingenesis.org/articles/2008/09/29/contradictions-introduction. See also Ken Ham, editor, *Demolishing Supposed Bible Contradictions* (Green Forest, AR: Master Books, 2010).

---

creationcolleges.org

In order to be mentioned on this site, the school's president (or an authority representing the college) has affirmed or endorsed the Answers in Genesis' statement of faith. In doing so, they are supporting the biblical-authority message of a young earth and literal six-day creation as described in Genesis. Each year, the college representative must reaffirm they are in agreement with this statement of faith. It should be noted that such affirmation by the college representative does not necessarily mean the entire college/university — including individual professors — will take the same stand.

AiG shares this college list with you in order to give you a good start in your search for a suitable Bible-upholding institution for your student. As we suggest in this book, parents and students need to conduct their own due diligence in their research, asking school representatives the right questions, with specific queries about Genesis. This will help them discern what is actually taught in the school's classrooms and how it lines up with Scripture.

1:1

answersingenesis

Appendix E

A Journey Toward Biblical Truth

Greg Hall

In this book we give examples of those who teach various concepts surrounding the debate of origins that are contrary to the Scripture. I wish I had been more transparent about my own personal compromises along this road in coming to the understanding I have today.

In my ministry, I have always believed in the inspiration, inerrancy, and infallibility of the Scripture. But I was also one for whom the evolution vs. creation debate seemed to be unnecessary. What did it matter how God created or in what time frame? I have reviewed sermons where I told my congregation that God is our Creator but also said that science has taught us that the universe is billions of years old and still in process of being created. I was a theistic evolutionist and so had no problem with that position just as so many academics do. I loved God and His Word, what was the big deal?

Then I began to be acquainted with some teaching that changed my ministry in a profound way. I would read R.C. Sproul, John MacArthur, Albert Mohler, Douglas Kelley, or Henry Morris and my mind began to change drastically. The origin of life debate was central to the authority of Scripture and our understanding of the nature and character of God. It all became acutely focused for me when attending the Centurions program with Chuck Colson and reading the work of he and Nancy Pearcy. Years later I became acquainted with Ken Ham of the Answers in Genesis ministry and all together began to realize that these men and women are right. The authority of the Scripture is at stake in this debate and, the truth is, the so-called "science" of evolution and long ages for the earth and universe is entirely incompatible with the biblical record. Naturalism is the religion of the age, and evolution is its dogma, and together they have devastated our culture. Biblical creationism is the only reasonable and true position for the believer.

Now while we are critical of compromised positions on these matters among Christian colleges, I can tell you about my experiences in the institution where I serve. I used to teach the senior capstone course. Several years ago, while I was formulating my thoughts on biblical creationism, I was teaching one day on the subject of the importance of the origins debate in our culture. I was trying the make the case for reading the Genesis account of creation in its literal, plain sense as God creating everything ex nihilo in six 24-hour days, just like the Scripture says. After I had been going on for a while a student raised her hand (a biology major I recall) and said, "You realize that the teaching of the biology department is evolution, right?" No, I didn't I had to admit.

I wonder how many times this account is repeated in Christian schools? I guess we just assume that the case for biblical creationism would at the very least be presented right alongside the teaching of the theory of evolution. In fact, you would think that the vast resources of those scientists who are helping the culture understand that the science behind evolution is very faulty would be brought into play in a helpful way to present the truth of biblical creationism to the Christian college student. At that time that was not the case. A compromise to be sure.

Since that time I have been meeting with members of our science faculty to discuss the origin issues. I have great conversations and find these academics are the ones very skeptical of the theory of evolution and very willing to get involved in understanding and presenting the biblical creation account. Among our religion faculty we have similar discussions. It is a very real issue for the leadership of our Christian schools to maintain this kind of interaction with faculty. Everyone is not always going to be on the same page, but I have found faculty very interested in talking about these important matters.

So when I join in the discussion of compromise in Christian schools do I intend to suggest that in my own personal journey or in the institution where I serve there is no such phenomena? Absolutely not. But there is in fact no more important issue for our times than whether or not we will accept biblical truth when it speaks about any matter. And it speaks clearly on the matter of the creation of all that exists by a sovereign God who spoke it into existence just like it says in Genesis 1 and 2. And I gladly join with those who believe in the literal truth of how God did it.

About the Authors

Ken Ham

Ken Ham is the president/CEO and founder of Answer in Genesis-U.S. and the highly acclaimed Creation Museum. He is also one of the most in-demand Christian speakers in North America. Ham, a native Australian, now resides near Cincinnati, Ohio, and is the author of numerous best-selling books. Ken hosts the daily radio program, "Answers . . . with Ken Ham," heard on more than 800 stations in America (and dozens more overseas) and is one of the editors and contributing authors for AiG's *Answers* magazine (a biblical worldview publication with over 70,000 worldwide subscribers).

Greg Hall

Greg Hall has served as president of Warner University since December of 1991. He earned his bachelor of arts in philosophy from the State University of New York, and his master of education and doctor of education in higher education administration from the University of Pittsburgh. Before coming to Warner University, Dr. Hall was the executive director of the Church of God in Western Pennsylvania for 7 years. He also served 14 years as a pastor in New York and Pennsylvania. He is a native of Jamestown, New York, and is an ordained minister.

Todd Hillard

Todd Hillard is a freelance writer from San Antonio, Texas, where he lives with his wife and five kids. A former youth pastor and missionary, he is passionate about taking the dreams and stories of others and bringing them to life on the written page. Todd was born and raised in the Black Hills of South Dakota. He received his BS in pre-med studies and psychology from the University of Utah and his MA in English from Arizona State University. He and his family lived in Turkey for two and a half years. He has 17 years of pastoral experience and has written more than 12 books.

Britt Beemer

Britt Beemer holds a BA from Northwest Missouri State University and has an MA from Indiana State University. In 1979, Beemer founded America's Research Group, a full-service consumer behavior research and strategic marketing firm. He currently serves as the director of research at America's Research Group, where he personally reviews all research and prepares and presents each strategic marketing plan. His work has been cited in the media, including the *Wall Street Journal*, the *New York Times*, Fox News, and many others.

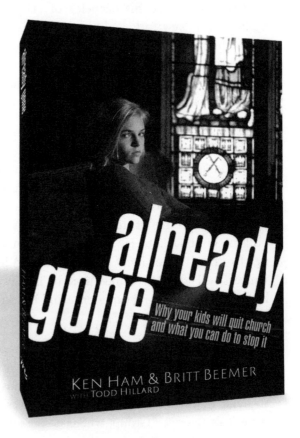